HISTORIC SANTA MARIA VALLEY
by Lucinda K. Ransick

A publication of the Santa Maria Valley Historical Society & Museum and the
Santa Maria Valley Chamber of Commerce

HPNbooks
A division of Lammert Incorporated
San Antonio, Texas

ISBN: 978-1-944891-25-1

Library of Congress Card Catalog Number: 2017931216

Historic Santa Maria Valley

author:	Lucinda K. Ransick
editor:	Michael Farris
cover artist:	Hattie Stoddard
contributing writer for "Sharing the Heritage":	Joe Goodpasture

HPNbooks

president:	Ron Lammert
project manager:	Daphne Fletcher
assistant project manager:	Alexandra Turner
administration:	Donna M. Mata
	Melissa G. Quinn
	Lori K. Smith
book sales:	Joe Neely
production:	Colin Hart
	Evelyn Hart
	Glenda Tarazon Krouse
	Christopher D. Sturdevant
	Tim Lippard

CONTENTS

♦

Main Street Santa Maria, c. 1900.

LEGACY SPONSORS

Through their generous support, these companies helped to make this project possible.

Allan Hancock College
800 South College Drive
Santa Maria, California 93454
805-922-6966
www.hancockcollege.edu

Andre, Morris & Buttery, PLC
2739 Santa Maria Way, Third Floor
Santa Maria, California 93455
805-543-4171
www.amblaw.com

Ca'Del Grevino
400 East Clark Avenue
Santa Maria, California 93455
805-937-6400
www.grevino.com

Diani Companies
351 North Blosser Road
Santa Maria, California 93458
805-925-9533
www.diani.com

Engel & Gray, Inc.
745 West Betteravia Road #A
Santa Maria, California 93455
805-925-2771
www.engelandgray.com

Historic Santa Maria Inn
801 South Broadway
Santa Maria, California 93454
805-928-7777
www.santamariainn.com

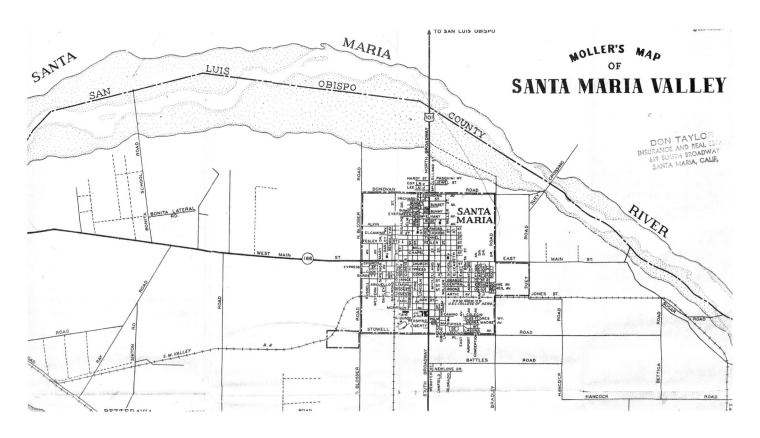

CHAPTER 1

THIS IS OUR VALLEY

The Santa Maria Valley, extending from the San Rafael Mountains to the Pacific Ocean, was the homeland of the Chumash Indians for about 13,000 years. These original American natives made their homes on the slopes of the surrounding hills, on the banks of the Santa Maria River, and along the central coast. About 2,000 years ago the Chumash created plank-built boats, called tomols, which they used for ocean fishing. In addition to this plank boat, the Chumash created fine basketry and cave paintings and made shells into currency. In all, they were a peaceful people with great reverence for the land and sea, and to this day they refer to themselves as the first people of our valley. Chumash elders tell us that "Chumash" means "seashell people." Boat builders and artists, the Chumash Indians enjoyed a more prosperous environment than most other tribes in California because of the generous resources provided by our propitious location.

The valley is bordered on the west by the Pacific Ocean and on the east by the San Rafael Mountains of the Los Padres National Forest. Prominent in the valley is Santa Maria, located 11 miles from the Pacific Ocean and situated north of the unincorporated township of Orcutt and south of the Santa Maria River. Guadalupe is approximately nine miles to the west. While Santa Maria experiences a cool Mediterranean climate, many microclimates influence the valley, making it superior for agriculture. The climate is mostly sunny, refreshed by the ocean breeze. A morning marine layer is common. Snow in the Santa Maria Valley is virtually unknown, with the last brief flurry recorded in Santa Maria in January 1949. The only recorded earlier snowfall was in January 1882. Annual rainfall averages 15 inches. The average summer temperature is 71 degrees, with an average winter temperature of 53. The Santa Maria Valley is hospitable, a definite sweet spot in California.

The Santa Maria Valley began welcoming explorers as early as 1769 when the Portolà Expedition passed through the valley during the first Spanish land exploration up the coast of what was then referred to as Las Californias province. White settlers were attracted here by the possibility of free land.

✦

George Moller's map of the Santa Maria Valley, c. 1954.

◆

*Above: A cave painting, located at
Chumash Painted Cave Historic Park,
off Highway 154.*
COURTESY OF ENCYCLOPEDIA BRITANNICA.

Top, right: James F. Goodwin.

*Below: The Thornburgh house, one
of the first houses in Santa Maria,
c. 1870.*

In 1821, after the Mexican War of Independence, the mission lands in the Santa Maria Valley were made available for private ownership under a Mexican land grant called Rancho Punta de la Laguna. The first settlement was made in 1840 when Teodoro Arrellanes and Diego Olivera took their grant of thirty thousand acres in the western end of the valley and called it Rancho Guadalupe. At the end of the Mexican War in 1848, California was ceded to the United States. Much of the valley's attributes was hidden. It would take some hardy, courageous pioneers to develop those hidden treasures and release the unlimited potential of the valley for themselves and future generations.

After California gained statehood in 1850, the area's reputation for rich soil began attracting farmers and other settlers. As they arrived in the valley, they found it practically treeless, giving the pioneers cause for trepidation for several reasons. Not only was there no shade, there was no wood to build homes or for windbreaks to protect their anticipated crops. Strong, persistent winds were a trouble to the first pioneers, but rows of trees were the answer. James F. Goodwin, who became known in the early days of the settlement as the "tree missionary," sold and gave away thousands of eucalyptus seedlings. Some of the giant eucalyptus trees seen today

a small cooperative in partnership with R.D. Cook, Samuel Lockwood and M.H. Stephens. This store was located on the southwest corner of Main and Broadway, and included the first post office. Mail came to the valley by stagecoach to Suey Crossing. Samuel Lockwood was the first postmaster. The little store was known as the "Grange Store."

FOUR CORNERS

Four of the valley's settlers (Rudolph Cook, John Thornburgh, Isaac Fesler, and Isaac Miller) built their homes near each other at the present corner of Broadway and Main Street. Each donated 40 acres at that junction to create the original boundaries of our town. The town had been known as Grangerville, leaving one to speculate that Santa Maria's first name was derived from the little store begun by Thornburgh. With the defining and refining of town boundaries, the township was surveyed in 1874 by G.W. Lewis, and a new name was sought. The newly platted town of Central City was recorded at the county seat on April 12, 1875. The four quarter sections of land

♦

Left: Thomas Garey founded the town of Garey in the valley southeast of Santa Maria in 1886. He moved to the valley when he was fifty-six.

Below: Rules for a stage trip as reproduced in a Los Alamos Days program.

are from those original seedlings. A determined group, those early pioneers had, by the end of the nineteenth century, transformed the Santa Maria Valley into one of the most productive agricultural areas in the state. Agriculture remains a key component of the economy for the entire region even today.

Between 1868 and 1874, post-civil war settlers began to arrive by wagon and on rail, recognizing both the potential of the valley and looking for a new start. Benjamin Wiley gained historical notation by becoming the first white settler to make a claim in the gap between the Spanish land grants established in the valley. He was followed by Joel Miller. Separated by only weeks, other first families of the valley arrived. Among them was John Prell, who arrived in November and located his farm early the next year, then built a small house, 12 by 14 feet in dimension, the first house of the valley. George Washington Battles, with his wife, Rachel, and family arrived next, followed by the Sibleys and the Holloways in the fall of 1868. By the end of that first year, there were 100 people living in the area, and more were making plans to come to the remarkable, fertile, Santa Maria Valley.

John Thornburgh, who came to the valley in 1869, arrived seeking relief from debilitating asthma. His wife Minerva Maulsby Thornburgh joined him, arriving by train, in 1871. So invigorating was the valley's climate that he regained his health and began a business, founding

Ten Commandments for Stage Passengers

The following list of rules was posted on all stagecoach station walls and on the ceiling of the coaches themselves.

Adherence to the Following Rules Will Insure A Pleasant Trip

1. Abstinance from liquor is preferred. If you must drink, share the bottle. To do otherwise makes you appear selfish. And don't overlook the driver.
2. If ladies are present, gentlemen are urged to forego smoking cigars and pipes, as the odor of same is repugnant to the weaker sex. Chewing tobacco is permitted if you spit with the wind, not against it.
3. Gentlemen passengers must refrain from the use of rough language in the presence of ladies and children. This rule does not apply to the driver, whose team may not be able to understand genteel language.
4. Robes are provided for your comfort during cold or wet weather. Hogging robes will not be tolerated. The offender will be obliged to ride outside with the driver.
5. Snoring is disgusting. If you sleep, sleep quietly.
6. Don't use your fellow passenger's shoulder for a pillow. He or she may not understand and friction could result.
7. Firearms may be kept on your person, for use in emergencies. Do not discharge them for pleasure, or shoot at wild animals along the roadside. The noise riles the horses.
8. In the event of a runaway, remain calm. Jumping from the coach may kill you, leave you injured, or at the mercy of the elements, highwaymen and coyotes.
9. Topics of discussion to be avoided have to do with religion, politics, and above all, stagecoach robberies or accidents.
10. Gentlemen guilty of unchivalrous behavior toward lady passengers will be put off the stage. It is a long walk back to Santa Barbara. A word to the wise is sufficient.

cornering Broadway and Main Street formed the heart of what is today Santa Maria.

Even before the platting of the town, Pleasant Valley School was built half a mile south of Main Street. It provided the first means of education in the valley. R. D. Cook who was an able carpenter, with the aid of a work party, built the 48-foot-long school in about three days. Martin Tunnell donated the property. Classes began in January 1870; Joel Miller was the teacher and among his first students were the four Cook daughters.

The town continued to develop, having left Grangerville behind and referring to itself as Central City. Isaac Fesler donated property for the Pacific Coast Railroad right-of-way. While this name made great sense to all, due in part to its location central to Sisquoc and Guadalupe, two other significant towns in the valley, it failed to work for the postal service. Mail was often being sent by mistake to Central City, Colorado. Santa Maria took its final identity when the *Santa Maria Times* published its first edition April 22, 1882. Although it wouldn't be until September 12,

1905, that the name was officially adopted. So, the town was Grangerville for roughly three years, Central City for approximately eight, and finally Santa Maria, a familiar name in the valley area, for as long ago as 1840 Don Juan Pacifico Ontiveros had named the "creek" (Santa Maria River) and his rancho at Tepusquet, Santa Maria. It would be decades later when the similarity with the name of Columbus' flagship resulted in the municipal logo being adopted.

Gaining steadily in population from those first days as Grangerville, the families in the immediate area consisted of the Millers, Cooks, Feslers, and Thornburghs, together with James McElhaney, from Arkansas; John Prell from Germany, who had become a United States citizen in 1863; Thomas Wilson from Scotland; the Charles Bradley family from England; Joseph Lockwood; the George Washington Battles family; and Ben Thurman, who came in 1869 and built a home. Most of the other families lived on the farms on the perimeter of the town such as the Cary Calvin Oakley family from Tennessee; the William Smith family from

✦

Juan Pacifico Ontiveros Adobe,
Tepusquet; erected 1857-8.

England; the Martin Luther Tunnell family, southerners of French descent arriving in 1868; the Frances Marion Bryant family from Maine, and then Minnesota; and the Trott family. These were the earliest families to settle and work the land in the years before 1870.

Reuben Hart arrived with the next wave of development. He was an industrious soul. He established the first water works for Santa Maria in 1880 at East Church Street and South Broadway. A windmill pumped the water from a well into a wooden tank. Later he pumped the water by steam power from an 88-foot well into an elevated wooden tank and ran water through pipes to the town. No small undertaking, Hart supplied the entire community with drinking and irrigating water. The town had grown to over 600 by 1886. This first water works would eventually serve 3,000 residents. Hart sold the business, but in 1912 the new owners failed and

◆

Above: The aftermath of a fire on Main Street in 1883.

Left: The Cook family, c. 1902. Back row (from left to right) Ella Cook Tunnell, Fred Lee Cook, Viola Cook Jones, John Tunnell, Rudolph D. Cook, Mary Cook Miller. Front row: Laro Jones and Therand Tunnell.

Hart saved the business by helping the city maneuver into purchasing the water works. In January 1916, for $74,000, Santa Maria would purchase and operate its own water works, thus controlling one of its most important utilities.

Hart also started a lumber yard, another first for the community. He improved streets, built curbs, assisted financially in the construction of churches, and served on the boards of early banks and other business enterprises. In 1888, he opened The Hart House. The new hotel was a superb accomplishment, an elegant showplace for all of central California. The Hart House was ornate and lavishly furnished, decorated in the Victorian Style of the '90s. It had beautiful chandeliers and fireplaces in the suites, ornately decorated high headboard beds, and lace curtains at the windows. It was opulent and beckoned travelers far and wide to stop at the ambitious town with its industrious spirit. Reuben Hart is remembered as the "Father of Santa Maria" for his massive development projects that benefitted the entire valley. Many other businessmen were to capture the driving ambition of this early settler. Santa Maria was on its way.

CHAPTER 2

THE MANY RICHES OF THE VALLEY

Exploration, expansionism, exceptionalism dominated the thoughts of valley pioneers as the old century died and the new one took off with optimism leaving oppression abroad, the destruction of war, and scarcity of goods or opportunity behind. With the gold rush of 1849 a fresh memory, valley residents found beneath their very feet a new cash cow to excite the senses and change their fortunes—oil!

Ushering in a new century was something older than the hills. Oil exploration had begun in 1888 as locals suspected the "brea seeps" were indicative of greater things. Originally used by the Chumash to line their tomols and later by settlers to create sidewalks, in 1895 these brea seeps were attracting local attention for a new purpose. However, late 19th-century attempts to find oil were shallow and often misplaced. Science and technology were key to enriching the valley, turning oil into a boom economy in the early 20th century. What had been secret under the soil was finally more discernable. In 1898, Union Oil Company sent geologist William Warren Orcutt to the valley as word 'seeped' out about this newly attainable resource. He began exploring the area, and in 1901 he urged Union Oil's president to purchase large land holdings in the Lompoc and Santa Maria area. Using his education as a tool for discovering the best places to locate wells, he believed there was great wealth in the hills, so the company, following his directions, leased 70,000 acres in the valley and vicinity. In October 1901, their third well on the Careaga lease came in at 150 barrels a day. In 1902, Union Oil discovered the large Orcutt oil field in the Solomon Hills south of Santa Maria, and a number of smaller companies also began pumping oil. The history of oil in the valley was just beginning. Two years later, Union Oil had 22 wells in production. Other significant discoveries followed: the Lompoc Oil Field in 1903 and the Cat Canyon field in 1908. Over the next 80 years, more large oil fields were found, and thousands of oil wells were drilled and put into production. Oil development intensified in 1934 with the discovery of the Santa Maria Valley Oil Field underneath the southern and western parts of the city of Santa Maria, which spurred the city's growth even further. From 1941-44 the Santa Maria area supplied much of the oil for the U.S. Navy's Pacific Fleet. Production was 45,000 barrels a day. By 1957 there were 1,775 oil wells in operation in the Santa Maria Valley. They were

◆

Investors reflected in oil reservoirs, c. 1904.

◆

Above: Field worker's housing on the Pinal Oil Lease.

Below: A Barca Oil Company 1904 Stock Certificate.

producing more than $640 million worth of oil or approximately 80,000 barrels per day. Oil became the biggest industry in the valley for a time. In 1986 oil prices dropped from $22 a barrel to $6 triggering a massive slowdown in the oil industry in the valley. By the 1990s, oil no longer reigned. Oil prices behave much like ocean waves, peaking and then toppling forward to crash, taking us all for quite a ride. The top price for oil was in June 2008 at $136.31 per barrel on the NYMEX. From there we see one of the sharpest drops in our history: oil closed at roughly $45 per barrel today (summer 2015).

ENLIGHTENMENT IN THE VALLEY

Roughneck behavior and a lack of parlor room manners seemingly permeated the valley. Whiskey Row was building its reputation. Grace Clark Armstrong, in reminiscences of her early

Santa Maria days, shared: "I will never forget the 13 saloons on Whiskey Row, no self-respecting women were ever seen inside." Truth was, most of the ladies even crossed and walked on the other side of the street to avoid the establishments that made Whiskey Row so notorious. The incredible number of men who first worked in the valley and the required hard work associated with their jobs at first seemed to eclipse any chance for a more cultured leisure finding a space; saloons dominated the night and the landscape. The only thing there were more of than saloons were spittoons!

The ladies soon rose to the challenge, and, while they couldn't rid the town of saloons, they were very successful at adding more tasteful options! Civilization would prevail and sophistication tiptoed its way into the valley as families grew, and a more refined way of life took a hold on the end of the day. From the night of the first party hosted by R. D. Cook, given in the first 'city' house built on the townsite of Santa Maria to raise funding for the first schoolhouse, cultured entertainment made its debut in the valley.

Santa Maria's first band was organized in 1881 with Augustus C. Schuster as leader and instructor. The band was known as the Liberty Band. Showman Harry Dorsey opened the Gaiety Theatre in 1910 presenting both vaudeville acts and motion pictures. It was the first showhouse in Santa Maria. He built the Santa Maria Theater in 1928. Chautauqua, extremely popular in the late nineteenth and early twentieth centuries, came to Santa Maria at Mrs. Richard's Empresario on South Pine Street. Young Santa Marians met for dances or movies here. A Chautauqua Assembly brought entertainment and culture for the whole community. It featured important speakers, teachers, musicians, entertainers, preachers and specialists of the day.

Big changes both in entertainment and business innovation arrived with G. Allan Hancock, who introduced the valley to great prosperity with his arrival in 1925. By 1930, five years after Hancock arrived, the population of Santa Maria had nearly doubled to 7,000. A musician since childhood, he had played cello with the Los Angeles Symphony. Hancock was delighted to find an informal musical group, and he immediately proposed starting a community orchestra. One of the first concerts, in which Hancock played the cello, was a benefit for the Minerva Club, raising funds for its new clubhouse at Lincoln and Boone streets. The clubhouse opened in 1928 and was designed by Julia Morgan, the architect for Hearst Castle.

LADIES' LITERARY SOCIETY

No club in Santa Maria has enjoyed a longer life than the Minerva Club. It was organized in October of 1894 by a group of 25 women devoted to the idea of making the town a better, more civilized place to live: intellectually, spiritually and morally. The ladies met on a Friday afternoon and originally called themselves the Ladies' Literary Society. The Minerva Club may have been named to honor Minerva Thornburgh, wife of one of the "founders," John Thornburgh. Minerva's strength and leadership, along with how well loved she was, makes this belief credible. Minerva died in 1898, and the club took her name in 1906. They were supremely active throughout the development of the Santa Maria Valley. Santa Maria's first library was a direct result of a letter written by the club to Andrew Carnegie in 1901. The desire for a library pressed the need for incorporation of the town. Incorporation was stipulated as part of the grant to receiving funding from the Carnegie Foundation. Santa Maria was incorporated in September 1905 and Alvin W. Cox was the first mayor. The library cornerstone was laid in 1908, and in 1909 the library was completed at a cost close to $10,000, a significant accomplishment for a town of about 2,000 people! Today's equivalent would be a value of about $12.7 million. The population in the valley continued to

grow and in 1939 a new library building replaced the Carnegie. It was dedicated on July 15, 1941, one of the last library buildings to be constructed on the west coast before World War II.

Meanwhile the original Carnegie Library served as a USO center and then a youth center under the Parks and Recreation Department. In 1966 after it was razed to the ground, deep feelings of nostalgia ensued and the footprint of the Carnegie was marked with 12 palm trees on the lawn facing Broadway. In 1990, it was decided that the "new" library was too small even after three renovations. The number of books, computers, and wiring had surpassed the capacity of this second library. The City Council approved a Library Master Plan in 1998 and the city applied for state grant funding in June 2002 in order to finance another new

✦

Above: A saloon on Whiskey Row, c.1874.

Bottom, left: The Santa Maria Concert Band, c.1905.

Below: Minerva Thornburgh, wife of Santa Maria forefather John Thornburgh, c. 1870.

♦

Above: The Carnegie Library converted for use as a USO center, 1943.

Top, right: Alfred Lutnesky, the local jeweler, had the first house with electricity in Santa Maria.

Below: A street scene of Santa Maria looking east c. 1910. The Santa Maria-Guadalupe electric car, tracks and power poles on Main Street. "Whiskey Row," where you could buy a glass of beer for a nickel, is on the far left.

library. This one was built on the parking lot immediately south of the Carnegie successor library. The city of Santa Maria built a $33 million main library which opened in August 2008 at approximately 60,000 square feet.

Santa Maria was well on its way to becoming a city of distinction. The pioneers of the valley were ambitious and farsighted, and their dream was that Santa Maria would one day be a leading Central Coast city. They knew it would take a good foundation to realize their vision and careful planning.

ELECTRIFICATION OF THE VALLEY

Electricity first came to Santa Maria in the early 1900s after the War of Currents Era (A series of events surrounding the introduction of competing power systems in the late 1880s). In

1879, Thomas Edison was able to produce a reliable, long-lasting electric light bulb in his laboratory. By the end of the 1880s, small electrical stations based on Edison's designs were in a number of U.S. cities, but each station was able to power only a few city blocks. The valley residents had their sights set high, and the demand for the benefits of electrification was rising. Resourcefulness was a prime virtue in this new energy industry. Still in its developmental infancy when Santa Maria Gas and Electric was built by W. J. Ballard and R. H. Ballard, electric service was rudimentary and unreliable—strong wind could disrupt service. In 1913 A. Emory Wishon established the Midland Counties Public Service Corporation and built a 70,000-volt electric transmission line from the San Joaquin Valley to the coast via Coalinga. This provided the coastal area with a supply of hydro-electric power and, by then connecting several other plants, made it possible to provide dependable service.

CHAPTER 3

TAMING THE VALLEY

The Midland Counties Public Service Corporation later merged with Pacific Gas and Electric, and the two companies served forty-nine of the fifty-eight California counties. Distribution lines were built to carry power to the farms and smaller communities. One of the first areas with power lines was Guadalupe. O.J. Reiner, a local contractor set the first meter to give service to that city. Another line was built to Orcutt supporting further oil field development. The first residence to be wired for electricity belonged to Santa Maria's first jeweler, Alfred Lutnesky.

The Santa Maria Realty Company, with Madison Thornburgh as president, Thomas B. Adam as vice-president, and John E. Walker as secretary, was organized on March 12, 1906. The two other stock holder-directors were Paul O. Tietzen and James F. Goodwin. This company preceded the Santa Maria Gas and Power Company, which was organized in January 1907 with the same officers and directors. In October of that year, the order was given to lay the gas pipe line from the Brookshire Oil Lease to Santa Maria and other districts in the valley. James F. Goodwin acquired the necessary franchise from the county permitting this construction. The Santa Maria Gas and Power Company merged with the Southern Counties Gas Company in the early 40s. At that time Santa Maria Gas had the distinction of being the oldest distributor of natural gas in California, having been founded by Goodwin and Tietzen at the turn of the twentieth century. In 1970 the Southern Counties Gas Company became part of the Southern California Gas Company. SoCalGas® has been delivering natural gas for more than 140 years now. It is the nation's largest natural gas distribution utility, providing energy to more than 20 million consumers through nearly 6 million meters in more than 500 communities. The company's service territory encompasses approximately 20,000 square miles in diverse terrain throughout Central and Southern California, from Visalia to the Mexican border.

There is no argument that the Santa Maria Valley was a busy, bourgeoning, hardworking place. Farming or ranching, ranchero or hacienda, it didn't matter; ultimately the first settlers of the valley had to get to market to buy and sell products. Rail, ship, and road transport or any combinations thereof; advancement was constantly being pursued. Innovation was a word injected repeatedly into the vocabulary of these first families and into the planning and execution of their town's development. Just as electricity and gas utilities propelled the striving valley forward, communications enjoyed revolutionary developments in the 19th century, and the valley residents wanted that too! The telegraph had made possible instant long-distance communication. More was learned about overseas markets for products produced locally; competition was met with timely information. Railroads used the telegraph to schedule trains so they wouldn't collide on the single tracks. Quick turnarounds on produce, goods, and materials made a tremendous impact on livelihoods. A communications revolution sped up and enabled commerce, fostered globalization,

◆

The Brookshire oil lease.

◆

Above: A crew erecting a telephone pole near Santa Maria.

Below: Switchboard operators for the Home Telephone Company, c. 1910. At the time the telephone company was in the First National Bank building on the corner of Church Street and Broadway.

and encouraged democratic participation. It was changing the face of the planet. Enhanced communications, together with the use of gas and electricity, provided a level of comfort before unknown by the masses, thus improving everyone's standard of living. Communications made its next big leap with the telephone. The earliest known date that for the telephone in Santa Maria was 1894. A directory published for the entire state indicated the city's first telephone was a toll station located in Marton's [sic] Grocery Store. In 1899 Santa Maria had a

few magneto telephones interconnected through a switchboard. Two young women, Grace and Florence Clark, were the first operators. The switchboard was located in the dressmaking shop of Mrs. L.L. Colvin inside the Hart House, later known as the Bradley Hotel. By 1906 there were 276 telephones in Santa Maria. Locally, service was known as Sunset Telephone Company, which had a small switchboard serving a few business customers. Robert Eastman Easton, young and energetic, entered the utilities field when he organized the Home Telephone and Telegraph Company. He arrived in Santa Maria in 1907.

The infrastructure of the valley was inviting to businesses and families alike: picturesque and contemporary. Most of the Santa Maria neighborhoods had Craftsman-style homes, straight streets, and square corners. Palm Court took another step forward in making Santa Maria a marvelous place to live. When the development was first planned, it was much different than the rest of the city. The Palm Court neighborhood, built in the early 1920s, had paved streets, underground utilities, street lights, landscaping and what was referred to as Italia architecture. In plain terms, it was upscale, modern, and classy!

With every Herculean leap forward, new challenges were created. Despite the sublime

and innocuous weather patterns of today, those early, hardy valley organizers faced down many natural trials, pushing them into the past and providing stability and security from nature's wrath with sound planning and investment.

TAKING ON THE ELEMENTS

A flood is credited with spurring the formation of a water conservation district program that was to provide relief for the entire valley. Routine flooding had plagued the valley since the early 1900s. Three days before the voters were to go to the polls in February 1937, a powerful flood struck yet again, ripping out the costly infrastructure of the valley's towns. Highways, bridges, and communications and power lines were destroyed. Cattle were drowned in the turbulent, swirling waters. Large areas of valuable irrigated land were inundated. The

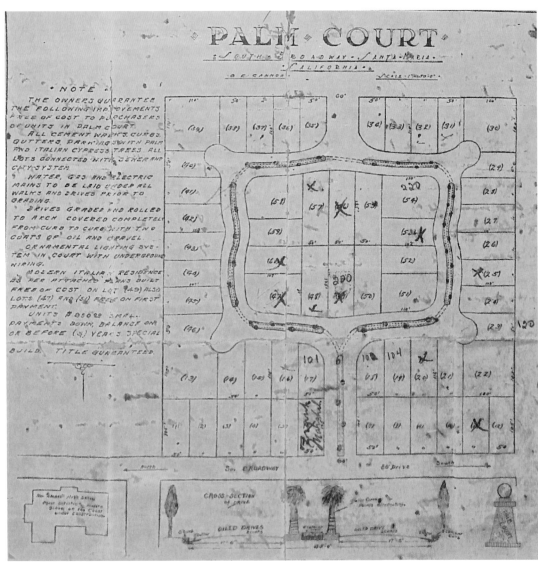

◆

Above: The Hart House was home to the first telephone switchboard in Santa Maria. The Hart House was built in 1888 on the corner of Broadway and Main Street. The vehicle was the first automotive stage between Santa Maria and Guadalupe.

Left: The original map of Palm Court.

residents needed no further convincing that something had to be done. Elected to serve on the first Board of Directors of the Santa Maria Valley Water Conservation District were M.B. O'Brien, E.J. Parrish, Guido O. Ferini, C.J. Donovan, Owen T. Rice and L. H. Adam. In the early 50s, it would be T.A. "Cap" Twitchell, son of pioneer resident Fremont Twitchell, to be credited with bringing to a positive conclusion the long fight for water control. As supervisor of this district, he worked indefatigably for the promotion of both the Vaquero and Cachuma Dams. Vaquero (Twitchell) Dam was built by the United States Bureau of Reclamation between 1956 and 1958. The dam and reservoir provide flood control and water conservation. The valley only receives significant amounts of rainfall during the winter, averaging about 14 inches per year. The water is stored in the reservoir behind Vaquero Dam during big winter storms and released as quickly as possible while still allowing

it to percolate into the soil and recharge the groundwater. The name of the Vaquero Dam was changed to Twitchell Dam in 1957 to recognize and perpetuate the memory of the man who did so much to bring this project to fruition ending the destruction, physical and economic, caused by the routine flooding of the valley.

Fires as well as floods had plagued Santa Maria in its first years. In September of 1883, at approximately 2 a.m., flames began streaming out of the workshop of T.A. Jones and Son on Broadway. Even with the first cry of "fire," it was evident that the whole building would be lost to the blaze. The entire male population turned out but realized almost immediately that their attention had to be given to saving adjacent buildings. There was no fire department, so, used to handling their own problems, they worked together covering roofs with wet blankets and drenching buildings with water. Saved from this fire were the Sedgwick House, the Music Hall, the

Goodwin and Bryant store and the office of the *Santa Maria Times*. The Jones store was a two-story frame structure 34 x 48 feet in size. It was a total loss, including its stock of about $1,000. This fire would be referred to for decades as "The Fire," while the next was to be known as the "Big Fire." In 1884 Broadway and Main was a tightly built 'tinder-box' of structures with board sidewalks and dirt streets. A fire broke out about 11 o'clock on Thursday evening, May 29. Smoke rose from the center of the block on the northeast side of Main Street. The fire moved rapidly and was aided by prevailing west winds that swept the fire into towering flames, demolishing buildings between the Odd Fellows Hall and the center of the block. In the morning, the lodge was the only remaining building. Santa Maria would have to begin again. This time brick buildings replaced the old wooden ones. Santa Maria started a fire department in 1904. Arthur S. MacLaughlin was named Fire Chief. He was appointed by the city Board of Trustees at a salary of ten dollars a month. A hand drawn hose cart, some hose, axes and nozzles made up the entire firefighting arsenal.

BACK TO BUSINESS

Undaunted by flood and fire, Santa Maria went back into business. The foremost business thoroughfare by 1890 was Main Street. It was 120 feet wide. Historians are of two minds as to why the street was so wide; one perspective is that it was to allow enough space to turn a six or eight horse hitch. The other suggested it was to prevent the rapid spread of fire that cities of this time were plagued by. The town covered an area three-quarters of mile square. Many of the

enterprises that flourished around the turn of the century lasted a relatively short period of time. There are others, such as Bryant and Trott Hardware Company and W.A. Haslam Company that endured the test of time and prospered into even the fourth generation.

Emmet Bryant began selling in Santa Maria in 1880. In 1882 he married Miss Laura Sharp, daughter to Hattie Sharp Hart and stepdaughter of Reuben Hart. They had three children: Ruby Cox, Elwood E. Bryant, and Lucille Stair. There would be seven grandchildren: Alvin Cox; Urban, Jane, Jack, and Marian Stair; and Lane and Glenn Bryant.

Mr. Bryant first went into business with James F. Goodwin. They leased the old Farmer's Union building from Reuben Hart. This business operated about three years before Bryant went to

◆

One of Santa Maria's first fire badges, found in an old outhouse near Chief Crakes' home.

♦

Above: A fire in downtown Santa Maria. Notice the flag pole on the right, c. 1914

Below: Bryant and Trott Hardware, downtown Santa Maria. The store was closed after 111 years.

keep books for Newhall Ranch, then to Los Angeles, before returning and beginning a hardware business with B.F. Bell. In 1890 Bell retired and George J. Trott, an uncle of Bryant, took his place. It would not be until July 1991 that Bryant and Trott, after more than 100 years of being in the hardware business in Santa Maria,

would close its doors. Bryant and Trott was located at 110 E. Main Street for more than 60 years. Emmett Bryant, the founder, died in 1939, and management was taken over by his son Elwood. Elwood died in 1966 and the business remained in the family and was run by his sons Glenn and Lane.

CHAPTER 4

OVERCOMING EARLY CHALLENGES

Business endured mostly due to the diligence of those first merchants who knew commerce was required to build a town. In the 1870s merchandise and essentials had to be hauled in by wagon from Port Hartford to "Central City." Conversely exports were delivered to Port Hartford or to Port Sal to be shipped to market. It could take several days to move materials across the distance. The Santa Maria Valley was a broad expanse unbroken by tree or shrub. West winds off the coast blew through uninterrupted. Those wagon trails were riddled with chuckholes, drifting sand, and, during the rainy season, the Santa Maria River could get too deep to cross making Port Hartford inaccessible. With a preponderance of elements working against them, it's a marvel that early businesses sustained themselves, even thrived. Businesses housed in those first wooden buildings were Santa Maria Meat Market, located on West Main Street; on Main Street, Eagle Drug Store, Central Drug Store, The Harness and Saddle Shop, The Boots and Shoes Shop, Hair Dressing Saloon, and Morris and Utley Milliners. Gas lamps provided lighting, and wooden planks formed curbs along dirt sidewalks. Central City boasted a population of 300 by 1882 and was a commercial center in the valley.

In 1889, William A. Haslam and Arthur Fugler formed a partnership and opened business as William A. Haslam and Company. Haslam was president and Fugler secretary. At first the store sold groceries and clothing and was known as the only place in town where a person could find whatever he needed or wanted. In 1906 the partners moved their business to the Odd Fellows building. The building was one of a kind. The beautiful staircase leading to the second floor and the hardwood floors throughout gave the place a special flair. The 18-inch thick walls proved to be superior to many of the earthquake-proof buildings of today. In 1912, Fugler decided to go into the real estate business and sold his interest in the store to Haslam. Most people carried accounts with the store, and, when the crops came in, the debt was paid. However, when times were tough and cash was short, Haslam's was known to carry townspeople from year-to-year. During the Great Depression, the company decided to give up the grocery department and to concentrate on dry goods alone. As the years trickled by, Haslam's opened six additional stores, one of which was one of the first stores in the downtown mall when it open in 1976.

◆

Wm. H. Langlois (left) and R. O. Walker (right), proprietors of Eagle Meat Market on South Broadway, 1895.

Coblentz and Schwabacher was another notable business in Santa Maria that came early and stayed late. The firm retired from business in 1932. Schwabacher was a German; Coblentz was a Frenchman. Their political views were in opposition, but their policy was that politics played no part in business. The two men were staunch friends and very much in agreement on how to run a business.

Post-World War II Santa Maria went on a growing spree, both geographically and economically. Just as the first valley residents came to the area for fresh perspectives and new starts, so did another generation burdened from

Top: Santa Maria Chamber of Commerce Banquet, January 25, 1921, at the U.S. Grill, 113 North Broadway. Since its inception in 1902, the Chamber's mission has been to better the valley's business climate, forge a strong community, and improve quality of life for residents. Through participation in Chamber activities, members were able to accomplish collectively what they could not do individually.

Middle: This 1915 plate is compliments of W. A. Haslam & Co., General Merchandise. The plate was donated to the historical museum by Mary Lundgren.

Bottom: This picture of downtown Orcutt has often been misidentified as La Graciosa.

the worries of war. Recently out of the military, three brothers having grown up in a share cropping family in Arkansas envisioned a brighter future. They brought their hopes to California with the courage to see it achieved. In 1944, Ed, Lawson, and Merrell Williams started a fruit stand in Wilmington, California. In a year the stand formed into a market. By 1949 the Wilmington

Above: The Williams Bros. Market on South Broadway where Michael's was located until 2015.

Right: Merrell Williams opened Merrell's Steak House.

store was sold and the three brothers headed for Santa Maria where they began their great adventure on the Central Coast by opening their first grocery market at 115 East Church Street.

For the next 40 years, Williams Bros. marketed to local communities by stocking locally grown produce and meats. A Santa Maria style barbeque wasn't complete without a trip to one of several Williams Bros. Markets for top block and locally grown pinquito beans. One brother opened his own restaurant, Merrell's Steak House. Until the mid-1990s, Williams Bros was a household name in the valley. The big chain stores were barely competition.

CHAPTER 5

PLANTING THE SEEDS OF FUTURE PROSPERITY

The Valley, with its dominant hand in agriculture, required the services and expertise of blacksmiths. The first shop was opened in 1874 by R. D. Cook. He sold to Reuben Hart in 1877. Inventing the gang plow is one of Hart's many accomplishments. The Roemer family began their business serving farmers and ranchers in 1890. Joseph Roemer set up business at Broadway and Chapel.

In 1916 his sons, Frank and Alfred, formed Roemer and Roemer with 57 employees working as blacksmiths, selling farm implements and automobiles, and providing woodworking among their many trades and services. The Roemer family continued to provide farm and ranch customers of the valley with fencing, feed, and other farm and ranch supplies into 2015.

Life in the valley was often hard and much of the work was dangerous. Dr. William T. Lucas, who arrived in 1879, and later Dr. Ormond Pinkerton Paulding, ministered to the sick, broken, and aged with amazing skill. Mrs. Lang's, a two-story sanitarium on South Broadway, served as a "hospital." Then Jessie Forbes Grigsby opened her 14-bed hospital with three day nurses, one night nurse and herself. Dr. Lucas treated patients at Grigsby. He also had his own office on the 200 block of North Vine. He was among the first to have an automobile; not much of a driver he was often heard shouting his vehicle to a stop. Physicians and nurses at the turn of the twentieth century were at the forefront of modern medicine. Small medical facilities came and went. There was a county hospital located off Morrison in the late 1920s just west of Buena Vista Park operating into the late 1970s as a full service medical facility; clinics operated at the site into the 90s. In 1940, eight Sisters of St. Francis of Penance and Christian Charity were assigned to Santa Maria to manage and staff a hospital urgently needed by our growing community of 8,000 people. Sisters Hospital first opened with 35 beds built at a cost of $130,000. Sister's welcomed their 1,000th baby in 1943, added an additional 15-room pediatric section in 1956, then a new wing with 85 beds in 1957 and a third operating room in 1959. Rapid growth for Santa Maria increased the need further between World War II and the 1960s. In 1961 Valley Community Hospital opened with 70 beds. For a brief period there was also Airport Hospital, located beside the train tracks off College Drive near Hancock College. Ground breaking for Marian Medical Center came in 1965 and the first patients were received in 1967. In 2012, Marian officially became part of Dignity Health and come to be Marian Regional Medical Center. From our first physician, Doc

◆

The Roemer and Roemer blacksmith shop, c. 1913.

Lucas, to today, the Santa Maria Valley has depended on excellent pioneer medicine to keep the valley residents healthy.

No matter how good the medicine, there was still the necessity for the inevitable. Wat Rodenberg's unexpected death as a result of a hunting accident, precipitated the need for a final resting place. In 1872 the Thornburg-Jones Cemetery filled this need. It soon became apparent however, that this location was too near to downtown. The Independent Order of Odd Fellows and the Free and Accepted Masons cemetery was started July 9, 1883, by local lodges. At that time the property was considered to be outside of the town far enough that it wouldn't be in the way of planned growth. In 1884 the Thornburg-Jones Cemetery began relocating graves to the new I.O.O.F. and F.&A.M. location. Removal of all remains was completed by 1886. Today the cemetery is part

of the Santa Maria Cemetery District, which was established August 6, 1917, and includes the small Pine Grove Cemetery in Orcutt. The Santa Maria Cemetery located at Stowell Road and College Drive is not exactly as "out" of town as was originally intended!

With a destination secured for eternal rest, end of life in the Santa Maria Valley gave wings to

some creative writing. Valley obituaries were often colorful, even poetic, if otherwise brief. Whether a loved one found his way to heaven through the pearly gates, crossed the great divide, took his wings, slipped into that last good night, met the grim reaper, or booked his tee time in heaven, an undertaker was needed to see to the final details of death and to care for the bereaved. The firm that first provided this service was founded in 1876. T.A. Jones and his son Samuel Jefferson Jones operated the mortuary under the business name T.A. Jones & Son, Furniture & Undertaker. In 1904 Albert Dudley joined them as a mortician. He bought out the undertaking part of the business in 1914 and changed the name to Dudley Mortuary. In 1930, Mr. Dudley's business sold to his son Russell. In 1972 he was joined by Jeffrey Hoffman. For over one hundred thirty years, Dudley-Hoffman Mortuary has provided trusted service for the families in the valley. They are recognized as the oldest continuous business in Santa Maria.

Another durable business in the valley was Union Sugar. The company arrived in September of 1887. By far the largest industrial complex built in the valley, the Union Sugar Company

beet refinery at Betteravia opened at the same approximate time as oil was king of the valley. The area where the factory found its footing, Betteravia, was so named after betterave, French for beet root. The Southern Pacific Railroad, contracted by the Union Sugar Company, built a spur from a point about three miles south of the Santa Maria depot to the site where the refinery was being erected. The Southern Pacific also laid rails in a standard gauge spur from Guadalupe to Betteravia, and so the beet refinery was served by two railroads. In 1899 the actual work of making sugar began. Union Sugar and the railroad had negotiated a rate of fifty cents per ton within forty miles of the plant. This would enable

✦

Above: A Southern Pacific sugar beet train at Gaviota.

Below: Women processing broccoli at Rosemary Packing Company.

farmers within that radius to be competitive in beet production from Los Alamos to Arroyo Grande and east to Sisquoc. Because Arroyo Grande had lost the refinery's location to Santa Maria, their farmers decide not to grow sugar beets. Farmers in Nipomo were contracted to make up that shortage. A giant in the valley, the company boosted the local economy, providing jobs and buying the locally produced sugar beets. It contributed millions of tons of beet sugar allotted to the US sugar industry, which was regulated by the federal government. Despite the Great Depression, market fluctuations, and war, Union Sugar produced beet sugar for more than 30% of the nation's sugar needs. The company was a division of Consolidated Food Corporation, which became a division of Sara Lee Corporation. In 1986 it became Holly Sugar. The plant would operate until the fall of 1993. Sugar beets took an entire growing season, crops with multiple seasons replaced the sugar beet slowly but surely and, by the time the plant closed, valley farmers had other cash crops.

Advanced development in irrigation triggered the valley's next great industry, produce: cauliflower, lettuce, carrots, broccoli. In the 1900s the Chinese were replaced by the Japanese in the

sugar beet fields as the dominant labor force. By 1910, a cooperative called the Guadalupe Japanese Association, which supported Japanese farm operations and had a branch in Santa Maria, helped turn the agricultural communities into commercial centers. Setsuo Aratani, a Japanese immigrant who arrived in 1917, began experimenting with growing vegetables and developed the means to ship to other states thereby pioneering the vegetable industry in the valley. Guadalupe's first packing plant, Guadalupe Produce Company, was organized by Aratani. He also created the All Star Trading Company, which imported fertilizer and sake from Japan. During the Japanese internment period, all of the Aratani properties in Guadalupe were lost except the All Star Trading Company, which reopened and continued its operations for decades.

The Minami family was another of the many Japanese families who farmed in the valley and were impacted by the attack on Pearl Harbor in 1941. Both H. Yaemon Minami and his older son, Yatato, were taken away and shuffled among different internment camps for five years. When they returned, they were able to recover 80 acres of their land that the bank had held in trust. The year 1949 proved such an exceptional year for the family farm that they increased from 80 acres to 2,000. They became one of the largest best-known farms in the state. Successful and generous the Minami family donated funding to open a new community/ recreational facility in 1979 that became known as the Minami Center in Santa Maria.

In 1912, L.D. Waller, a native of London and skilled in raising flower seeds, founded the Waller Seed Company in Guadalupe. Shortly after the company opened, Dr. John Franklin, an avid horticulturist, and Paul Giacommi became partners with Waller. The company became known as the Waller Franklin Seed Company.

◆

Above: A produce box label from H.Y. Minami & Sons.

Below: Workers washing flower seeds.

Award winning flower seeds and vegetable seeds were sent worldwide for decades. Acres of marigold rows would swell the fields at the Waller Franklin Seed Company's flower fields in Guadalupe. Initially planting only 30 acres, increasing demand for the company's exceptional product pushed them to expand to 350 acres by the 1930s.

Of all the successful businesses in the valley, strawberries sit top. Commercially grown strawberries have been the valley's top crop for the past several decades (grapes are rapidly catching up). There are many farms throughout the valley, and together they boast more than 7,000 acres of strawberries. The Sheehys were the first family to begin commercial strawberry farming in the Santa Maria Valley. The Sheehy brothers, Kenneth and Rod, partnered with Ned Driscoll and Tom Porter to form the valley's first commercial strawberry operation in 1944. Strawberries remain a dominant crop in the valley today and are California's number one crop in value per acre, with state farmers growing the bulk of the nation's strawberries on less than one percent of the state's total farmland. In 2012, strawberries starred in Santa Barbara County's agriculture sector, which was worth nearly $1.3 billion in total production value. Driscoll's has been growing strawberries for over 100 years in the Santa Maria Valley.

Another industry not to be overlooked in the history of the valley is the dairies. Young men from European countries, with few job opportunities, founded the dairy industry in the valley. Swiss-Italian and Portuguese dairymen were the backbone of all the dairy businesses right up until the last diary (DeBarnardi Dairy),

✦

Above: Kenneth Sheehy and son, Robert, loading strawberries onto the first air transport of berries out of Santa Maria, 1947. The airplane was a WWII surplus C-47.

Below: A barbeque held at Sunset Laguna Dairy Farm in the mid-1940s.

◆

Above: Farming at Union Sugar, Betteravia, California; December 1912.

Top, right: The Santa Maria Valley had a strong dairy industry.

Below: The space shuttle Enterprise *at Vandenberg Air Force Base, 1984.*

in the valley closed in 2005. The Santa Maria Valley's dairy industry is a result primarily of the Swiss. During the 1930s, arguably the pinnacle of the diary days, there were more than 60 dairies in the Santa Maria area. Most dairies were manned by Swiss-Italians with an "i" at the end of their names: Dolcini, Pezzoni, Tognazzini, Righetti, Lanini, Scolari, Zanetti, Maretti, Signorelli, Morganti, Turri, Spazzadeschi, Donati, Manni, Ambrosetti, Pinoli, Diani, Freddi, and Rollini, to name a few! The dairy industry was a seven day a week, no holiday business. Cows don't not produce milk on the weekend or holidays, dairymen remind! Milking is an everyday event. Perhaps this is why some generations "moooved" on to new trades and crafts.

The Santa Maria Valley preserved some of its original roles while transforming others. The valley's top crops by dollar value are: strawberries, wine grapes, broccoli, head lettuce, and avocados. The valley seemingly transcends time: advancing, growing, and evolving. Santa Maria is 'the little town that could' in a valley that recreates itself over and over while retaining its simplicity and balance.

Always a leader in agriculture, transformative in the transportation of produce, pioneering in aeronautics for decades as first a training ground for World War II pilots and then home to the many businesses supporting the rocket industry and Vandenberg Air Force Base, the Santa Maria Valley moves ever forward, redefining itself while maintaining a precious balance with tradition. Today our rolling hills are landscaped by mile after scenic mile of grapevines, producing some of the best wines in the industry. Owing to the cool growing climate, the valley is best known for its Pinot noir, Syrah, Chardonnay, and Pinot Blanc. Santa Maria Valley is an American viticulture area; this appellation is the oldest in this portion of California. In this region, grape growing dates back to the Mexican colonial period of the 1830s. Today, vineyards in the valley encompass 7,500 acres. Forging ever forward, the valley is robust with new industry for new generations while still serving our ageless, famous, Santa Maria Style BBQ.

CHAPTER 6

GROWING UP IN THE '60S, SANTA MARIA STYLE

Santa Maria had a population of 20,000 in 1960. John F. Kennedy was campaigning for president. Viet Nam was raging in the background of political dialog. The Civil Rights movement was taking shape and "women's lib" was a new term in the vocabulary of the nation. Hippies dotted the entire country, but feasted on summer in 1969 at Woodstock Music Festival in upper state New York. The world is waking up to the Berlin Wall, listening to the Beatles, and before the decade finished, Martin Luther King, Jr., John F. Kennedy, and Robert F. Kennedy would be assassinated. It was a transformative time to grow up in. The Santa Maria Valley will join the space race and grow with optimism.

In its first 55 years the Santa Maria Valley thrived, and, from 1950 to 1960, Santa Maria's population doubled, reaching over 20,000 souls. By the time Santa Maria Class of 1960 graduates, SMUHS will need triple the staff and have double the students. Righetti High School (RHS), will be built in the suburban community of Orcutt in 1963 to relieve overcrowding at Santa Maria High School, and RHS will graduate its first class in June 1964. Righetti's boundaries serve students from the areas of several elementary school districts, which include the community of Orcutt, portions of the city of Santa Maria, the city of Guadalupe, and the towns of Los Alamos, Sisquoc, Garey, and Casmalia, as well as a large portion of rural northern Santa Barbara county. It derived its name from lifetime resident and community leader Ernest Righetti, for his invaluable service to the valley and work on various school boards. Pioneer Valley High School, Santa Maria's third high school, opened in August 2004. The Saints of SMUHS could scarcely have known the future of their town in the heady days of the 1960s. Santa Maria had been a one high school town since 1884.

Santa Maria High's campus is located just blocks from the center of downtown. Established in 1884, Santa Maria Union High School secured this prize location and is a historic setting sprawling over 40 acres. Ever aware of their history, Santa Maria High's campus has a patio dedicated to Ida M. Blochman, teacher and botanist who collected botanical specimens extensively in the Santa Maria

◆

A postcard of Santa Maria High School, 1908, published exclusively for T. A. Jones & Son.

Valley. Some of SMUHS physical exteriors include Old Main, Wilson Gym, the Patios, the Home Ec., and the Old College. By 1962, Santa Maria Junior College, which was originally co-located on the Santa Maria High School campus enjoyed a new identity and location when Allan Hancock released Hancock Field, buildings and all, to the Junior College's trustees. When the first increment of new buildings opened, Allan Hancock College spread its wings, displaying a new name at its own site, giving the high school some much needed relief.

HANCOCK AND THE COLLEGE

Right: The Santa Maria High School campus in 1962.

Below: George Allan Hancock with baby chickens at Rosemary Farm.

Captain George Allan Hancock was one of the west's wealthiest men. His wealth was based on oil from the family's historic Rancho La Brea. La Brea was a Mexican Land Grant acquired in 1880 located near Los Angeles.

Hancock was a Renaissance man. Among his many triumphs was the founding of California Bank, later to become First Interstate Bank. He founded Rancho La Brea Oil Company and donated millions of dollars and large parcels of land to the University of Southern California. He also established the west's first educational television station and was a founding father of the Automobile Club of Southern California. Hancock was world renowned in the field of marine science and was also a farmer, dairyman, horseman, cattle and poultry rancher, oil and gas prospector, banker, manufacturer, merchant mariner, ship owner, pilot, train engineer, packer, trucker, aviator, scientist, explorer, educator, and musician.

In the Santa Maria Valley most farmers utilized dry farming techniques. Arriving in Santa Maria around 1925, Hancock introduced new irrigation methods which sent the valley into another boom time. Few men have personally directed such a diversity of interests and activities as Hancock. He established and was president of Santa Maria Farm Company, Santa Maria Valley Railroad, Santa Maria Ice & Cold Storage Company, Rosemary Farm, Rosemary Packing and La Brea Securities Company.

The College of Aeronautics, started by Hancock, trained thousands of pilots for duty during World War II. Allan Hancock College grew and was groomed as a consequence of its namesake's love of education and flying. Hancock rescued the struggling junior college from the back end of the high school campus and launched aeronautics into a new era from this location. In 1939 the junior college became the

first in California to offer its students an opportunity to learn to fly. The aeronautical training included a ground school and was done in cooperation with the Santa Maria School of Flying.

G. Allan Hancock's influence guided the college's pathway after a slow start. The roaring 20s had inspired Santa Maria educators to establish a junior college as part of the Santa Maria Union High School District. A tough and ferocious bulldog was made its mascot. The college's first curriculum of courses paralleled those offered by the University of California. Emphasis was on letters and science with an initial enrollment of six. The junior college struggled, housed in rear rooms at the high school. When the dark days of the 1930s brought a screeching halt to the flamboyant 20s, enrollment began to increase and included business, vocational courses, and later aviation. When Hollywood movie-maker Cecil B. DeMille filmed his first version of the Ten Commandments, he chose locales near here for the scenes. Santa Maria

✦

Above: Early packing was done in this Rosemary Packing Corp. warehouse with trucks bringing crates of vegetables from the fields. An earth ramp was made to lift the trucks up to the level of the dock.

Below: Hancock College of Aeronautics, Santa Maria, California, 1939. Cadets lined up for inspection before the hangar flight line.

Junior College students, under the direction of Miss Ethel Pope, created two enormous brassieres to adorn papier-mache sphinxes which were placed on sand dunes near Guadalupe and filmed in the epic. Miss Pope was director of the drama department at the junior college and is responsible for launching its outstanding dramatic reputation.

World War II received pilots from the school and although the enrollment dropped during the war years, the school gained stature in the community. At the end of both WWII and the Korean War, men returned home and found post war education at the college. Hancock helped the college continue toward its destiny and in the early 1960s Allan Hancock College

became a fully accredited two-year school. The college continues to provide quality education for valley students and much more. Santa Maria and the valley have been entertained and informed with culture, art, and current events almost since it opened the campus. Lecture series held on college grounds were of such exceptional quality that renowned speakers were often times booked. Art festivals, musical productions and foreign films, were part of the wide variety of programming that graced the campus. A performing arts complex that seats 448 was built; it featured modern lighting and sound. We know it today as Pacific Conservatory of the Performing Arts, PCPA. The Pacific Conservatory Theatre not only provides

COMMUNITY THEATRE

professional theatre year round for the Santa Maria Valley but also trains acting and technical craft workers for careers in theatre. The valley was, and is still today, treated to, and spoiled by, the vision of those first Santa Maria Valley guardians of culture.

The Santa Maria Civic Theatre, founded in 1959, edged in ahead of PCPA on the timeline, providing an additional choice for valley residents desiring a cultural experience. In 1961 the

✦

Above: What goes up must come down for redevelopment! The site of the Bank of Santa Maria, seen here in January 1928, later became home to Security First National Bank.

Below: The fire department hard at work.

Below: President Richard Nixon
during a visit to Santa Maria in 1960.

group was incorporated in the state of California as a non-profit educational organization. The civic theatre association produced four to five "Broadway" plays each year, casting local talent to perform at the association's own theatre. In 1964 "SMCT" purchased their present building from the Pacific Telephone Company and converted it to a black box theatre. The original building had only one rest room and no dressing rooms. The seats were salvaged from the burned out Santa Maria Theatre which was built in 1928. Members stripped, repainted, reupholstered, and installed the seating. The first stage lights were made from empty coffee cans painted black. From this resourceful beginning to today, decades later, the Santa Maria Civic Theatre provides local thespians with an enthusiastic audience. SMCT claims to be the longest running continuous performance group of any community theatre in the area between Ventura and Monterey. In 56 seasons the "SMCT" has produced more than 200 productions entertaining over 85,000 theatre goers in the valley.

With a plethora of educational opportunities and cultural experiences in their own backyard, Santa Maria High School graduates perceived their future was as bright as any star. Optimism was in bloom throughout the valley despite the Cold War atmosphere surrounding them nationally. As the 1960s carried on, there were

approximately 15,000 homes in Santa Maria and another 19,000 around the valley. There was an enthusiastic industrial development program being conducted by the city, and Santa Maria was attracting new and diverse industries. Once again its strategic location was enabling new industry to affordably capture major markets like Los Angeles and San Francisco from the hospitality and convenience of the Santa Maria Valley.

CHAPTER 7

SPORTS IN THE VALLEY

With a mostly male-dominated work force in the first half century of the valley's development, it should come as no surprise that sports have been a major distraction for those hard working men. As early as the 1800s, baseball was a passion and a release after long hours and hard labor. Industrial leagues formed and some small diversion from Whiskey Row was created. The Santa Maria Stars and later the Santa Maria Indians semiprofessional teams included players who made it into the big leagues throughout the United States. Other sports like swimming, basketball and football also found valuable players home-grown in the Santa Maria Valley.

Sports was a passion for many in the valley. Setsuo Aratani, a baseball enthusiast, took a team from the valley to Japan in 1927. They played 30 games and won 27. John Madden coached football at Allan Hancock College and is a former NFL football player, former Super Bowl-winning head coach (with the Oakland Raiders), former commentator for NFL telecasts, and the featured expert on a video games series bearing his name. The valley has provided excellent athletes and coaches to professional sports. Many got their start playing in little league or high school here in the Santa Maria Valley.

Les Webber was a professional baseball player, a right-handed pitcher over parts of six seasons (1942–1946, 1948) with the Brooklyn Dodgers and Cleveland Indians. He compiled a 23–19 record

✦

Standing third from left is "Lettuce King" Setsuo Aratani of Guadalupe, California. His packing labels read, "Home Run King," and "Safe at Home." Aratani's company team competed throughout California and would travel to Japan in 1927.

in 154 appearances, mostly as a relief pitcher, with a 4.19 earned run average and 141 strikeouts, Webber played one game for the 1948 World Series Champion Indians. He died in Santa Maria at the age of 71.

Teddy Davidson went from the sandlots of Santa Maria Little League all the way to the majors to pitch for the Cincinnati Reds and Atlanta Braves in the 1960s. He was attending Allan Hancock College when he was signed by the Reds.

James R. Lonborg, born in Santa Maria in 1942, was drafted by the Boston Red Sox in 1963. His pitching debut was in April of 1965. During his career he played for the Red Sox, Phillies, and the Brewers before retiring in 1979.

Bryn Nelson Smith was an alum of Allan Hancock College and a former professional baseball player who pitched in the Major Leagues from 1981-1993. Selected in the 49th round in 1973 as the 779th player, Smith signed by the Baltimore Orioles as a free agent, was traded three years later and made his Major League debut with Montreal, then on to the St. Louis Cardinals in 1989 before finishing his career in Colorado in June 1993, after becoming the first winning pitcher in Colorado Rockies history, defeating Montreal, 11-4, on April 9, 1993. He pitched seven shut-out innings, at age 37. Bryn attended Alvin Elementary and Fesler Junior High, before enrolling in Santa Maria Union High School where he graduated in 1973.

He is said to be one of the best defensive third basemen in the 1990's. Born in 1967 Robin Mark Ventura attended Righetti High School in Orcutt and was picked tenth in the 1988 Major League Baseball Draft by the White Sox. In 1988, a member of the U.S. Olympic team in Seoul, he hit .409 to help the U.S. win the Gold Medal. The same year he won the Golden Spikes Award, a Major League Baseball Players Association award honoring players with exceptional athletic ability and exemplary sportsmanship. He won six Golden Gloves, an award handed out to players who have a superior fielding season. A total of 18 Gold Gloves are awarded each year with Gloves going to one player at each position for both the National League and American League. Ventura was inducted into the Oklahoma State University's Hall of Fame in February 1998. Robin Ventura played for the Chicago White Sox, New York Mets, New York Yankees and the Los Angeles Dodgers before

Above: John Madden, Hancock College assistant football coach, 1961.

Right: Chicago White Sox Manager Robin Ventura, 2012.

retiring and being named the 39th manager for the Chicago White Sox on October 6, 2011.

William "Bill" Bertka, the former Santa Maria Golden Dukes, was the Hancock College men's basketball coach from 1954-57. He finished with a 43-game winning streak and the state championship, before he left to coach at Kent State. Bertka is the current veteran Los Angeles Lakers head scout.

It was high school coach Bob McCutcheon who spotted a tall, lanky, boy standing in line to

TED DAVIDSON • PITCHER

REDS

EXPOS

JIM LONBORG • PITCHER

RED SOX

◆

Top, left: Les Weber.

Top, right: Teddy Davidson.

Bottom, left: Bryn Smith.

Bottom, right: James Lonborg

register as a freshman at SMUH, in September 1954. John, "Rudy" Rudometkin was born in Santa Maria in 1940. He attended Alvin and Cook Street Schools and El Camino Junior High before he was noticed in that high school line. He spent one year playing basketball at Allan Hancock College before attending the University of Southern California. He made both high school and college history, breaking and making records

of all kinds. Rudometkin went on to become a professional basketball player, for the New York Knickerbockers (1962–63, 1963–64, and part of the 1964–65 seasons) and San Francisco Warriors (signed as a free agent on February 2, 1965) in the National Basketball Association (NBA). He was selected in the second round as the 11th pick in the 1962 NBA Draft by the Knicks and spent three seasons playing in the league. Rudometkin was nicknamed "the Reckless Russian" by Chick Hearn, the legendary Los Angeles Lakers broadcaster who used to broadcast USC men's basketball games before transitioning to the NBA. In May 2001, John "Rudy" Rudometkin IV was inducted into USC's Hall of Fame.

Mark Brunell graduated from Saint Joseph High School in Orcutt. He was selected by the Green Bay Packers in the fifth round of the 1993 NFL Draft. Brunell was a three-time Pro Bowl selection with the Jacksonville Jaguars. He also played for the Washington Redskins, New Orleans Saints, and New York Jets. In 2009, he earned a Super Bowl ring as the backup quarterback and holder for the Saints' Super Bowl XLIV winning team.

The valley also produced its share of amateur athletes for the Olympics. John Paulsen and Eugene Lenz were world class swimmers competing in the Summer Olympics in 1932 and 1960, respectively. Paulsen graduated from Santa Maria High in 1933 and Lenz in 1955. Lenz attended Miller Street School and El Camino Junior High before he enrolled in SMUHS. Eugene Lenz was inducted into Cal Poly's Hall of Fame in 1987. He held 14 school records and was Cal Poly's first All-American Swimmer, winning the California State College Swimming Championship in three different events in four years.

Sports careers were launched from a range of platforms in the Santa Maria Valley. The infrastructure for success was in place; all you needed was a dream and a willingness to work hard.

◆

Right: John "Rudy" Rudometkin, Hancock College, 1959.

Bottom, left: Mark Brunell starting quarterback for the St. Joseph High School 1985-87.

Bottom, right: Eugene Lenz, Olympic swimmer, 1932.

CHAPTER 8

VANDENBERG AIR FORCE BASE

After its transfer from the Army to the Air Force in 1957, Camp Cooke became Cooke Air Force Base. On October 5, 1958, Cooke Air Force Base became Vandenberg AFB, the nation's first ballistic missile training center. The transition from army camp to missile base solidified in December 1958 when Vandenberg AFB successfully launched its first missile. Vandenberg launched the world's first polar orbiting satellite, Discoverer I, on February 28, 1959. The Discoverer series of satellites provided other significant firsts for Vandenberg. In August 1960 the data capsule was ejected from Discoverer XIII in orbit and recovered from the Pacific Ocean to become the first man-made object ever retrieved from space. A week later, on August 19th, the descending capsule from Discoverer XIV was snared by an aircraft in flight for the first air recovery in history.

Shrouded in a cover story of scientific research, Discoverer was actually the cover name for Corona, America's first photo reconnaissance satellite program. The publicized Discoverer series came to an end in January 1962. The cover story for Discoverer had simply worn out.

Santa Maria was experiencing the early days of the Cold War. An atmosphere of fear pervaded the American population and one of paranoia for the United States Government. Our parents and grandparents had endured WWII and the attack on Pearl Harbor. Now it seemed in the 1960s that we needed to prepare for a nuclear version of global war. Intercontinental Ballistic Missiles, (ICBMs) were a rapid response weapon with a mission and strategy to handle just that. Vandenberg AFB was a centerpiece to preventing Soviet attacks. Vandenberg was so strategic to national defense that President Kennedy came to get a firsthand view of its potential. Located roughly 22 miles from Santa

♦

A double missile launch at Vandenberg Air Force Base.

Cpl. Joe Di Maggio Playing At Camp Cooke, Calif.

◆

Top, left: A postcard from Camp Cooke, 1944. Baseball great Joe Dimaggio spent part of his World War II service at Camp Cooke.

Top, right: With eyes to the sky: President Kennedy, Secretary of Defense Robert McNamara, and General Thomas Power watch a missile launch at Vandenberg Air Force Base, March 23, 1962.

Maria, VAFB's mission and growth would positively impact the entire region. The Santa Maria Valley doubled in population as the base became more and more valuable to national defense. Shrouded in secrecy, there was no hiding or denying that the new air force base was bringing a different future to the valley. Vandenberg's location provided a site at which a launch could reach polar orbit without the booster rocket ever flying over a populated area. A launch from California's central coast doesn't fly over another landmass until it reaches South Pole. Launches from Vandenberg fly southward, allowing payloads to be placed in high-inclination orbits such as polar or Sun-synchronous orbit, which allow full global coverage on a regular basis and are often used for weather, Earth observation, and reconnaissance satellites. With satellites in polar orbits, over time the entire planet could be viewed. The result was a bird's eye view of possible Soviet threats to our nation, well worth a presidential visit in the 1960s.

The economic effect on the valley by Vandenberg AFB was tremendous. An Air Force report on one month, May 1964, tallied spending in Santa Maria and the nearby communities as $308,083 by active military personnel and $259,418 by civilian contractors associated with the base. Adding to this monthly influx, it was further reported that by 1966 nearly 41% of the Vandenberg work force,

who resided off-base, were living in the Santa Maria area. Santa Maria was facing another growth spurt and welcoming it with open arms and big plans. Set-backs did come but Vandenberg's location placed them in position for the next big development in our pursuit of the stars. The valley developers took bigger and bigger steps to ensure they were ready for the future.

In 1972, Vandenberg was selected as the West Coast Space Shuttle launch and landing site. Excitement for the base's new mission was expansive, and the valley reveled in the exciting news. Once again disappointment knocked. SLC-6 was still being prepared for its first shuttle launch, targeted for 15 October 1986, when the Space Shuttle Challenger disaster occurred on January 28, 1986, just 73 seconds into flight, grounding the Shuttle fleet and setting in motion a chain of events that ultimately led to the cancellation of all west coast shuttle launches.

Before the tragedy, the valley was blooming and booming as a space center and technology hub. In 1968 even the *Santa Maria Times* placed a reference to Vandenberg's main mission technology under its title, "Missile Capital of the Free World." Just as quickly as the excitement took off in the early 1960s, it crashed in the mid-80s leaving the valley to recover from a significant and devastating loss. So much infrastructure had been prepared over that period for this high flying industry, and it came to an abrupt and screeching halt in an instant. Business and housing values tumbled in free fall, and the valley stiffened to the disappointment.

CHAPTER 9

SANTA MARIA COMES OF AGE

BROADWAY

One of the first highways designated by the BPR (Bureau of Public Roads) in 1925, US 101 stretches from San Diego north to the Canadian border. U.S. Route 101 is one of the last remaining and longest U.S. Routes still active in California and is the longest highway of any type in the state. Originally it ran through the middle of Santa Maria as Broadway. The relocation of US 101 bypassing downtown Santa Maria on the east solved traffic problems for many local residents for many years and helped to induce growth of the city to the east, but it was a death knoll for many tourist-serving businesses on Broadway. Santa Maria was lined in the early 1960s with hotels and motels that watched their business become dependent on exits and off ramps to bring guests past their doors.

◆

Broadway looking north in 1965.

LET IT GROW

The valley economy in the 1960s had its eyes in the sky with the Space Race, but agriculture continued to be important back here on Earth. In 1961 the fastest growing field was the frozen food industry. Field-to-Freezer vegetable industry was a business phenomenon. Like a new ice age, frozen water was the single thing that allowed for so much in the way we could distribute food. Ice expanded the agricultural markets for Guadalupe, Santa Maria, and Lompoc in the valley. Efficient valley farmers were just as savvy and competitive in the economy as the factories, freeways, and the gigantic missile base that was eating up the workforce and escalating the population. The business of growing and freezing lima beans, broccoli, peas, and other vegetables reached 50 million pounds annually. Agriculture was redefining itself, replacing the human and horse labor of the nineteenth

✦

Top: Colonial Motel.

Middle: John Inglis freezer plant on the west side of Santa Maria.

Bottom: The Highway 101 off-ramp at Stowell Road looking North, c. 1995.

century with new procedures and new machines. Ag was a healthy competitor in the economy, in spite of new housing that covered hundreds of acres, even with the air base's rapid development as a missile center, and notwithstanding a land gobbling freeway that deviated from Broadway, trekking to the east of Santa Maria and consuming agricultural rich land on its way to the Santa Maria River.

Owen Stewart Rice was certainly one of Santa Maria's favorite sons. Rice and his father merged their interests into Owen T. Rice and Son, which eventually became OSR Enterprises and has been farming in the valley for more than 100 years. Competition for agricultural land came from

multiple directions. In late 1963 Columbia Records opened a vinyl record pressing plant in Santa Maria smack in the middle of a former bean field owned by Rice. A $6-million pressing plant and warehouse; the facility was also used as the shipping center for the Columbia Record Club. At one time described as the biggest record manufacturing plant in the western United States, Columbia was in business for eighteen years before a steep decline in demand for records closed its doors in 1981.

The valley began as an agrarian society and nothing could steal the prosperity of the earth from these dedicated farmers. Making space for new industry while cultivating the fields was

◆

Above: The $6-million Columbia Records plant on E. Stowell Road, 1963. To the right is the Southern Counties Gas Company plant.

Below: Bean and grain harvest stored along the Pacific Coast Railway on North Depot, c. 1907.

commonplace and common sense to the valley residents. After G. Allan Hancock made irrigation successful in the 1920s, there wasn't anything to stop the growing prosperity on the rich lands of the valley. More than half of the lima beans produced for the United States markets were grown in Santa Barbara County, most of them in the Santa Maria Valley. This amounted to more than 5,300 tons of tiny lima beans, more than $53 million in vegetables, and over $6 million in strawberries in 1973.

Pinquito beans are believed to be a cross between a pink bean and a small white bean. How they came to be grown in the Santa Maria Valley remains a mystery. Some say the beans were given as a gift by a Mexican cowboy to an early Swiss-Italian settlers. Others suggest that a lady brought the plants with her when she migrated to the valley from Europe. The only certainty is that pinquito beans flourish in the fertile soil and mild climate of the Santa Maria Valley, which is the only place where pinquito beans are commercially grown. Pinquito beans are an essential component of the traditional Santa Maria Style Barbecue menu.

LOCAL HANGOUTS, HAUNTS, AND HIDE-AWAYS

Park Aire was a drive-in movie theater. A drive-in theater is a form of cinema structure

consisting of a large outdoor movie screen, a projection booth, a concession stand and a large parking area for automobiles. Within this enclosed area, customers viewed movies from the privacy and comfort of their cars. Some drive-ins had small playgrounds for children and a few picnic tables or benches. Drive-ins reached peaks in the 1960s. Originally, a movie's sound was provided by speakers on the screen and later by an individual speaker hung from the window of each car, which would be attached by a wire. This system was superseded by the more economical and less damage-prone method of broadcasting the soundtrack at a low output power on AM or FM radio to be picked up by a car radio. Park Aire provided a perfect social gathering spot. Eating and cars went together like "love and marriage" in the late '50s and early '60s. If you had a car, you had everything you needed to grow up. Motoring from Leo's Drive In and Fountain to Rick's Rancho was a well-worn circuit, followed by cruising over to the Park Aire for the "entertainment." After the movie places like Bill's Take Out, built in 1953 at the corner of North Broadway and El Camino Street in Santa Maria were popular. One could get a Billy Burger for change. In '53, Broadway was still Highway 101 and these popular Drive Ins were great turn-arounds for teens with carloads of friends cruising around connecting with each other, pausing along the way at other great haunts like Foster's Freeze and A&W.

Growing up in the '60s was fun!

✦

The exterior and interior of Rick's Rancho, c. 1955.

◆

Above: The A&W Root Beer stand.

Middle: Velva Freeze.

Bottom: Fay's School of Beauty.

CHAPTER 10

THE CHANGING FACE OF THE VALLEY

CENTRAL CITY REDEVELOPMENT PROJECT

Downtown merchants were uncertain of their prospects and prosperity in relationship to the multi-million dollar, nine square block, shopping mall that redevelopment fans proclaimed was the heart of the Central City project. Thomas P. Weldon, Jr., initiated the Housing and Urban Development (HUD) project in 1970 to rid Santa Maria of the 'blight' that was Whiskey Row. He was followed by Gordon Gill in 1974. Complaints were made and misunderstandings developed into deep mistrust as the project began displacing the old to make way for the new. The merchants hired local attorney Rodney Melville to sort out the way forward. When the dust settled, it was clear that merchants and developer were at odds. Local businesses would not be able to buy into the mall as they believed had first been proposed. Merchants uniformly agreed that if the project had been originally represented the way it turned out, then this development would never have taken place. Nevertheless the project moved forward, blocking downtown business with road closures, restricted parking and other improvements. Owners of businesses on Main and Broadway held their breath hoping to survive the redevelopment project that had once looked so promising for them. There was plenty of name calling, some for the developer Ernest W. Hahn who seemed rigid in his business model. It was Gordon Gill who sat in the hot seat and delivered the bad news to merchants, and it was Thomas Weldon, Jr., who took the brunt of criticism for the reported misinformation that divided merchants from the developer.

Many merchants began to face the prospect of going out of business after believing they had been assured that they could buy back their own land and buildings. Now it appeared they had cleared the way for their own competition. The city council continued to try to bring the ends together. The summer of 1974 was confusing, as all parties learned the ins and outs, and ups and downs, of government redevelopment projects. Urban renewal projects are unique in their development because, in

normal development of a regional center, like a mall, the developer will purchase a bare piece of ground and install the improvements and construct buildings. In an urban renewal project, many things must occur: land must be planned for the development, followed by appraisals of all land within the area; followed by acquiring the land and relocating every individual, family and business before construction can begin. Despite the many hiccups, the project went forward successfully. Santa Maria Town Center is recognized as the largest enclosed shopping center on the Central Coast of California, with about 600,000 square feet. It consists of 25 acres of retail space, over 65 stores, and 3,200 parking spaces. It opened in 1976 with Gottschalks and Sears as anchors. May Company California, later Robinsons-May and now Macy's, was added in 1990. Gottschalks closed in 2009. In 2012, the mall was sold to Spinoso Group, who began renovations on the former Gottschalks wing. The old Gottschalks building was razed to the ground and a movie theater rose in its place. This new wing has plans to include entertainment venues such as a soccer training facility, batting cages and other sporting venues. The Central City Redevelopment project is still under perfection!

Above: Gordon Gil, 1967.

Below: Beginning in the late 1960s, Santa Maria entered into a period of redevelopment that would last for decades.

♦

Top and middle: Numerous businesses were sacrificed to the Santa Maria down town redevelopment project which started in January 1968. Redevelopment continued into the 1980s with the removal of Weaver's Camera Shop, Et Cetera, the Christian Science Reading Room, Gardner and Wheaton's Rexall Drug Store, and the Santa Maria Theatre.

Bottom: Hilary Burke adds stacks of petitions to those carried by George Smith. A total of 13,700 signatures were collected, with 11,298 needed to certify an election on the county split.

COUNTY SPLIT

The only topic that drew more discussion in the 70s than the Downtown Project was something called the "County Split." In the 1970s, the north and the south of Santa Barbara County were at such odds there seemed a chance that the county might splinter. The panel in charge of depicting the county's possible destiny was Los Padres Formation Review Commission. It was an inequity of county resource distribution that drew sharp criticism from North County residents. North County felt it had been drained of financial resources in order to build facilities in the South County. The commission was on a mission to bring forth the facts and realities of the two-county proposal.

First in evidence is the need for a county seat in the new Los Padres County. While Los Alamos

enjoyed consideration briefly, it was soon decided that locating the county seat on Foster Road in the center of Orcutt was the best solution. Next in consideration were the tax hikes that would ensue with a county split. Ultimately it would be the dollars that would make sense to voters, legislators, and the feuding factions. Splitting the county was not going to save either the old or the new county any money. In fact there would be at least a modest increase in spending for both leading to tax hikes for all concerned. Since the whole ruckus had arisen over money, it seemed logical that in the final analysis it would be money on which the decision would ultimately turn. The big positive for the split was when it was

Oxnard). Conclusions were that a proposed new county was viable and that it will be more expensive to run two counties than one.

Pro-split forces were facing a tough fight in the November elections. The biggest visible support for the county split was the Santa Maria Chamber of Commerce, which long had felt the South County had restricted the North County growth. By the numbers a split would provide Los Padres County with 41% of Santa Barbara County's population, 51% of its land and 35% of its assessed valuation.

The commission submitted in late June its official report, a 300 page document for voters to review for resolution on the November ballot. The official language for the split read like this (July 13, 1978 *Santa Maria Times*), "For the formation of Los Padres County with authority to levy a maximum property tax rate equal to that of Santa Barbara County for general purposes, unless otherwise provided by law." Yes or No. The paperwork done, the next few months were devoted to rhetoric on the part of both sides. The "split debate" raged on. Measure A, as the split was proposed to voters approached its moment of truth. At midnight on November 7, 1978, results showed 9,393 votes for the county split and 7,623 against it among voters of 62 precincts in the Fifth District. It was clear that the "split" had won the heartland of what was hoped to be Los Padres County. But it suffered a resounding defeat in the rest of North County. In Santa Ynez and Lompoc the vote was 4,448 for and 11,094 against. North County had defeated the split on its own; South Coast votes were of no consequence in the face of these numbers. Citizens to Preserve Santa Barbara County had prevailed; Los Padres County was never born, but the idea of a split was not forgotten.

ALL-AMERICA CITY

Santa Maria was named as an All-America City on June 20, 1998. The All-America City Award is given by the National Civic League annually to ten communities in the United States. It recognizes groups whose citizens work together to identify and tackle broad challenges and achieve uncommon outcomes. Winners can be neighborhoods, towns, villages, cities, counties, or regions. The All-America City Award is the

determined that the new county could stand on its own without problems, but there would be no savings to bank. The extensive commission study was covered broadly in the press as well as in every coffee shop, barber shop, and location where two or more gathered.

The commission's job was to examine the facts and report to the voters. The law required that two commissioners come from the proposed county (Helen Pedotti and W. Mark Durley, Jr.), two from the remaining county (Mary K. Wright and John Kay), and one from outside the county (Chairman John Flynn of oldest community recognition program in the nation. The program was created in 1949 and, since its inception, more than 600 communities have been named All-America Cities. Each year, interested communities may submit a comprehensive package based on published criteria. Deserving communities are named as finalists, and the year's ten award winners are named from that pool of applicants.

Being named as an All-America City does not mean that we have a perfect and flawless city. The designation honors the way people care for their community and take charge of their future prosperity. It recognizes partnerships and progress, creativeness and cooperation, resolve and pride, qualities that create the cornerstone of American citizenship.

While Santa Maria's designation extends into perpetuity, the City of Santa Maria maintains its All-America City Committee to create and coordinate community-based projects which address the 10 components of the All-America City Civic Index. The ten components are Citizen Participation, Community Leadership, Government Performance, Volunteerism and Philanthropy, Inter-Group Relations, Civic Education, Community Information Sharing, Capacity for Cooperation and Consensus Building, Community Vision and Pride, and Inter-Community Cooperation. The City intends to remain deserving of this designation in perpetuity.

A WOMAN MAYOR IN SANTA MARIA

In 1960, the world of American women was limited in almost every respect, from family life to the workplace. American women who worked in 1960 were largely limited to jobs as teacher, nurse, or secretary. Women's Lib a passé term today, became a ceiling cracking rant of the 1970s. Politics remained solidly "man's" work through the '70s in Santa Maria. In 1973 in Santa Maria, Frances Beaver, the first woman president of the Santa Maria Valley Chamber of Commerce made her bid to become the city's first woman mayor. She was 58 years old, the owner of a highly successful Santa Maria real estate business since 1959 and had lived in Santa Maria for the past 30 years. The only woman council member since the city's incorporation in 1905 was Sadie

◆

Sadie West, the first woman to serve on the Santa Maria City Council.

West, a building contractor who served on the council in the '30s. The idea of women in politics was new and rare having only just received the right to vote via the 19th Amendment which was ratified by Congress August 1920. The March 5th ballot of 1974 was the first time that the mayor would be elected by popular vote. After a few snafus by other potential candidates, only Elwin

Mussell, with two terms on the council, and Frances Beaver were certain to be on the ballot. There was no woman mayor in the city's 68 year history. As fate would have it, a woman mayor wouldn't be elected until Alice Patino in 2012, Santa Maria's 107th year. Mayor Patino, a homegrown Santa Marian and only the second woman ever elected to the City Council, captured 50 percent of the 14,516 votes cast in the mayor's race to notch a solid victory over fellow challengers Mike Cordero at 34%, Marty Mariscal at 9% and Dan Gebhart at 6%. Frances Beaver only managed to capture 30% of the vote in 1974 in her bid to be the first lady mayor of Santa Maria. Sadie West, a council member around eighty years ago, was the first woman to grace the City Council. Alice Patino was appointed to the council in 1999 and subsequently elected. Hilda Zacarias followed in 2006, Terri Zuniga in 2012, and Etta Waterfield captured one of two open seats on the council in 2014 with 33.31% of the votes to become the fifth councilwoman.

LOOKING FORWARD

To some degree, we are all pioneers. Each generation marvels at the sparsity of conveniences and comforts the previous group endured. If you pounded out your senior paper on a manual typewriter or know how to write your name in cursive, you understand the concept and you are a pioneer by someone's standards. The valley has been home to some families and businesses for multiple generations; it continues to evolve, welcoming new families to integrate with the firmly established. The valley is a colorful festival for feasting the senses from our rolling hills that transition from the dry earth tones of summer to the lush green ones of winter. At the foot of those hills, flat land sweeps forward, speckled red with strawberries. Cruising California Highway 135 on any given weekend one sees in the landscape innumerable swatches of grapevines bobbing in and out of every crease. It can be hard to stay on the road with so much to take in, but stay alert; deer cavort along the roadside, a safe distance from the beef that grazes serenely atop the ridgelines, trodding along well-worn paths. The sky is filled with sunshine and some pretty serious raptors and scavengers! Through the valley, change is the only constant as you slip into the cooler breezes near our coastline. If you live here, you never want to leave and if you visit, you are going to want to live here!

Above: Alice Patino, mayor of Santa Maria.

Below: The beauty of the Santa Maria Valley.

CHAPTER 11

VALLEY TOWNS, RANCHEROS & PLACES OF COMMERCE

At the end of the 19th century, the valley was rich with towns, farms, and homesteads. No one town was any more likely to fail or succeed than another. Influences that affected the outcome of these "upstarts" of civilization in the valley were as varied as the personalities connected to them. A handful are thriving today, others are ghost towns, and some have vanished altogether.

◆

Suey School, 1893.

LA GRACIOSA

La Graciosa, which was located south of present-day Orcutt, was the valley's first town. It had a store and saloon in 1868 and a post office which began service in 1872. Soon after the post office, a voting precinct was established, the townsite was surveyed, and 40 lots were laid out and put up for sale. La Graciosa's residents had wrongly assumed that they were building on government land; inopportunely, La Graciosa was laid out on the Todos Santos y San Antonio land grant. Businessman and land baron Henry Mayo Newhall acquired both Rancho Suey and Todos Santos y San Antonio in 1877. He served suits of ejectment on all the inhabitants adding $40,000 in damages as a kicker. Townspeople packed up and moved away, and La Graciosa was no more. Those early displaced pioneers' descendants can revel in the final disposition of the land that included the valley's first town of La Graciosa. In 1882, H.M. Newhall died and management of the Ranchos Todos Santos Y San Antonio passed to his sons who, a year after his death, formed Newhall Land and Farming Company. In 1942 they were forced to sell the land to the United States Government for the creation of a wartime army training base, Camp Cooke. The Newhall's lost their claim and Todos Santos Y San Antonio became government land.

BICKNELL

Bicknell is a ghost town mostly located on the old Careaga family ranch in proximity of the Orcutt Oil Field south of Santa Maria. The town was named for John Dustin Bicknell, an attorney, real estate agent, and investor. Bicknell was a company town built for oil workers in the early years of the 20th century but abandoned in the mid-1930s, becoming a ghost town in the valley.

◆

Above: Bicknell, 1923.

Below: Guadalupe Home, 1912.

GUADALUPE

Diego Olivera and Teodoro Arellanes were grantees of Rancho Guadalupe in 1840. The grant extended along the Pacific coast and encompassed present-day Guadalupe. Following the drought of 1864, Rancho Guadalupe passed into the hands of the family of José Joaquín Estudillo and his wife, Juana Martínez de Estudillo. In 1866, Juana Martínez de Estudillo, whose mother was a sister of Teodoro Arellanes, bailed José Teodoro Arellanes son, Antonio Arellanes, out of foreclosure, by acquiring Rancho Guadalupe. In 1867, José Joaquín Estudillo's son-in-law, John B. Ward, who was married to Concepcion Estudillo, started farming operations on Rancho Guadalupe. He built a two-story adobe and is credited with constructing the valley's first fences. Fences were unknown in this part of the country. The first ones were made of willow

wood and cottonwood tied together with rawhide. These fences were called 'worm' fences. Ward's time on Guadalupe was short. The following year, 1868, Guadalupe Rancho fell into receivership yet again. In 1870, Teodoro LeRoy, established ownership.

LeRoy quickly sold off portions of the rancho starting the first influx of dairymen and farmers to the valley. The town of Guadalupe was soon laid out. Guadalupe in 1874 was a village of about 100 dwellings, six stores, one fruit shop, two hotels, five saloons, a post office, a Wells Fargo & Company express office, two livery stables, and a blacksmith shop. Guadalupe was settled by pioneers of many unique backgrounds: European, Chinese, Filipino, Japanese, and Mexican. The small town was incorporated as the city of Guadalupe on May 19, 1946. The city name honors Our Lady of Guadalupe, the title given to the Virgin Mary. Today the city has a population of approximately seven thousand. Guadalupe is economically and socially tied to the city of Santa Maria, which is ten miles to the east.

POINT SAL

Point Sal, near the city of Guadalupe, consists of approximately 80 acres and includes just over 1 1/2 miles of ocean frontage. Lands above the beach and rocky shoreline have extremely steep slopes, and landslides are prevalent. The area was given its name by George Vancouver in 1792 in honor of his friend Hermenegildo Sal. The point was discovered accidently by Ensign Sal in a dense fog which still often pervades and engulfs the point. In 1864 Eliza Clayton married Charles Haskell Clark. Her father purchased and bestowed Point Sal on them as a wedding gift.

They settled on the land and built a wharf in 1871. Point Sal throve with activity when C. H. Clark and W.D. Harriman opened Clark's Warf to receive lumber to help build the nearby town of Central City. All of the lumber for the first houses in the Santa Maria Valley was from boats at Point Sal. By 1874 farmers from Guadalupe and nearby could haul their harvest, mostly grain, for shipment from this newly constructed wharf. Although it was wrecked during a storm in 1876, it was immediately rebuilt. As many as 120 wagons, pulled by four-, six-, and eight-horse teams, could be seen daily during the grain harvesting season, moving slowly from the valley to Point Sal and coming back. A little town, Morrito, briefly flourished on the point, with two or three cottages, several store-houses, a boarding house and a post office. A school was located nearby as well. The wharf was 800 feet long and 20 feet above the water, but the breakers literally ripped it to splinters in 1876. The point remained in service until about 1882 when Clark and Harriman sold it to the Pacific Coast Railway.

CHUTE LANDING

Chute Landing was about a mile to the north of Clark's Wharf and fifteen miles distance from then Central City (Santa Maria). It consisted of an elevated framework projecting from a cliff more than 60 feet with an elevation of 80 feet. When it opened for shipping, freight to San Francisco was fifty cents cheaper per unit via

◆

Above: A gold mine 2.5 miles from Point Sal.

Below: Grain and gypsum were shipped from Chute Landing, north of Casmalia. The ship is the Bonita, c. 1878.

Chute's Landing than by rail. In 1881, 8,000 tons of grain were shipped from the chute landing. After the Pacific Coast Railway reached Santa Maria in 1882, Pt. Sal and Chute's Landing were no longer needed, the harvest could now be carried by rail to Port Harford (Port San Luis) affordably. The wharves' purpose gone, the residents abandoned the area for work and prosperity in other locations in the valley.

BETTERAVIA

Today, Betteravia is a road in Santa Maria. A few longstanding valley residents remember the town of Betteravia and its significance in the valley at the end of the 19th century. There was great importance and extreme excitement associated with the beet root. Betteravia, located six miles west of Santa Maria, was born when the Union Sugar Company selected the area to build the biggest industrial complex the area had ever known to refine sugar from sugar beets. The Union Sugar Company, incorporated in September 1897 and with headquarters in San Francisco, chose its name to signify the union of the Santa Barbara and San Luis Obispo county sugar production areas. Betteravia was a company town that existed for nearly ninety years. At one time this community supported a population of 350 residents. Community

infrastructure consisted of 65 cottages, a hotel, a church, a schoolhouse, a post office, an amusement hall, a general store, a gasoline station, and a fire department. The sugar beet was a major regional agricultural and railroad freight crop in both Santa Barbara and San Luis Obispo counties during the 20th century.

In 1950, the Union Sugar Company decided it no longer wanted to remain in the renting business and gave notice to all residents to evacuate. Homes were sold for an average of $50. Most of the homes were bought by their occupants and relocated. About 1988, the plant, then owned by Imperial Holly (aka: Imperial Sugar), suffered a dust explosion and fire, which resulted in the injury of eight employees, seven critically. After the explosion the decline was rapid. The sun set on the town of Betteravia; following the closure of the sugar plant in 1993, Betteravia became known as a ghost town with many vacant and demolished buildings echoing the past alongside rusting equipment and a missing lake.

GAREY

About 1889 a pioneer nurseryman from Los Angeles, Thomas A. Garey, organized a land company which bought land on the east side of the valley. Very large orchards were planted around the townsite that would bear his name.

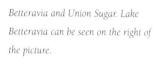

Betteravia and Union Sugar. Lake Betteravia can be seen on the right of the picture.

Garey is located about 10 miles southeast of Santa Maria and 5 miles north of Sisquoc. The town consisted of a hotel, a blacksmith shop, a store and, of course, a saloon. The trees of the orchards did well for the first few years, and the fruit was an excellent quality, but the dry years of 1897-98 were their undoing. There was no means for irrigation and the trees were eventually lost. After the orchards failed at Garey, some of the land was planted to beans, alfalfa, and grain; by 1905 Union Sugar had leased a large portion to grow sugar beets. Garey never developed as a town. In 1894, for a brief period, the Southern Pacific Railroad, having reached San Luis Obispo, was studying routes through the central coast. One of the proposed routes surveyed was through Garey. It would have made for a shorter route than the one finally accepted, but challenging the mountains through Gaviota Pass to the coast, was an obstacle that dissuaded the SP, and so the route, though longer, went through Guadalupe and south through the Casmalia Hills, bypassing even Santa Maria by nine miles. In the 2010 United States Census Garey had a population of 68; not a ghost town, but close.

CAMP COOKE

Camp Cooke was a coastal army base that opened in October of 1941. Cooke was a Civil War hero, Major General Philip St. George Cooke. There were 36,000 men stationed at the camp during the height of its service. The United States Army stationed and trained 170,000 troops at Camp Cooke 1941-46. The Army acquired vast acreage southwest of Santa Maria extending from Point Sal to Jalama Creek and including most of Rancho Todos Santos y San Antonio. Responding to war in Europe and to Japanese aggression in China and the Pacific, the United States was rapidly expanding its armed forces and military facilities. Eventually Camp Cooke housed the 6th, 11th, 13th and 20th Armored Divisions, the 86th and 97th Infantry Divisions, and the 2nd Filipino Infantry Regiment. In 1944-46, a prisoner of war camp was operated for captured German soldiers and Italian belligerents. In 1945, 9,000 inmates were at a maximum security Army disciplinary barracks under the command of Camp Cooke officials. Later this became the Lompoc Federal Penitentiary.

The years from 1946 to 1950 were so quiet that Camp Cooke looked like a ghost town. In, August of 1950 troops began training for the Korean War, and the camp was busy again until 1953. The camp closed and was transferred to the United States Air Force in 1957. The transformation of the army camp to a ballistic missile training center began. It was projected that the center would bring thousands of people and hundreds of thousands of dollars into the valley. The new facility was christened Vandenberg Air Force Base October 5, 1958. Camp Cooke was in the history books.

◆

Above: Loading sugar beets onto trucks at Betteravia.

Below: Personnel from Camp Cooke and the Santa Maria Army Air Base playing Donkey baseball during World War II. Admission was by supplying an item for the scrap drive.

◆

Above: A tent city at Camp Cooke, March 1944.

Below: A well-known landmark of Sisquoc, the Sisquoc Mercantile Company.

SISQUOC

Sisquoc is located east of U.S. Route 101 about 15 miles southeast of Santa Maria and 5 miles south of Garey. The Chumash Indians called this area "Sisquoc," which meant "gathering place," or alternatively "quail." There are many references to the Chumash language in the naming of towns and rivers in the valley; determining a single translation is an inexact science! Dating back to the 1850's Sisquoc was part of a Mexican land grant. The post office named Sisquoc opened in January 1881 with Frederick Wickenden as postmaster. Sisquoc has a fire station, a church, a preschool-8 school, called Benjamin Foxen, home of the Bobcats, and a store. Sisquoc has a microclimate with mild weather year round. First used as a stock area, then for wheat, fruit orchards and beans. The population was 183 at the 2010 census. The town is at the intersection of Palmer Road and Foxen Canyon Road, at the southwestern edge of the floodplain of the Sisquoc River. Sisquoc is predominantly an agricultural land use area, well known for vineyards and strawberry fields, while the hills to the south and west contain the Cat Canyon Oil Field. Wildlife near Sisquoc includes bobcats, coyotes, mountain lions, rabbits, and gophers. The families of Sisquoc have remained for generations.

BLOCHMAN CITY

Blochman City was an educational phenomenon located on the Palmer Oil Company lease in Cat Canyon. It was customary in the early days for an oil company to build a camp when oil was discovered and a field ready to develop. Housing was built for married men, bunkhouses for the single ones. Boarding houses, stores, and schools also appeared in these make-shift 'towns.' Blochman City was a progressive way to give practical experience to students at Blochman School. Bina Fuller and Teresa Bruce believed their students would need practical experiences to compete in the real world. Ranging in ages from 6-16 and grades 1 through 9, with the support of their community, Blochman City was born. The classes constructed actual buildings in which business would take place. The oil lease on which the school was located agreed to lend the land for this city. Boys learned how to survey and prepared streets and lots upon which buildings would stand. Merchants in nearby communities donated construction materials and even merchandise for the store shelves. The streets, it was decided by the students, were to be paved and curbed. Regulation sized curbs were constructed; the students made the forms and poured the concrete themselves. Blochman City had ten buildings: post office, bank, store, health department, city hall and newspaper office, florist shop, information center, a museum and two model homes. Each building measured about 8 x 10 feet.

Each business had its own bookkeeping system. Paper money was circulated to pay students who earned by working in the city. There were numerous positions of authority from postmaster to bank president. With the money earned, students purchased food samples and other supplies. They were also encouraged to save money to purchase their own property. A miniature forest was planted around the city. The children took care of the forest and also constructed a park which included a pond with water lilies.

To study and better understand our voting system, students learned to use ballots to elect important positions like mayor, police chief, or chamber of commerce president. These elected officials met to solve city problems as they arose. All work had to be done outside of regular school hours.

A Blochman School District still exists today, but the innovative, progressive student city is only a memory, relegated to the pages of history. It does however provide evidence that a good teacher can provide an extraordinary education to students, no matter the location, with community support.

SAN RAMON CHAPEL

The San Ramon Chapel was built in 1875 by Frederick Wickenden at the request of his wife,

◆

The Blochman City school project received national attention when it was featured in the Saturday Evening Post *in 1946.*

Ramona Foxen Wickenden, in Foxen Canyon, two miles east of Sisquoc. It was a dry year, Wickenden had 5,000 sheep and there was no grass. He drove the sheep north to save the herd. In the Salinas Valley they found grass and had their lambs. Wickenden continued on to Redwood City where he sold the 5,000 sheep for a dollar apiece. With the money, he purchased redwood boards at the mills and shipped them to Port Harford. He purchased enough boards to add eight rooms to the Wickenden Adobe and to build the chapel. In 1879 the chapel was officially dedicated as the San Ramon Chapel and services were held once a month. Because the chapel's structure stood on stilts, the services were often disrupted by cold and wind. Attendance dwindled, and eventually the chapel was only used for baptisms and special ceremonies.

In July 1966, the San Ramon Chapel became the first official landmark in Santa Barbara County. On August 31, 1975, the chapel was dedicated as State Historical Landmark #877. Mass was celebrated by Father Bertin Foxen, following the dedication. This also marked the chapel's 100th birthday. In November 1976, Father Anthony Runtz, pastor of St. Louis de Montfort Church in Orcutt, agreed to restore regular services. Since that time, mass has been held every Sunday.

Thanks to the hard work and dedication of the community, the chapel has literally been brought back to life. In 1979 the San Ramon Preservation Committee was formed and incorporated as a nonprofit organization. Its job is to maintain the chapel and to preserve its historical integrity.

LOS ALAMOS

Twelve miles from the chapel is the town of Los Alamos. Los Alamos is relatively isolated. It is about 10 miles to Buellton, Solvang, and Los Olivos to the southeast, Guadalupe, Orcutt and Santa Maria to the northwest and Lompoc and Vandenberg Air Force Base to the west and southwest; respectively. The large Cat Canyon Oil Field is in the hills to the northeast, the Zaca Oil Field to the east-southeast, and the Orcutt Oil Field is in the hills to the northwest of the town. San Antonio Creek passes through the town on its way to the ocean. Los Alamos is Spanish for "the cottonwoods."

In 1839, José Antonio De la Guerra y Carrillo, a son of José de la Guerra y Noriega received the Rancho Los Alamos Mexican land grant. In 1876 during the centennial of the United States, Thomas Bell along with his nephew John S. Bell, and Dr. James B. Shaw, all from San Francisco, purchased acreage from Rancho Los Alamos and neighboring Rancho La Laguna. Los Alamos

◆

Above: The William Gewe home in Los Alamos.

Left: One of the early Los Alamos houses is the John Leslie home on Bell Street, c. 1940.

prospered and grew quickly, serving as a popular stagecoach stop from 1861-1901. In 1880 the Union Hotel opened to serve overnight travelers. In 1881 the Careaga brothers and Gaspar Orena became large land owners purchasing approximately 17,000 acres and 4,000 acres, respectively, of the Los Alamos Rancho. Another

early pioneer was Mr. C.H. Pearson, who arrived as he often set the time frame, "When Los Alamos had only a half-dozen houses." William Gewe came in 1882 and bought out the blacksmith shop owned by Pearson. Gewe purchased a block of land on which he built a two-story home and a substantial blacksmith shop with equipment and machinery more up-to-date than most in the area. From 1882-1940 the narrow-gauge Pacific Coast Railway ran to Los Alamos from San Luis Obispo. More economic prosperity pervaded the area when oil was discovered at the Orcutt field in hills north of Los Alamos in 1901 and in the Purisima Hills south of the Los Alamos at the Lompoc Oil Field in 1903. Between those years, in 1902, Los Alamos was shocked by a tremendous earthquake that nearly emptied the town with its devastation. Most buildings were reduced to rubble, and it was reported that not a chimney remained standing in the Los Alamos Valley. Aftershocks reduced any remaining structures over the next four days. No loss of life was reported which was attributed to the fact that there was no brick construction of homes or commercial buildings. The oil fields were completely disrupted, but eventually Los Alamos returned to its pre-quake way of life.

The town flagpole at Centennial and Bell Street was dedicated in 1918, the same year as Santa Maria's. The Los Alamos Chamber of Commerce was active from 1920 through 1932 and instrumental in forming an electrification district, obtaining telephone service, paving streets and providing mail service. Today residents still pick-up their mail from the Post Office downtown, as no home delivery is available.

Most recently the growth of the Santa Barbara County wine region, and the popularity of the acclaimed 2004 film *Sideways* which highlighted various wine tasting rooms, has helped the small town of Los Alamos to endure. Los Alamos is also home to the last standing Pacific Coast Railway station, and to fine dining establishments, and antique stores.

Of great historical interest is a commonly told tale that took place in the hills above Los Alamos in the early years following the Mexican-American War. Legend describes the hills as headquarters for the bandito Salomon Pico and his hard-fighting, quick-shooting band of outlaws. Commanding a view of the surrounding country, the mountain was a safe retreat in 1856 when enraged ranchers and tradesmen determined to rid the country of the desperado. Pico was hated for his banditry by the newly arrived settlers of the valley and the prosperous prospectors who traveled with gold filled pockets but was protected from capture and prosecution by others as a defender of his people. Pico's victims were usually wealthy "gringo" travelers who were slain by knife, gun or rope. Often their bodies were left lying in the road to strike terror into the hearts of others and bolster Pico's reputation. Most of the early-day Californians were not easily terrorized and such was the rising temper of the people that Pico found it "urgent" to leave his hideout. It has

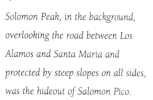

◆

Solomon Peak, in the background, overlooking the road between Los Alamos and Santa Maria and protected by steep slopes on all sides, was the hideout of Salomon Pico.

been widely speculated that Pico's escapades are popularized and romanticized in the character "Zorro." Like Zorro, Pico lived a dual life: ranching by day and defending justice by night, riding a powerful steed and trusting to the loyal support of his people. Some of the stories from his outlaw years connect clearly with certain aspects of the Zorro legend, others not so much. How much Salomon Pico contributed to the legend of Zorro is pure conjecture. It doesn't stop tourists and treasure hunters from scouring the hills looking for buried gold and other booty presumed hidden in the hills above the little town of Los Alamos; Solomon Peak was (mis)named in remembrance of the notorious bandit.

CASMALIA

Casmalia, which is situated in the Santa Maria Valley twelve miles southwest of Santa Maria is located on the 1840 Mexican land grant, Rancho Casmalia. In early Casmalia most of the local residents were employed in agriculture. A ruinous two-year drought caused ranchers and farmers to suffer devastating losses and Casmalia disappeared from the scene.

In 1861 the first stage connecting San Francisco to Los Angeles was inaugurated, and a line running from the Dana Rancho in Nipomo through Foxen Canyon and Los Olivos carried travelers to Santa Barbara. In 1877 the through-stage route was changed and ran south to Guadalupe, passing near Casmalia on its way to La Graciosa and Los Alamos before reaching Los Olivos. A formal town was founded by Antonio Tognazzini in the mid-1890s and was named Someo, after the village of origin of the Tognazzini family, Someo, Switzerland. When the

post office was opened, however, it was named Casmalia, rather than Someo, because of a name conflict with another California town named Someo. After oil was discovered at Orcutt, oil crews arrived on the Casmalia scene. In 1896, in order to complete its coastal route, the Southern Pacific Railroad was pushing its tracks south from San Luis Obispo through Casmalia and housing was needed for section crews. That same year, on November 10, 1896, Casmalia's first post office opened with Frank A. Vandoit as the postmaster. The first through-train arrived in 1901, and until 1937 Casmalia was a flag stop on the railroad. In the early 1900s approximately 1,500 people lived in the picturesque western town of Casmalia. Over the years, the residents of Casmalia have scattered until approximately only two hundred hardy souls remain.

ORCUTT

Orcutt was a hub of activity at the turn of the 20th century. It was the company town of the Union Oil Company and a major trading and supply center for north Santa Barbara County's oil district. Oil was stored in huge tanks in the town awaiting transportation. In April 1904, there was so much activity that it became necessary to create and lay out the townsite to support the burgeoning oil industry that had been brought on by the efforts of William W. Orcutt. E.W. Clark, General Manager of the Pacific Coast Railway. Clark decided on the name of the town in favor of Orcutt. Orcutt himself was not enthusiastic about the idea. He was heard to remark that while he did not wish to be discourteous in declining the honor, the idea reminded him "of the practice of naming cheap

◆

The Southern Pacific Railway near Casmalia. Oil sumps can be seen in the foreground. In the background is the Dave Thompkin Ranch known as El Rancho San Antone.

Orcutt Depot (P.C. Narrow Guage R.R.) 1907
Pinal Horses

cigars after cheap actresses." The idea went forward without Orcutt's blessing and not long after the name was established, an event so remarkable took place that the town name was on the lips of oilmen everywhere. On December 2, 1904, Hartnell No. 1, the first producing well on Hartnell property, came in with a roar, shooting gas and a column of oil up over a height of 150 feet. Oil flooded the gullies and creek beds. Uncontrollable, Old Maude, as Hartnell No. 1 became known, spouted 12,000 barrels of oil every day, gushing over one million barrels in its first 100 days. Old Maude was the largest oil producer the world had ever seen. Despite advances in science that made drilling for oil less speculative, Old Maude was an accident. A drilling crew hauling heavy equipment across rugged terrain toward a selected location for drilling abruptly changed plans when equipment fell from the back end of the wagon. Rather than putting the rig back together and continuing, they decided to make their work easier by drilling on the spot. Old Maude came in as a spectacular gusher, flooding the canyon with oil as crews struggled to contain tens of thousands of barrels of black gold running downhill by hurriedly constructing earthen dams. The origin of the name "Old Maude" has not been definitively determined; some sources attribute it to the name of a mule, others to a favored town prostitute. Whatever the origin, Old Maude is

still noted as one of the all-time top producers of oil in the world. Orcutt was a boom town, and its population continued to grow through the 1970s, reaching 22,000 by the decade's end. Orcutt is today still an unincorporated township and remains proud of its rich and colorful history.

RANCHO TEPUSQUET

Rancho Tepusquet was a 8,901-acre Mexican land grant given in 1837 by Governor Juan B. Alvarado to Tomás Olivera. The grant extended along the Sisquoc River and encompasses Sisquoc and Garey, northeast of Los Alamos. Tomás Olivera married María Antonia Cota in 1816. By her previous marriage, María Antonia Cota had daughters María Martina Osuna, who married Juan Pacifico Ontiveros of Rancho San Juan Cajón de Santa Ana in 1825, and Eduarda Osuna, who married Benjamin Foxen of Rancho Tinaquaic in 1831. Tomás Olivera was superintendent of three mission ranches: La Purisima, Santa Ynez and Santa Barbara. Olivera died in 1848.

With the cession of California to the United States following the Mexican-American War, the 1848 Treaty of Guadalupe Hidalgo provided that the land grants would be honored. As required by the Land Act of 1851, a claim for Rancho Tepusquet was filed with the Public Land Commission in 1852, and the grant was patented to María Antonia Cota *et al*, heirs of Tomás Olivera. In 1855, the heirs of Tomás Olivera sold Rancho Tepusquet to stepdaughter María Martina Osuna and son-in-law Juan Pacifico Ontiveros. Juan Pacifico Ontiveros moved to Rancho Tepusquet in 1856 and constructed an adobe on the property, where he lived until his death.

RANCHO TINAQUAIC

William Benjamin Foxen, a native of Norwich, England, was a sea captain who came to Santa Barbara County in the early 19th century. Foxen married Eduarda Osuna, the stepdaughter of Tomás Olivera of Rancho Tepusquet, in 1831. In 1837, Foxen was granted the two square league Rancho Tinaquaic. The grant comprised most of what is known as Foxen Canyon, northwest of

Los Alamos. In 1846 during the Mexican–American War, Foxen guided John C. Frémont over the Santa Ynez Mountains at San Marcos Pass helping Fremont, who was acting under orders from Commodore Robert F. Stockton. He lead his military expedition of 300 men to capture Santa Barbara. There was a torrential rainstorm on the night of December 24, 1846, but, in spite of losing many of his horses, mules and cannons, which slid down the muddy slopes during the rainy night, his men regrouped the next morning and captured the presidio and the town without bloodshed. A few days later Frémont led his men southeast toward Los Angeles, accepting the surrender of the leader Andrés Pico, cousin to Salomon Pico, and signing the Treaty of Cahuenga on January 13, 1847, which terminated the war in Upper California. A plaque commemorates Foxen's contribution to Fremont's success.

✦

A home at the mouth of Tepusquet Canyon.

SHARING THE HERITAGE

Historic profiles of businesses, organizations, and families that have contributed to the development and economic base of Santa Maria Valley

◆

Guadalupe State Beach surf.

COURTESY OF GREG IGER.

The Pages Drill Team parades down
Broadway, 1963.

Quality of Life

Healthcare providers, foundations,

universities, and other institutions that

contribute to the quality of life in the Santa Maria Valley

MASONIC HESPERIAN LODGE #264

'Heart of Santa Maria' 66 Years Ago—First Santa Maria Store

Santa Maria's first mercantile establishment and Masonic Temple, from an old wood-cut made in the early eighties, owned by S. J. Jones. The building was located on the northeast corner of North Broadway and East Main and fronted on East Main street. The building, according to Pioneer Jones' recollection, was erected by Miller & Lovett in 1873, and from it, they distributed the first mail to Santa Marians, brought in from the stages at Suey crossing. Miller & Lovett sold to Kreidel & Fleisher, later M. Fleisher & Co. Sam Fleisher and others still own the property. The Fleisher store played a prominent part in the early life of Santa Maria. Another prominent early-day mercantile firm here was that of Kaiser Bros., according to Pioneer Jones. They located at 115 or 117 East Main, coming here from Guadalupe. Later they built where the Security-First National bank branch is now located and then sold out to Wilheimer & Coblentz. Later the firm became Coblentz and Schwabacher. When the Santa Maria bank occupied the corner, Coblentz & Schwabacher moved to the location now occupied by the Bowies Furniture Co., where they remained in business until a few years ago.

MAIN AND BROADWAY IN EARLY 80's

One of Santa Maria's early-day mercantile establishments, and Masonic Temple, from an old wood-cut made in the early eighties, owned by J. C. Jones. The building was located on the northeast corner of North Broadway and East Main and fronted on East Main street. Jones says the trees were the artist's imagination, drawn in to keep the buildings from looking so bare. The Fleisher store played a prominent part in the early life of Santa Maria. It later became the Coblentz & Schwabacher store.

♦

Left: Masonic Temple newspaper feature, May 5, 1939.

BOTH ARTICLES COURTESY OF THE *DAILY TIMES*.

In the Middle Ages, the term "freemason" was awarded to highly skilled stonemasons who were hired as free agents to build castles and cathedrals in England and Scotland. Because of the inherent danger of their work, stonemasons formed local organizations called lodges to take care of sick and injured members as well as the widows and orphans of those who were killed on the job. Eventually, men who were not skilled stonemasons wanted to join the group for the many advantages it offered. These men were known as accepted masons rather than working masons. This is how the group began to shift from a craft guild to a fraternity.

The fraternity spread throughout Europe and the American Colonies and freemasonry became very popular in colonial America. George Washington was a Mason, Benjamin Franklin served as the head of the fraternity in Pennsylvania, as did Paul Revere and Joseph Warren in Massachusetts. Other well-known Masons involved with the founding of America included John Hancock, John Sullivan, Lafayette, Baron Fredrick von Stuben, Nathanael Greene, and John Paul Jones.

Another Mason, Chief Justice John Marshall, shaped the Supreme Court into its present form.

Over the centuries, Freemasonry has developed into a worldwide fraternity emphasizing personal study, self-improvement, and social betterment via individual involvement and philanthropy.

Hesperian Lodge came into existence on June 4, 1881, when sixteen local members of the Guadalupe Lodge #237 came together to form what became the Hesperian Lodge #264 F. & M. in "Central City" today known as Santa Maria.

The name "Hesperian" was chosen for the Lodge although the reasons why are fairly unknown. However; through generational word of mouth, it has been said that the majority of its founders all had attended "Hesperian College," and therefore they took the name Hesperian as a college fraternity memory.

Originally known as Grangerville, the town's name was changed to Central City in 1874, as it was half-way between Guadalupe and Sisquoc on the Pacific Coast Railway. Four local ranchers each donated forty acres of land adjacent to what are now Broadway and Main Streets. These men were Isaac Fesler, Rudolph Cook, John Thornburg, and Isaac Miller, whose last names are still on the streets around the city's center. In 1885 the name was changed to Santa Maria

because the postal service sent many residents' mail to Central City, Colorado by mistake.

Although the membership in the Hesperian Lodge is too extensive to list, it is important to note some of their first members that not only helped shape the lodge as we know it today but also were the movers and shakers of early Santa Maria. Their contributions to the Santa Maria Valley are undeniable:

- Charles Armstrong
- Henry Clay Bagby
- Major Baker
- Charles Bradley
- George Gilbert Brown
- George Doane
- Albert Allen Dudley
- Asa Hoffman
- Charles Gardner
- John Harrison
- Haydon Herman Heller
- John Houk
- Matt Howerton
- Irving Nolan McGuire
- Isaac Miller Thomas Nance
- Addison Hervey Orr
- Ormond Pinkerton Paulding
- Thomas Preisker
- Madison Thornburg
- Henry Clay Tunnell
- William Hulbert Tunnell
- Fremont Twitchell
- John Walker
- Alfred Weilheimer
- John Winters

On October 12, 1882, the Hesperian Lodge No. 264 F. & A. M. was chartered.

In December 1883, Santa Maria's first brick building was put up by T. A. Jones to replace a two-story wooden structure that had gone up in flames September 3 of the same year. The second story of the new building became a lodge room for the Santa Maria Masons, the office of Judge Thornburgh and a reading room for WCTU. *The Santa Maria Times* moved in the following January.

On May 12, 1905, the Masonic Hall Association purchased the lot on the northwest corner of South Broadway and West Church Streets. On September 30, 1905, the corner-stone was laid and on May 1, 1907, the new Masonic building was dedicated. This building

was used continuously until April 30, 1930, when it was declared unsafe.

On August 4, 1930, the Hesperian Lodge began meeting in the just-completed Pythian Castle Hall located at the northeast corner of West Church and South Lincoln Streets. That same year, the Hall Association purchased a large residential lot with a large house situated on it located on the northeast corner of East Cypress Street and South Vine. The house was divided into two sections and rented out until a new temple was built there in 1955.

Ground for the new lodge was broken February 21, 1955, and the cornerstone was laid the following May 28. The first meeting was held in the lodge's new location the following November 28.

✦

Above: The lodge located at the northeast corner of East Cypress Street and South Vine.

Two views of the old Masonic Temple at Broadway and Church Street

Top, building is shown prior to the 1925 earthquake; the cornerstone is behind woman in sweeping skirt. Shown in August 1961, bottom, is the same building, one story shorter and with the famed B & B Coffee Shop on the first story; by this time, the Masons had moved to another temple

Lodge, established the present Santa Maria Cemetery. Many of the city's schools, including Righetti High School, had cornerstones laid by the organization. Masons continue to serve the community, with major events including sponsorship of Public Schools Week and the annual spelling bee, now under way. They also sponsor youth groups for young men and women.

Above: Masonic Lodge newspaper feature, 1961.

Cornerstone to be unveiled

Continued from Page 3

● An envelope containing cards and letterheads of merchants in the city of Santa Maria.

● Copies of several newspapers.

● A sketch showing the history and foundation of the town of Santa Maria.

● A 50-cent silver coin from 1905.

The Grand Lodge of the state of California will perform the removal ceremony with the help of local Hesperian Lodge officers. Officials of the Grand Lodge also were on hand when the original cornerstone was installed.

The cornerstone materials, if located and still intact, will be displayed at the Santa Maria Valley Historical Society, 616 S. Broadway, at a later date.

Prior to the opening ceremony, a luncheon will be served in the Masonic Temple, 700 E. Lakeview Road, Santa Maria. For luncheon reservations, contact Wendell Swanson, master of the Hesperian Lodge, 934-3309, or Charles W. Floyd, 934-0655, 8 a.m. to noon.

Hesperian Lodge No. 264 was founded in Central City in 1881, a year before the city became known as Santa Maria. Fifteen Masons assembled on June 4, 1881, at Kriedel and Fleisher's Hall. The general merchandise was downstairs, with the Masonic Hall established on the second floor of this wooden building.

Eighteen Masons from Guadalupe Lodge No. 237 and representatives from Magnolia Lodge No. 242 and King David Lodge No. 209 became charter members. Other charter members included names that now are part of Santa Maria's history and streetnames: John Lafayette Tunnell, John Gotlob Prell, Addison Hervey Orr, Henry Stowell, William Wilson Stilwell, John Edgar, Thomas Clayton Nance, Joseph Kaiser, Robert Braun, John W. Grant, Charles Wesley Martin, William Laird Adam, Frederick Franklin Field, Madison Thornburg, Samuel Kriedel, Edgar Henry Stowell, James Franklin Goodwin, Marks Fleisher, Martin Van Buren Robbins and Charles B. Dutcher.

The Masonic Hall Association was incorporated on Dec. 23, 1904, for the purpose of building the Masonic Temple. M. Thornburg was the president. By 1905, Fremont C. Twitchell was master, and William H. Tunnell senior warden.

The Santa Barbara earthquake of June 29, 1925, dealt a blow to the Masons' plans for the second floor of the elegant, high-windowed new three-story building on Church and Broadway. Unsafe for large assemblies due to earthquake damage, the floor was turned into office space.

In the late '30s the Masons were able to begin to purchase a new plot of land at Cypress and Vine streets, finally building a second Masonic Temple in 1955. They ultimately met another obstacle, as they were in the path of the eastside downtown renewal. They say the site of their second temple is now under Sears in the Santa Maria Town Center.

The move to the present temple on Lakeview Road came in 1975. Some of the emblems, the central altar, pedestals and other parts of the lodge's trappings have been moved from temple to temple. The wool carpeting, first purchased for the "second temple," is still in use on the floor at the Lakeview facility.

The Masonic Lodge is dedicated to assisting in the development of the community. The lodge, with the local Odd Fellows

In 1972 the lodge received notice that its property on Cypress and South Vine stood in the way of the development of the Towne Center East Mall. It was time to move again.

The lodge found a temporary site for its meetings at 725 East Foster Road where it remained for about a year.

In the meantime, negotiations were being held between the lodge and Elwin Mussell, owner of property at 700 Lakeview Road. Groundbreaking for the new lodge took place October 14, 1974, and the cornerstone was laid on April 25 of the following year.

On July 7, 1975, the first meeting of the Hesperian Lodge took place in its new building on Lakeview where it continues to meet today.

November 20, 1990, the site of the first Masonic Lodge (on South Broadway, across from the Robinson/May Complex), was designated as a City of Santa Maria Landmark.

Hesperian Lodge is committed to keeping up the tradition of giving back to the community. Its members spend endless hours through various programs they have within the Masonic community to help contribute to the Santa Maria area.

Throughout the year Hesperian Lodge is used for numerous events and occasions for the community: Santa Barbara County Elections, United Blood Services, Santa Maria Chamber of Commerce, Santa Barbara County Speech Therapy and Youth In Harmony.

Ellis Hickman Rice Memorial Masonic Scholarship, awarded each year by the Hesperian Lodge, is pleased to offer $1,000 scholarships to local high school seniors who will graduate within the boundaries of the Santa Maria Valley area. The winners of theses scholarships are selected by a committee made up of Hesperian Lodge members.

Everyone has heard of all the wonderful things Shriners Hospitals do for children, however, many do not realize that all Shriners are Masons! The Shrine Club of Santa Maria is dedicated to helping raise awareness and support for Shriners Hospitals. Their members are often seen throughout the community in parades and holding barbeques to raise money in order to help more children. Through their diverse efforts, many of our local children have been recipients of the care given by Shriners Hospitals.

As part of their continued efforts to support local education, the Hesperian Lodge holds an annual Spelling Bee for fourth through sixth grade students. The Masons have sponsored the Spelling Bee since 1975. It hosts up to 200 local students each year in April to commemorate their commitment to public education. First, Second and Third place plaques are awarded to the top three students of each grade.

On April 11, 2015, Hesperian Lodge took a small corner of their property and dedicated it to those who paid the ultimate price to guarantee our religious and Masonic freedoms. Veterans Memorial Garden is a place where one can reflect and contemplate, not that they are no more, but live in thankfulness that they were. We hope you will take just a moment to visit our garden, pause, reflect, and then leave uplifted,

knowing that the day each of our fallen comrades died was but the birthday of eternity.

The Masons are very committed to the youth. They have established three different youth organizations: Job's Daughter, DeMolay, and Rainbow Girls. Each organization is specifically designed to help mentor youth while helping them become active within their communities.

Many of these kids you will find volunteering in the community. They have been known to deliver stuffed animals to the local hospital for the kids or serve dinner at the homeless shelter, or even help build fences for the Santa Maria Open Space Association.

But it is not all about work, they also like to have plenty of fun. The Masons are very active in helping raise money to send the kids on special trips to the movies, bowling, camping, laser tag, or even Disneyland!

MASONIC RETIREMENT HOME & CARE CENTER
MASONIC CHILDRENS HOME
SHRINERS HOSPITALS FOR CRIPPLED CHILDREN & BURN INSTITUTES
SCOTTISH RITE-CHILDRENS HOSPITAL & LANGUAGE DISORDERS PROGRAM
EDUCATIONAL SCHOLARSHIPS, LOANS/GRANTS
KNIGHTS TEMPLAR EYE BANK

OES
FREE CANCER DRESSINGS CANCER RESE
CONVALESCENT RELIEF HEART RESEAR
YOUTH: RAINBOW JOB'S DAUGHTERS DeM
MUSCULAR DYSTROPHY RESEARCH
MUSEUMS AND LIBRARIES
MENTAL RETARDATION RESEARCH

MINERVA CLUB

The hearty pioneers who settled the Santa Maria Valley in the late 1800s encountered a wild and desolate landscape filled with challenge and hardship. There was not a tree in sight. Water had to be hauled long distances. The nearest trading posts were twenty-five miles away and the roads were rutted trails. Despite the hardships, many could see the hidden opportunities available to those who worked hard and risked all. Although gritty determination was required to survive and build on this land, the early settlers included pioneer women whose domestic labors were enhanced by an interest in music, literature, and art. It was in this environment that twenty-five pioneer women gathered in the home of Mollie Smith on October 8, 1894, for the purpose of organizing a ladies' literary society.

These women were hungry for companionship and knowledge to help themselves, their families and their community enjoy a richer and more meaningful life. The twenty-five founders decided to name their organization the Ladies Literary Society of Santa Maria. Four years later, the name was modified to the Women's Literary Club of Santa Maria. In honor of a revered founding member, Minerva Thornburg, the club's name was changed in 1906 to the Minerva Library Club of Santa Maria.

The word 'library' was dropped in 1954 and the organization became the Minerva Club. One of the oldest clubs in California, the Minerva Club's rich 122 plus year history is intertwined with the development and growth of Santa Maria.

In addition to enriching their lives, members were instrumental in establishing the first lending library. Fostering education has always been of interest to Minerva. Since those early days, they have developed a generous scholarship program and continue to be involved in numerous civic activities. The Minerva Club grew rapidly in its early days. Within three months, membership had more than doubled to fifty-three. Members were sharing their newfound ideas, news and knowledge with their families and neighbors. For women living in an isolated frontier, the Minerva Club supplied companionship, education and a vision of an enriched life. From its beginning, the Minerva Club has been noted for its outreach. Within months of its founding, the club presented its first program for the community. A musical with "literary entertainment" was held at McWilliams Hall. This was followed by club-sponsored appearances by professional entertainers, serious lectures on issues of the day and musical programs.

One of the Minerva Club's proudest and most important achievements was the establishment of Santa Maria's first public library. A small lending library was organized shortly after the club was formed. In 1896 club members spent $66.99 to purchase a bookcase holding ninety books. A local merchant allowed the club to place the bookcase in his store and library cards were sold to the public. The library was moved to the post office in 1900 and other moves followed as the lending library grew. During this era, philanthropist Andrew Carnegie was making grants to localities wanting to build a public library and members of the Minerva Club jumped at this opportunity. The club organized community support for the library and urged the city council to incorporate and

open negotiations. A Carnegie Library was built on city-owned land on Broadway and when the library opened in 1909 the Minerva Club donated more than 600 books for its shelves.

The club began looking for a permanent clubhouse in 1902 and the effort came to fruition in 1925 when Mr. and Mrs. J. F. Goodwin donated land at the corner of Boone and Lincoln Streets. After extensive fundraising, a design submitted by famed architect, Julia Morgan, was selected. Construction began in June 1928 and official opening ceremonies were conducted four months later. The "Grand Ol' Dame" has been enlarged and remodeled several times through the years and members are dedicated to preserving the historic structure, which is on the U.S. Registry of Historical Places. The club motto, "Higher Knowledge and Better Morals" was carved into the wood beam over the stage in 1938.

During the early 1900s, the town's first park was set aside. Minerva raised funds and planted trees and flowers at Buena Vista Park. With no irrigation system, members hand-watered plants to ensure their survival. Minerva was instrumental in bringing the Campfire organization to local girls. First-class flower shows were held drawing crowds and planting the seeds for the county fair. Plays and fundraisers were held to buy adjacent lots for clubhouse parking.

The club's tradition of recognizing students began in 1917 when the entire senior class was honored. A yearly luncheon for honor students began a few years later. In 1952 the club began awarding scholarships. The first scholarships, totaling $500, were funded by the profits from the sales of the club's cookbook, selling strawberry shortcake at the county fair and personal contributions. The Minerva Club Trust Fund

✦

Above: Mr. and Mrs. James F. Goodwin donated the lot at the corner of Boone and Lincoln Streets to the Minerva Club in 1927.

Bottom, left: The clubhouse was designed by Julia Morgan and is pictured here in 1929 soon after completion.

Bottom, right: Julia Morgan was the architect for William Randolph Hearst.

emphasis on local talent and speakers. Ladies enjoy making and nurturing friendships. Club membership includes retired teachers, realtors, lawyers, nurses, homemakers, ladies still working, and granddaughters of original pioneers. The club ladies do more than play bridge, arrange flowers and sip tea. Members work together to help Santa Maria continue to grow and prosper through education, support of the arts and by being fierce guardians of local history. Truly, Minerva Club is a bastion of gentility in an ever-changing world.

❖

Above: Pie booth at the county fair, c. 1938.

Right: The club sponsored well attended floral shows, c. 1947.

Below: The Minerva Club as it appears today. The building is on the National Registry (inset) of historic places as well as the State of California and the City of Santa Maria.

was organized after receiving a generous bequest from the Maxine and Burns Rick Estate. Since 2001 the Trust has awarded nearly $353,000 to local high school seniors attending college. In total, the club has awarded $370,000 in scholarships since 1953.

The roles of women have changed dramatically since those pioneer ladies first met more than a century ago. The Minerva Club remains a vibrant, growing organization offering a wide variety of activities to members. Programs are interesting with an

Established in September 1955, the purpose of the Santa Maria Valley Historical Society is to provide a center for collection, conservation, interpretation, and research concerned with the history of the people of the Santa Maria Valley, while making this knowledge and interpretation available to the community. The Santa Maria Valley Historical Museum is located at 616 South Broadway, Santa Maria, California.

media to be taken out of the library area. Many items are rare and unduplicated. Our photo library offers over 10,000 photographs digitally preserved and easily searchable. The obituary database has reached beyond 8,000 listings.

The museum's research library offers a vast array of materials related to the development of the Santa Maria Valley. Also included in the holdings are a selection of materials on the valley's first families, American Civil War Era documents, and anthropological and archeological materials related to the people of the valley and California. We welcome visitors to come in, browse, and enjoy our research room. We do not allow books, magazines or other

The historical society is a nonprofit governed by a board of directors. From its first days, when Ethel May Dorsey originally envisioned it, the society and museum have thrived due in general to the generosity of its members and the support of the City of Santa Maria. Over its history the society has benefitted from hundreds of volunteers and their thousands of donated hours. Every major accomplishment can be attributed to the tenacity and benevolence of this faithful cadre of volunteers who have worked diligently through the decades of the society and museum's existence.

We invite everyone to become members and to embrace the heritage of our wondrous and beautiful valley.

CITY OF SANTA MARIA

Located along California's beautiful Central Coast, the City of Santa Maria is the largest and most populous city in Santa Barbara and San Luis Obispo Counties. Santa Maria's population grew from about 40,000 residents in 1980 to over 103,000 by 2015. Santa Maria has a business-friendly reputation, a moderate cost of living, and offers a wide range of choices for recreational, cultural and social pursuits.

To meet growth, the city maintains and improves its infrastructure with new public facilities such as its police and fire stations, library, as well as numerous other recreational facilities. Downtown's Santa Maria Transit Center provides convenient bus service throughout the community, including to the expanded Marian Regional Medical Center.

The city is recognized with national, state, and local awards. Santa Maria was named as an All-America City on June 20, 1998—one of only ten cities from across the nation to receive this coveted designation that year. This is one of the nation's oldest and most respected community recognition programs. The All-America City Award, sponsored by the National Civic League, recognizes exemplary grassroots community problem-solving and is awarded to communities of all sizes that collaboratively tackle challenges and achieve results. The designation honors the way people care for their community and take responsibility for their future. It recognizes partnerships and progress, creativity and collaboration, perseverance and pride.

The city has earned five prestigious statewide recognition awards—the coveted Helen Putnam Awards of Excellence for innovative programs. Established in 1982 by the League of California Cities, this program recognizes outstanding achievements and innovative solutions by city governments to improve the quality of life in their communities in the most effective manner possible. The city programs honored were in the categories of public safety, health and wellness, internal administration, public trust and ethics and community involvement, and financial management and planning.

At the local and regional level, the city consistently is recognized for its leadership and collaborative spirit in long-range water issues, law enforcement assistance, and other municipal

operations. The city also partners with the Santa Maria Public Airport to jointly fund Economic Development services in an effort to recruit new companies to the area and retain existing employers. In addition local leaders have initiated an ongoing revitalization effort to make downtown more appealing, encourage more events, and welcome more businesses.

The city partners with the Serve Santa Maria program to beautify and improve the community. Over the years, thousands of volunteers have donated tens of thousands of hours of time and labor to beautify parks and schools with new plants and murals, litter pick-up, even making repairs at the homes of seniors and those unable to do home improvement projects by themselves.

Every year, Santa Maria welcomes thousands of people to the Santa Barbara County Fair, and hosts the famous Elks Rodeo and Parade. The Rodeo Parade, along with the annual Rotary Holiday Parade of Lights, and the West Coast Kustoms Cruisin' Nationals and the Cruisin' for Life event are just a few of the community-oriented events along Highway 135 (Broadway) corridor. In addition, hundreds of families attend the city's summer concerts in the parks, and the annual Grapes and Grains festival each fall.

Santa Maria also counts among its attractions five museums, over two dozen city parks, the acclaimed PCPA at Allan Hancock College for live theater, and the city's state-of-the-art public library. Then there is the food! In addition to numerous authentic Mexican restaurants, Santa Maria is known for its copyrighted tri-tip BBQ, award-winning wine country and sweet juicy strawberries.

Agriculture remains a major industry with many sophisticated infrastructure expansions such as advanced hydroponic greenhouses and large produce coolers. Additionally, Santa Maria enjoys an expanding economy based on a healthy combination of commercial and manufacturing development, education, health-care, retail trade, tourism, oil production, banking, and nearby Vandenberg Air Force Base.

The City of Santa Maria remains focused on providing excellent public services while creating and maintaining a beautiful city with contemporary amenities for its residents and businesses—as it extends a helping hand to commerce and a warm welcome to visitors.

✦

Above: Fire Station No. 1, located at the intersection of Cook and Pine Streets, was built in 2002 and is one of six city fire stations.

Below: The Abel Maldonado Community Youth Center opened in November 2001 and features a multipurpose room, computer lab, meeting rooms, fitness facility, and many other youth-related services.

Bottom: As seen from Broadway (Highway 135), the Santa Maria Public Library is a community anchor, providing information and computer access since its opening in 2008.

Santa Maria Recreation and Parks

◆

Top, left: Abel Maldonado Community Youth Center, 600 South McClelland Street.

Top, right: Pioneer Park, 1150 West Foster Road.

Bottom, left: Preisker Park, 330 Hidden Pines Way.

Bottom, right: Paul Nelson Aquatic Center, 600 South McClelland Street.

The quality of life in the Santa Maria Valley is greatly enhanced by its many beautiful parks and the recreational activities provided by the Santa Maria Recreation and Parks Department

The department operates 254 acres of developed parkland in twenty-seven neighborhood and community parks, as well as part of the 1,774 acre Los Flores Ranch Park. The department also operates ten community centers, including the Abel Maldonado Community Youth Center, Hagerman Softball Complex, Paul Nelson Aquatics Center, Elwin Mussell Senior Center, and Veteran's Memorial Community Center.

As in most American cities, the concept of municipally owned parks and recreation facilities was little recognized until well into the twentieth century. The earliest mention of parks in Santa Maria is a request by the parks superintendent in 1914 for a pay raise from $25 to $35 per month. The council approved the raise, but only on the condition that the superintendent would furnish one horse for park maintenance purposes.

A further search of city records reveals that recreation is not mentioned in any form until the summer of 1934 when a local printer,

Elwin Mussell, requested the city council initiate a summer recreation program and employ a summer playground director for $300. Following the request, the school superintendent and a teacher volunteered to serve as playground directors without pay. The council, however, did approve the expenditure of $175 to purchase equipment for what became the first playground program in Santa Maria.

Three years later, in January 1938, Skip Winas was employed by the City of Santa Maria and the school district "to take charge of" recreation activities in the city. The city's first recreation center—with programs for young people—was established in 1941 in the Carnegie Library.

During World War II, the chairman of the Parent Teacher Association (PTA) Recreation Committee expressed the PTA's "serious concern" over the lack of any planned recreational program in the city. The council soon announced that a five-member recreation committee would be appointed and a custodian of equipment would be hired. Then, in 1943, the pool manager, Paul Nelson, was appointed the first full-time recreation director. Nelson made a strong

◆

Top, left: Los Flores Ranch Park.

Top, right: Los Flores Ranch Park burros, Solomon and Mojave and friends.

Left: Los Flores Ranch Park grass filled valleys.

contribution to Santa Maria, both as an outstanding swimmer and through his efforts in building a strong recreational program. Joe White succeeded Nelson in 1952 and, at this time, the city's park and recreation functions were combined to form the Santa Maria Recreation and Parks Department.

Today, the recreation and parks department provides more than 3,000 programs for all ages in the areas of recreation classes, sports leagues, health and wellness activities, community special events and educational enrichment classes.

Santa Maria now has twenty-seven city parks, including more than 254 acres of grass, trees and playing fields, two public swimming pools, gazebos for summer concerts, plenty of places to barbecue, an 11-acre lake where visitors can fish, and another park with a replica of the good ship Santa Maria. More parks are being developed to bring residents even more outdoor recreational opportunities.

Santa Maria also has a regional park in Los Flores Ranch Park, nestled in the Solomon Hills, just south of Santa Maria. Once owned by Chevron and serving as the hub of the local petroleum industry, the 1,774 acres of rolling hills was sold to the city in 2009 to serve as the future integrated waste management facility and will provide 100 years of solid waste capacity. Recreational uses and the IWMF operations have been carefully coordinated so that both uses will co-exist. More than 1,100 acres have been reserved for recreation use and will provide regional open space and a rare mix of environmental education, recreation, land preservation and eight miles of easy to difficult multi-use trails through oak trees, grass filled valleys, invigorating wetlands, and other flora and fauna habitats. Hikers, equestrians and cyclists are able to take a quiet and relaxing stroll or an invigorating ride through the varied terrain while viewing an abundance of wildlife and panoramic vistas from the hills to the sea. Los Flores Ranch is the only park in the area that has access to multi-use trails and is the first recreation open space in the Santa Maria Valley.

To learn more about Santa Maria's parks and the city's recreational activities, check the website at http://www.cityofsantamaria.org/city-government/departments/recreation-and-parks.

LOS ALAMOS:
THE VALLEY OF THE COTTONWOODS

Below: Tom Coe, the stagecoach
driver (bottom photo) is buried in the
Los Alamos Cemetery.

Old and new came together as cowboys drove their herd through the street past the gas station and telephone poles, and cattle passed through Los Alamos for the last time. The west was changing, and, with it, the tiny community.

Stretching from two miles east of Los Alamos to eight miles west of it, for tens of thousands of years, rain washed soil from the surrounding hills into the Los Alamos Valley. Completely isolated from the ocean, the valley kept this fertile soil for itself. Before the Spanish named the valley for the cottonwood trees that line San Antonio Creek, which passes to the north of town, Chumash Indians had a village here.

Spanish land grants of Rancho Los Alamos and Rancho La Laguna shared the valley between Jose Antonio de la Guerra y Noriega and Octaviano Gutierrez. In time these land grants were divided and sold. Two of the buyers, Thomas Bell and James Shaw, gave half a square mile of each of their ranches to the town of Los Alamos.

A survey map of the town in 1876 clearly shows the road from the east to the west ends of Los Alamos entering and leaving on Main Street. Businesses were established on this street as it was planned to be the primary route through the town. The Wickenden brothers had a general merchandise store there. But Bell Street became the county road leaving Main Street to residences and the churches.

William Benjamin Foxen, Don Guillermo as Hattie Benefield relates in her biography *For God and Country*, bought the Tinaquaic land grant, just north of Los Alamos, from Victor Linares in 1837. Foxen was the first English settler in northern Santa Barbara County. His descendants are buried throughout the Los Alamos and Santa Maria Valley cemeteries and include members of the Arata, Castro, de la Guerra, Ontiveros, Simas, and Wickeden families as well as many others. A review of the pioneers of the Santa Maria Valley includes Glines, Patterson, Pico, Scolari, and Shaw, all of whom were pioneers of the Los Alamos Valley as well.

Ranching in the valley soon found itself sharing the land with dairy farming and agriculture. The discovery of oil on Careaga Ranch west of town brought new industry into the valley.

By the time of the last cattle drive through Los Alamos, there had been 3 cemeteries, 2 jails, 3 hotels, 2 blacksmith shops, 2 banks, a dozen saloons and as many gas stations. There had been schools at Harriston, Careaga, and in town. Los Alamos was a major stagecoach stop followed by a depot for the narrow gauge railway. The Wells Fargo office was followed by the Greyhound depot.

Few remember the mail boxes outside the first post office; the cinema; Dick Carroll's rose garden at the school; Marge and Leonard Farrow's café (now an antique shop); or Bill Zenger's Courtesy Café (shared with the town library, which was run by sisters Agnes Pearson and Elizabeth Clark, both buried in the Los Alamos Cemetery) at what had been Pearson's Cheap Cash Store. Who remembers dances at the Men's Club most weekends, the rifle club where we were taught to shoot 22s in the old railway station, or bus trips to swimming lessons at Paul Nelson Plunge in Santa Maria and to see *The Ten Commandments* at the Arlington Theatre in Santa Barbara? In school, we had square dancing for recess every Wednesday morning, and Mrs. Reed loved baseball, so we listened to the World Series in her eighth grade classroom every spring.

No one is left to remember the fire that burned down the school or the one that burned down the Union Hotel. There was the earthquake in 1902 that almost completely destroyed the town. There was the robber fleeing up the coast who was captured in town.

Today you can see many of the old buildings. Pearson's is still standing. So is the Leslie house. The Foxen home, on Foxen Lane, burned down almost 100 years ago, but others, such as the Bell, Moore, and Jensen homes, still stand. The narrow gauge railway station (the last of its kind in California) and the Depot Hotel are still here, but who knows where the St. George Hotel was? Vestiges of the past remain in the T&T Garage; Jake and Nellie Taylor's Shady Rest Motel, albeit as The Bakery; and the bank, which is now a deli, is still on the corner of Bell and Centennial.

Who will remember you, Los Alamos, when tract homes are the rule and the last cattle drive has been forgotten?

◆

Above: Harriston Post Office.

Below: Tract homes in the town of Los Alamos.

ALLAN HANCOCK COLLEGE

♦

Allan Hancock College broke ground in 1996 on the Lompoc Valley Center, which opened in 1999. The center became a reality with legislative funding secured by California Superintendent of Public Instruction Jack O'Connell (second from left), who posed with Dr. Ann Foxworthy, college superintendent/president (far left), Lompoc Mayor Joyce Howerton (second from right), and Trustee Richard Jacoby (far right).

Allan Hancock College, a California public community college located in northern Santa Barbara County, has been ranked one of the best community colleges in the state, and one of the top 150 community colleges in the nation, according to the Aspen Institute in 2011, 2014 and 2016.

The main campus of Allan Hancock College is located on 105 acres at 800 South College Drive in Santa Maria. The college also has campuses at the Lompoc Valley Center, Vandenberg Air Force Base, and in Solvang.

Allan Hancock College gives students the opportunity to begin working on a bachelor's degree, prepare for a career, or upgrade skills. The college offers associate degrees and certificates in more than 100 areas of study and is particularly well known for its English as a second language program, professional theatre and public safety training programs. Hancock has a high standard for providing superior support services for its students, including counseling and tutoring to help students achieve their dreams and fulfill the college's motto of "Start here. Go anywhere."

The college was founded in 1920 when the Santa Maria High School District established Santa Maria Junior College. Classes were held at Santa Maria High School until 1937 when voters approved a bond issue to build a college wing on the northeast corner of the high school campus.

As enrollment expanded, the college moved in 1954 from the high school facilities to Hancock Field, which had housed the original Santa Maria Airport, Hancock College of Aeronautics, and the University of Southern California's School of Aeronautics. The name of the school was changed to honor Captain G. Allan Hancock, a prominent state and local community leader who owned the land and facilities at the airfield. That same year, the community voted to establish the Santa Maria Joint Junior College District. In 1963 the Lompoc Unified School District and Santa Ynez Union High School District were annexed to the community college district, and the district was renamed the Allan Hancock Joint Community College District.

Allan Hancock College first offered classes beyond the main campus in 1952 when it started classes at the Camp Cooke Army Barracks, which is now Vandenberg Air Force Base. A center was opened at the air base in 1957. The college started offering classes in the Santa Ynez Valley in 1971 and in Lompoc in 1974. With legislative funding

secured by California State Superintendent of Public Instruction Jack O'Connell, the college completed construction of the Lompoc Valley Center in 1999 to better serve students in that area.

The face and landscape of the college took a dramatic turn in 2006 when community voters approved the issuance of $180 million in general obligation bonds to improve facilities and technology at the school over a ten-year period. Since its passage, Measure I funding has transformed the college's facilities and technology and allowed the college to better serve the needs of the district.

Nearly $20 million in technological improvements have modernized and streamlined college processes and upgraded both hardware and software in labs and classrooms. Nearly $130 million has funded or partly funded nine major capital construction or renovation projects. Decades old classrooms, labs, and administrative spaces have been replaced by state-of-the-art equipment and buildings. The Allan Hancock College Measure I Citizens' Oversight Committee formed in October 2006 to help ensure bond revenues were expended only for the purposes authorized by law.

New facilities from the bond include the Community Education, Science, Early Childhood Studies, Student Services, and Administration buildings, a new state-of-the-art track and field facility, as well as the Industrial Technology Complex. The college's fire, law enforcement, emergency medical services, and environmental health and safety programs train at the new state-of-the-art Public Safety Training Complex. Located at the Lompoc Valley Center, the $38 million facility includes a high-speed track, shooting range, six-story burn tower, and more features to provide hands-on training.

One of the most unique fixtures of Hancock is PCPA. Since 1964, PCPA has been presenting exemplary theatre and providing excellent training with a resident company of theatre professionals. In 1965, voters approved a school bond for the construction of the Marian Theatre, and the 448-seat venue opened in the summer of 1968 with a production of *Camelot* featuring Laird Williamson. In 1971, PCPA was invited to perform a production of *Hamlet* in Solvang's Hans Christian Andersen Park. The rest as they say is history, because PCPA has called Solvang its summer home ever since. Three years after its debut in Solvang, the community built the Solvang Festival Theatre,

a project completed in just fifty-eight days. PCPA expanded once again in 1992 with the inauguration of the Severson Theatre, a flexible "black box" theatre adjacent to the Marian Theatre. PCPA remains the only resident professional company on California's Central Coast and the only training program of its kind offered at a community college. With more than 100 acting and technical students per year, PCPA is known for producing exemplary artistic experiences for the community while preparing thousands of actors and theatre technicians for a career in theatre.

Much of the college's success is due to the stability of its leadership. The Allan Hancock College Board of Trustees, which is currently comprised of six elected members, governs on behalf of the communities they represent within the district. Over the years, many trustees have provided a consistent voice by serving for three or more terms. Both Ernest Righetti (1946-1979) and Owen Rice (1950-1979) were trustees for nearly thirty years, and managed the college's relocation and expansion. Carol Anders (1998-2010) and Henry Grennan (2000-2012) oversaw the use of Measure I funds and prioritization of projects. Elected in 1994, Larry Lahr has served on the board for more than twenty years and provided guidance and leadership over Measure I projects and state budget cuts. Today, Trustee Lahr is joined by Tim Bennett, Bernard Jones, Gregory A. Pensa, and Hilda Zacarías.

Dr. Ann Foxworthy, the first woman selected to be the college's superintendent/president, served in that position from 1992-2004. She was instrumental in introducing online instruction and registration to Hancock, oversaw the expansion of the college to include the Lompoc Valley and Solvang centers, and helped restructure the Allan Hancock College Foundation.

During his tenure as superintendent/president from 2005-2012, José M. Ortiz, Ed.D., oversaw the passage of Measure I and capital projects created with the funding. He successfully completed an accreditation reaffirmation and secured prestigious grants.

Trustees appointed Kevin G. Walthers, Ph.D. as the college's ninth superintendent/president in 2013. Since his hiring, several major facilities have come on-line, the college has received large donations and grants, and the college has twice been recognized by the Aspen Institute as one of the top community colleges in the state and country.

In every sense, Allan Hancock College is a college for the community. More than ninety-eight percent of its students come from the local area. The college puts great emphasis on the success of its students and challenges them to excel. In return, Hancock students consistently enjoy one of the best transfer rates to University of California and California State University campuses, including Cal Poly, San Luis Obispo, and UCSB.

The college has more than 1,200 full- and part-time employees, which makes Hancock one of the twelve largest employers in Santa Barbara County. The college has an economic impact of $200 million per year.

Notable alumni include actors Kathy Bates, Jessica Chastain, Harry Hamlin and the late Robin Williams; NFL running back Cameron Artis-Payne, television producer Tim Kring, former Major League pitcher Bryn Smith, San Luis Obispo County Sheriff Ian Parkinson, former Santa Maria Valley Chamber of Commerce Executive Director Bob Hatch, as well as numerous state and local leaders.

For more information about Allan Hancock College, visit www.hancockcollege.edu.

♦

Since district voters approved a $180 million bond for capital improvements in 2006, the college has opened numerous state-of-the-art facilities, like the Industrial Technology Complex, Student Services building (pictured), Public Safety Training Complex and new sports complex.

SMOOTH, INC.

For more than forty years, the Santa Maria Organization of Transportation Helpers—best known by its acronym, SMOOTH—has served the public transit and specialized transportation needs of seniors, the disabled, and economically disadvantaged residents of the Central Coast.

As the Consolidated Transportation Service Agency (CTSA), SMOOTH also provides referrals, planning, and support for community transportation projects in the region. SMOOTH operates three distinct divisions for direct services. The Transit Division includes Guadalupe Transit and the County Health Care Clinic Shuttle. The CTSA division includes services with Tri-Counties Regional Services, Senior Dial-a-Ride, City Recreation and Parks transportation for disabled adults, and Special Trip Services. SMOOTH's Non-Emergency Medical Transportation makes up the third division.

A nonprofit 501(c)(3) corporation, SMOOTH was first organized on March 27, 1974, to develop a transportation service to help senior family members and neighbors live independently and avoid premature institutionalization. Sixteen community organizations were represented at the planning meeting, including civic clubs,

grant organizations, social service programs, the City of Santa Maria, local faith-based groups and professional groups. During the next meeting on August 22, 1974, local attorney Jon Gudmunds offered the unanimously approved name, Santa Maria Organization of Transportation Helpers—SMOOTH.

The first SMOOTH vans were purchased with funds provided by the Altrusa International Club, the Community Action Commission (CAC) and community contributions. The fleet included a wheelchair lift that was later used for the 'Senior Bus' service, which provided daily trips from neighborhood bus stops and senior residences.

The City of Santa Maria initiated its first public transit system in 1976 and formed a relationship with SMOOTH that would last until 2003.

The 1980s was a period of sustained growth for SMOOTH with the development of three contract services. The County Public Health Care Clinic Shuttle, SMOOTH's longest continuing contract, began in 1982, providing van service to medical appointments in Santa Barbara. In 1983, SMOOTH began a weekly service, which operated until 2002 for

Above: Photograph from the November 24, 1975, issue of the Santa Maria Times.

Right: SMOOTH's state-of-the-art office and maintenance facility, dedicated in 2008.

Opposite, top: Early "Senior Bus" and SMOOTH Board, c. 1975.

Opposite, center: SMOOTH, Inc.'s first wheelchair lift equipped van, c. 1977.

Opposite, bottom: One of SMOOTH's contemporary vehicles, purchased with grant funds from the Santa Barbara Foundation.

sight-impaired individuals attending the Braille Institute in Santa Barbara. Then, in 1986, SMOOTH began providing door-to-door transportation to Santa Maria for residents of Guadalupe. This service was replaced in 1999 by a formal transit route, the Guadalupe Flyer, and then joined in 2000 by the in-town Guadalupe Shuttle. Guadalupe Transit now has the distinction of having the highest passenger trip per capita in northern Santa Barbara County.

A pivotal event occurred in 1999 when SMOOTH was designated the CTSA by Santa Barbara County. SMOOTH was charged with providing specialized transportation for residents and social services who were 'falling through the cracks' with traditional transit programs.

A fleet of four small vehicles provided 15,786 passenger trips its first full year in service and the CTSA program has grown to thirty vehicles providing more than 75,000 trips per year. The growth was the result of the purchase of sixteen new cutaway buses in 2002 through a federally-funded grant administered through the office of Congresswomen Lois Capps.

In 2003, recognizing hundreds of seniors were in need of a public dial-a-ride service, SMOOTH initiated the Senior Dial-A-Ride (SDAR) in Santa Maria. One of the first SDAR passengers commented, "There were times when I could not afford a taxi to get to the pharmacy or grocery store and I would do without. Now, the bus costs me just $4!"

In 2012, SMOOTH began providing daily Non-Emergency Medical Transportation for Medi-Cal patients to dialysis and medical appointments in Santa Maria and Lompoc. This is SMOOTH's fastest-growing operating division, increasing by forty percent during its first three years of service.

SMOOTH has weathered a number of challenges in a very volatile industry during its forty-two years of service. Despite statewide insurance crises, state budget crunches, spiraling fuel costs and economic recessions, SMOOTH has maintained its focus on serving seniors, disabled and economically disadvantaged residents. It is this focus that remains the benchmark for services that will take the company into a bright future.

MICHAEL W. MOATS, MD INC.

When Michael W. Moats graduated from medical school and completed his dermatology residency, he was recruited to Santa Maria by Dr. Bruce Howard because the city was in a growth spurt and underserved by dermatologists. Thirty-eight years later, Dr. Moats continues to provide sound, ethical dermatological care to the community.

The practice provides most general dermatology and cosmetic services utilizing board certified dermatologists, certified physician assistants and registered nurses.

Dr. Moats received his undergraduate degree from UCLA, and then graduated from UCLA Medical School in 1974. He completed his dermatology residency at USC. He is a Fellow of the American Academy of Dermatology and a Board Certified Dermatologist. He is also a member of the Pacific Dermatologic Society and the California Dermatologic Society.

Dr. Moats began his practice in Santa Maria in 1978 with one employee, Pam Cordero, who functioned as both the sole front and back office employee. Dr. Moats found that starting a private practice, which is really a small business, without any business experience was a challenging experience, particularly dealing and complying with regulatory agencies.

"We tried to maintain pace with scheduling and still give personalized service," Dr. Moats explains. "But beginning a practice without knowledge of government regulations of small businesses required a sharp learning curve."

The practice has grown from the original 1 employee to 13 employees and 3 providers. A cosmetic dermatology department, Moats Laser & Skin Care, was organized twelve years ago by Dr. Moats and his wife, Susan. Currently, Moats Laser & Skin Care is the top provider of Botox and dermal fillers in Santa Barbara County and San Luis County.

Cosmetic services provided by Dr. Moats include laser hair removal, IPL, laser skin resurfacing, LightPod V650, BOTOX® Cosmetic, JUVEDERM® Ultra Plux XC, JUVEDERM® Voluma, Restylane®, and Radiesse®. Aesthetic procedures include chemical peels, SilkPeel Demalinfusion, DeraFrac™, Chemical peel alternatives and Jane Iredale Mineral Makeup.

Dr. Moats. has been voted 'Best Place to Look 10 Years Younger' by the local newspaper six years in a row.

The practice's patient base extends from Santa Barbara to Paso Robles, with most patients coming from North Santa Barbara County and South San Luis County.

Facilities have expanded several times because of the practice's growth. The current location is 525 East Plaza Drive, Suite 200 in Santa Maria and on the Internet at www.moatslaser.com.

Dr. Moats joined Dr. Bruce Howard to establish the Central Coast Dermatological Society and Journal Club, both of which meet once a month to help further continued medical education. Dr. Moats has also attended the annual meeting of the American Academy of Dermatology for thirty-eight years and multiple other educational meetings to stay abreast with current topics in dermatology.

Dr. Moats was appointed Assistant Clinical Professor of Dermatology to train medical students. He is also on staff at Marian Regional Health Center and currently provides clinical rotation for one month to teach dermatology practice to each of the six family practice second-year resident physicians at the hospital. Dr. Moats is one of the six longest practicing physicians on staff at Marian Regional Health Center.

Dr. Moats is a member and past president of Santa Maria Noontime Kiwanis Club and a member of Santa Barbara Breakfast Rotary.

He has served on the Santa Maria Planning Commission, including seven years as chairman; and is a founder and director of the Community Bank of Santa Maria. He was elected to the Santa Maria City Council in November 2016.

An avid marathon runner, Dr. Moats has completed forty-three marathons, including Boston three times. Dr. Moats and his wife, Susan, have resided in the Santa Maria Valley for thirty-eight years where they have raised their four children. They have seven grandchildren.

SHEPARD
EYE CENTER

✦

Above: The original Shepard Eye Center in the early 1980s.

For nearly half-a-century, Shepard Eye Center has pioneered the latest and most innovative eye care for residents of the Central Coast.

Throughout its history, the eye center has been guided by its mission statement: "To provide a wide range of eye care with excellence in order to deliver both the best outcomes and the finest experience. We always operate in the best interests of our patients while showing the highest degree of caring, ethics and respect to our patients and each other."

Shepard Eye Center was established in 1967 by Dr. Dennis D. Shepard, an ophthalmologist who opened a solo practice in Santa Maria. Dr. Shepard, who holds several patents on eye surgical devices and other medical equipment, brought the very latest in eye care to the Central Coast. Dr. Shepard's wife, Francisca (Franzi), a talented businesswoman, was instrumental in the growth and development of the eye center.

Although no longer active in the day-to-day operation of the center, Dr. Shepard still keeps a close eye on the practice he established.

Among his many achievements, Dr. Shepard was the first to bring modern cataract surgery to the Central Coast. Prior to 1972, no doctor between Los Angeles and San Francisco had implanted an artificial lens inside the eye after cataract surgery. In those days, cataract surgery was a dreaded procedure requiring weeks of recuperation, followed by thick, 'coke-bottle' glasses or contact lenses. Today, Shepard Eye Center surgeons can perform cataract surgery on most patients with no needles, no stitches and no patches in its outpatient surgery center. A variety of advanced artificial lens options are available.

As the practice grew, Dr Shepard began to add additional ophthalmologists, and in 1983 he and Franzi built Shepard Eye Center at 1414 East Main Street next to Marian Medical Center. A year later, Dr. Shepard opened one of the first ambulatory surgical centers in California, providing surgical services outside a hospital setting. The new center soon attracted patients from all over the West Coast for state-of-the-art cataract surgery.

The staff continued to grow in the late 1980s, including the addition of a retina specialist, Dr. Stan Galis and several optometrists.

Dr. Stephen Bylsma joined the practice in 1993 and Dr. Rami Zarnegar in 1997. Dr. Shepard's son, Daniel Shepard, MD, followed in his father's footsteps as an eye surgeon. With additional training in retina surgery, he joined the practice in 2002.

◆

Left and below: The Shepard Eye Center at 910 East Stowell.

In 2004, Shepard Eye Center expanded into Lompoc and added optometrist Ken Kendall as the managing partner. Dr. Randall Goodman joined the group in 2005, and they opened a new large eye center in Lompoc in 2007 at 425 West Central Avenue.

Building on its reputation for innovation, Shepard Eye Center doctors were first to perform LASIK surgery in Santa Maria. The center now offers vision correction surgery that corrects a variety of problems, including nearsightedness, farsightedness and astigmatism using laser techniques such as Custom LASIK, the Implantable Collamer Lens (ICL) and natural lens replacement using bifocal implants.

In addition to its state-of-the-art surgical procedures, Shepard Eye Center provides its patients a full range of services from eye exams, glasses, contact lenses, glaucoma treatments, cataract surgery, retina care as well as being a leader in eyelid surgery. Their goal is to continue to offer world class eye care to the Central Coast.

The staff of Shepard Eye Center now includes 3 board-certified comprehensive ophthalmologists, 2 board-certified retina specialists, 5 optometrists and 70 support staff.

After renovating the historic Columbia Records building, a large new Shepard Eye Center opened at 910 East Stowell in 2015. The new expanded modern clinic has facilities

located all on one floor and is equipped with the very latest technology and equipment. The clinic includes a full service optical shop, eighteen exam rooms and a surgical suite for cosmetic and LASIK surgery.

After nearly fifty years, Shepard Eye Center in Santa Maria and Kendall-Shepard Eye Center in Lompoc remain committed to providing exceptional care. They pride themselves in offering our community an experience that combines the highest degree of professionalism with warmth, openness and understanding.

Boys & Girls Clubs of Santa Maria Valley

Boys & Girls Clubs of Santa Maria Valley (BGCSMV) has been in the forefront of youth development for half-a-century, working with young people from disadvantaged economic, social, and family circumstances. BGCSMV is dedicated to ensuring that our community's young people have greater access to high-quality programs and services that will enhance their lives and shape their futures. These programs foster a sense of belonging, competence, usefulness, and influence that builds self-confidence and leads youth members to great futures.

The organization was originally founded in 1966 after the Valley Merchants Association sent Santa Maria Police Officer Bill Bernhardt to Los Angeles to attend a law enforcement conference. Speakers at the conference recommended that cities entertain the idea of opening a Boys Club. The Valley Merchants Association, searching for a community relations/service project, contributed the initial $1,800 in startup money. Community leaders like Jack Gilliand and Sue Sword persuaded Officer Bernhardt and Bob Magee, then editor of the *Santa Maria Times*, to organize the club. The club's original location was the former Kirk Lumber building on West Main. It did not take long for the organization to outgrow that location. In the mid-1970s, the Donati family donated the land and the club moved to its current Railroad Avenue location in Santa Maria.

Programs for girls were added in 1985 and the organization's name was changed to Boys & Girls Club of Santa Maria. In 1990 a foundation was formed to support ongoing operating costs associated with BGCSMV. This foundation now has over $1 million in assets and continues to financially support BGCSMV's mission every year under the guidance of a volunteer board.

BGCSMV now serves 1,400 registered youth in day-to-day programming and an additional 6,900 youth via its various sports programs. Our clubs are designed exclusively for youth ages six to eighteen. BGCSMV operates 2 traditional clubsites (1 in Santa Maria and 1 in Guadalupe) and 7 ASES-funded sites in the Guadalupe Union and Santa Maria Bonita School Districts. There is also a clubsite located in the Evans Park Public Housing Complex in cooperation with the housing authority of the county of Santa Barbara. Three of the ten sites are open year-round.

Boys & Girls Clubs of Santa Maria Valley is a place of hope and opportunity. Our priority outcome areas are: to lead youth to academic success, help them adopt healthy lifestyles, and assist them in building character and citizenship skills. These priority outcome areas were created to ensure that every child graduates from high school on time with a plan for their future.

We keep our fees low and affordable, so that all young people have access to the club. However, it costs BGCSMV $1,169 annually to provide services to one child. Your financial support helps keep kids off the streets and in our clubs. Give today at www.bgcsmv.org or call 805-922-7163.

Dr. Gerald Ebner, a beloved Santa Maria physician, estimates that he has delivered more than 10,000 babies during his long career.

Dr. Ebner's OB-GYN practice began in 1979, following completion of his service at Vandenberg Air Force Base. He and another Santa Maria physician opened the first out-of-hospital, physician-owned birthing center in California in response to the emerging trend of family participation in pregnancy and birth. Dr. Ebner's son, Aaron, was the very first delivery on Father's Day, 1984. The birthing center closed after a few years as hospitals began providing similar birthing experiences.

His wife, Susan, an OB-GYN nurse practitioner/sonographer, has been at Dr. Ebner's side throughout his long career. They married while both were at Vandenberg Air Force Base in 1977 and, working together, have been able to accomplish much over the years.

Dr. Ebner served as chairman of the board of Valley Community Hospital for ten years. Always a progressive thinker, he became an early pioneer in female pelviscopy surgery, which allows more complex surgeries to be performed through a small umbilical incision, thus reducing anesthesia time and post-op recovery.

After more than forty years of service to the area, Dr. Ebner semi-retired in 2012. However, many of his patients had grown with him from puberty to menopausal years and refused to let him retire. He continues to practice part-time and his main focus recently has been bio-identical hormone replacement and other female aging issues.

"Santa Maria Valley has been a wonderful area in which to live, raise a family and practice medicine," says Dr. Ebner. "Very few things can compete with the satisfaction I've experienced with families experiencing the birth of their children, or improving the medical quality of a woman's life."

Working together Dr. Ebner and Susan have accomplished much to be proud of over the years, but they are especially proud of their blended family: Tom Kriz, David Ebner, Damon Ebner, Charlotte Ebner, M.D., Alex Ebner, Aaron Ebner, Jody Ebner Janovick and their nine (so far) grandchildren.

DR. GERALD EBNER, M.D.

◆

Left: Dr. Gerald Ebner.

Below: Dr. Ebner and his wife, Susan.

PARK AVENUE SMILES

DR. CAROLYN BALDIVIEZ, DDS

✦

Dr. Carolyn Baldiviez, DDS.

Park Avenue Smiles is home to Dr. Carolyn Baldiviez, DDS. Dr. Baldiviez went into private practice in 1996 when she purchased Dr. Oye's practice. She was the second female general dentist practicing in Santa Maria. In 1999, she purchased Dr. Beaver's practice and moved to her current location at 111 East Park Avenue in Santa Maria in 2005.

Dr. Baldiviez graduated from University of the Pacific School of Dentistry in San Francisco in 1994. She received her Bachelor of Science degree in Biology from Loyola Marymount University in 1991. Dr. Baldiviez was born and raised in Santa Maria and is a 1987 graduate of St. Joseph High School. She is blessed to be able to practice dentistry and raise her children, Caitlyn and Noah, in her hometown with her husband, Vincent Martinez, Esq., who is the managing partner of Twitchell and Rice, LLP. Dr. Baldiviez has enjoyed the opportunity to provide services for many people she has known her entire life and their families, as well as many new members of the Santa Maria community.

Park Avenue Smiles is a state-of-the-art practice providing services for all ages and includes preventative and restorative services, digital x-rays, cosmetic procedures, implant restorations, sleep appliances, TruDenta® headache and facial pain treatment, and Invisalign. Dr. Baldiviez' practice has a small hometown feel and is located in a renovated home that was originally built in the 1940s. The growth of the practice mainly comes from the referrals they are blessed to receive from patients. The greatest compliment received is through these referrals. New patients are always welcome.

At Park Avenue Smiles, Dr. Baldiviez and her team focus on providing the Santa Maria community with high-quality dental care in a warm, friendly and comfortable atmosphere. They feel it is absolutely essential to build trust with their patients by listening carefully to any questions and concerns and by working to address them. Kindness and caring are the cornerstones of Park Avenue Smiles' approach to dentistry, and it is what you can expect every time you visit the office. As dentistry continues to change, they will continue to grow and change as well, while always treating their patients in a manner in which they would want to be treated, providing the best dental care. Park Avenue Smiles is located on the Internet at www.drbaldiviez.com and at 111 East Park Avenue in Santa Maria.

St. Joseph High School, a college preparatory school in the Archdiocese of Los Angeles, is a vibrant learning community rooted in the Josephite Fathers' philosophy of 'Spirit of Family.' Faith development is emphasized through daily prayer, weekly adoration, theology classes, Masses, prayer services, and retreats.

St. Joseph High School opened in 1964 thanks to the inspiration of His Eminence James Francis Cardinal McIntyre who believed strongly in education and in the need for a Catholic high school in the most northern point of the Los Angeles Archdiocese. Cardinal McIntyre invited Josephite Fathers from England and Belgium, along with their sister community, the Daughters of Mary and Joseph, to administer the school. Their presence can still be felt on campus today.

The school serves students from the Santa Maria and Santa Ynez Valleys, Nipomo, Arroyo Grande, and Lompoc, as well as international students from China and numerous countries in Europe. The population of the student body ranges from 400 to 500, with approximately forty staff members.

The college preparatory curriculum at St. Joseph High School not only results in an average of ninety-nine percent of graduates going on to college, but these students also experience success in higher education. Graduates attend many of the top universities across the nation including Duke, Stanford, Notre Dame and UCLA. The school has been recognized with the National Blue Ribbon School Award and has continually received full-term accreditation from the Western Association of Schools and Colleges as well as the Western Catholic Educational Association.

St. Joseph High School offers twenty-two varsity sports, twenty-four clubs and organizations, and a comprehensive service program to balance the educational experience that results in the development of the whole person. Christian service is essential to each student's education and St. Joseph High School students can be seen throughout the community serving at various events, or volunteering at agencies, schools and parishes. More than 11,000 service hours are donated annually by the students.

St. Joseph High School is proud to have provided a lasting and valuable educational experience to three generations of students thus far. In keeping with the Spirit of Family, graduates continue to offer their time and talents back to the school and to their various communities, working in and contributing to all facets of business and industry. The strategic plan of St. Joseph High School will enable students for generations to come to receive a faith-based college preparatory education in keeping with the school's motto "To Image Christ in Mind, Heart, Body, and Soul."

✦

Top, left: Left to right, leading the procession for the dedication of the school on February 4, 1968, Fr. John Mayhew, Fr. Emil De Mol, Fr. Vincent McCabe, Cardinal McIntyre, and Msgr. Kieran Marum.

Above: St. Joseph High School's Crest and Motto on display in the school's front office.

Below: A statue of St. Joseph the Worker, Patron Saint of St. Joseph High School, adorns the grounds of the school.

LARRY LAVAGNINO

A REVIEW OF HIS LIFE

❖

Larry Lavagnino, mayor,
City of Santa Maria, 2003-2012.

Join me as I try to give you the essence of my wonderfully happy life.

I was born on October 2, 1935, in Santa Maria, California. I did the usual kindergarten and elementary school routine. I have always given the Sisters of St. Francis credit for building a solid foundation for my life, which I still use on a daily basis. They took a five-year-old boy and taught him to read and write, taught him right from wrong and to treat everyone with respect. I graduated from Santa Maria High School in 1953, without great distinction I might add! After my freshman year at Loyola University, Los Angeles, my father thought I might be more successful joining the Navy. I loved the Navy. They took a kid and turned him into a man.

In 1965, I went to work for Curtis Tunnell, who represented the Santa Maria area as 5th District Supervisor on the Santa Barbara County Board of Supervisors. Upon his retirement

in 1975, I continued to assist his successor, Harrell Fletcher. It was sixteen years that laid the foundation for future accomplishments.

After another sixteen years of working for large companies such as Southern California Gas Co. and Western LNG, I retired in 1994 at the age of fifty-nine, but not for long. I was appointed to the Santa Maria Planning Commission in 1995 and was chairman of the commission in 1996. In 1996 the city council appointed me to a vacant seat on the city council. In 2003, I was once again chosen by the council, this time, to be the mayor of the City of Santa Maria.

From 2003 to my retirement in 2012, I spent the happiest days of my life as mayor of my hometown serving the citizens of Santa Maria. During my time as mayor, I ran twice for re-election, receiving over seventy percent of the votes both times.

One of the things that I am proudest of is my family. My loving wife, Donna, never complained once about my absences representing the over 100,000 people living in the City of Santa Maria. I was always proud standing next to her at the many functions we attended over the years. All of our children have made us very proud. I have read that parents are considered successful if their children do great things and are honest and true. With that criteria, Donna and I have been very successful.

I loved every minute I served as mayor. I always remained true to my roots. My parents never saw me become mayor, but in my heart, I know they would have been very proud, but very surprised. Now, as I wind down my life, I have already decided on the heading for my tombstone. "LIFE WAS GOOD." And, it truly was.

I have to agree with my dad, life is good—especially when you live it like he has. I have never met anyone more honest, more caring or more dedicated to their job than my dad. I know he gave much deserved credit to the Sisters of St. Francis, but my grandfather, Larry Lavagnino, Sr., also played a huge role in providing the example to my dad of what a good man looked like. A good man opens doors for others, offers his seat to a woman, is fair in his business dealings and gets involved in the community. My grandfather was a much respected member of the Santa Maria community, working over forty years for the Bank of America and volunteering for almost every service organization in town. Even though he passed away in 1980, I still have people that approach me with stories of how he helped their family.

I did what most young Santa Marians do when they get old enough, I moved away in search of the big city and all the excitement that goes with it. I found myself in Phoenix, Arizona working in the aerospace industry. I spent the better part of fifteen years climbing the corporate ladder until one day I received a phone call that my dad been hospitalized with some heart trouble. After returning to Santa Maria to visit him, I fell in love with the place. I decided that it was time to move back and start over in my hometown. One of my first stops was the local bank where I was lucky enough to be waited on by a beautiful young woman named Marian, who ended up becoming my best friend and wife.

Soon after my arrival, I happened to meet the Mayor of Santa Maria, Abel Maldonado, who was running for State Assembly. We quickly became friends and after his election,

he offered me a job as his district representative. In 2003, Congressman Elton Gallegly tabbed me to head up his new district office in Solvang. I spent seven great years, honing my skills at constituent service and building relationships within the community.

Finally, in 2010, I decided that it was time to attempt my own run for office. After spending twelve years working on state and federal issues, I came to understand that local government is the most effective and so I ran for a seat on the Santa Barbara County Board of Supervisors. Amazingly enough I won and was even re-elected in 2014. I love what I do!

As is the case with many long time Santa Maria families, my grandfather laid down a path, my father followed it and improved upon it and now it is up to me and my kids to honor those that came before us by living lives they would be proud of—yes, life is good!

"I FOLLOWED IN MY FATHER'S FOOTSTEPS."

✦

Steve Lavagnino, member Santa Barbara County Board of Supervisors.

DIGNITY HEALTH–MARIAN REGIONAL MEDICAL CENTER

Marian Regional Medical Center's history began in 1940 when the Sisters of Saint Francis founded Our Lady of Perpetual Help Hospital with an unwavering mission to further the healing ministry of Jesus. In 1943, just three years after its inception, the hospital celebrated the birth of the 1,000th baby.

By 1957 the facility had opened a new wing and increased the patient capacity to eighty-five acute-care beds and fifteen bassinets. Growth in the Santa Maria Valley advanced the need for expanded medical services, hence the Sisters broke ground on a new 125-bed hospital on East Church Street. The ten-acre parcel was generously donated by local philanthropists Captain Allan and Marian Mullin Hancock. In 1967, Marian Hospital opened under the leadership and direction of Sister Marilyn Ingram, O. S. F. and had admitted more than 5,000 patients within two years.

The evolution of the facility continued through the latter half of the twentieth century, marked by innovation and expansion. The change of name in 1987 to Marian Medical Center reflected the hospital's commitment to comprehensive care and specialty services. These services included the Marian Heart Center, Imaging Services, Cancer Care and a clinical affiliation with UCLA, the opening of Marian Extended Care Center, and the development of Home Health, Hospice, and Infusion Services.

As Marian entered the twenty-first century, demand once again exceeded the capacity of the existing hospital, and plans for a new facility commenced. As these plans were underway, Marian continued to expand with Plaza Diagnostic Imaging Center and Plaza Surgery Center. To accommodate the need for increased Emergency Services, Marian opened the Patient Care Center. Furthermore, a state-of-the-art Neonatal Intensive Care Unit was opened in 2010 to provide expert care and advanced technology to the increasing newborn population.

Throughout the years, Marian has evolved from a small community hospital to a comprehensive regional medical center. Demand increased for the latest technological advancements, programs, and services that would allow our community to receive exceptional care locally. In 2012, Marian opened the doors to a new, state-of-the-art, 191-bed facility, marking a new era in healthcare for the Santa Maria Valley. The new facility includes a designated Receiving Center to treat ST-segment elevation myocardial infarction (STEMI) heart attacks, a twenty-one-bed level III Neonatal Intensive Care Unit, Level III Trauma Center, and a Cardiac Catheterization Hybrid Suite, among many other services.

Marian is also home to Mission Hope Cancer Center, the first and only integrated oncology facility on the Central Coast. The comprehensive center combines cancer treatment, imaging, research, education, and outreach services along with advanced technology and dramatic improvements in patient comfort.

Years ago, Marian made a commitment to the community to offer the most advanced technologies, the latest in medical breakthroughs, and the highest trained physicians and medical professionals. As we continue to evolve, we remain true to our promise; then, now, and always.

Santa Barbara County represents one of the most philanthropic regions in the United Sates of America and the Santa Barbara Foundation, established in 1928, has helped to nurture this quality in each successive generation. With their south county headquarters situated in the Léni Fé Bland building in downtown Santa Barbara, the foundation endeavors to build philanthropic capital, strengthen the nonprofit sector and solve community challenges throughout all of Santa Barbara County. The foundation continues to be the largest grant maker in Santa Barbara County and has a proud tradition of supporting students throughout Santa Barbara County with scholarships.

Established by Major Max Fleischmann, heir to the Fleischmann Yeast Company, with $250,000 worth of Standard Brands stock, the foundation's original purpose was to provide free band music to the people of Santa Barbara. As the Great Depression of the 1930s deepened, he and the trustees widened the scope of support. The foundation quickly became the central charitable organization in the community, leading efforts to upgrade substandard housing, fund hospitals, create employment and ensure the region's water supply.

The foundation's endowment, which consists of gifts from hundreds of donors throughout Santa Barbara County has grown from Fleischmann's original gift of $250,000 to over $310 million today. The number of nonprofits that have been funded by the foundation has grown to over 600 and staff has increased from three employees in 1991 to twenty-four employees in 2016.

The scope of the foundation's mission has evolved throughout the years. In recent decades, the foundation has made investments in the community in the areas of health and human services; education and youth development; arts, culture and humanities; environment and animals; and public, societal and community improvement. In 2015, the foundation awarded grants totaling nearly $22 million and provided $1.6 million in student scholarships.

Recognizing the need to expand the reach of services in the northern part of Santa Barbara County, the foundation is opening a north county headquarters in Santa Maria in the fall of 2016. The foundation will also be providing enhanced nonprofit educational opportunities in Lompoc and Santa Maria, expanding donor services, and continuing philanthropic partnerships.

The Santa Barbara Foundation offers donor advised funds, committee advised funds, charitable gift annuities and specializes in complex gifts of real estate, business shares and gifts funded with illiquid assets. Additionally, donors who desire to make a gift that will provide them a guaranteed income stream as well as satisfy their philanthropic passions may be interested in setting up a Charitable Gift Annuity. The Foundation is licensed by the State of California to administer this type of gift and a number of donors have made significant contributions to their favorite charity using this planned giving vehicle.

The Santa Barbara Foundation endeavors to become ever more vigilant at fulfilling our mission as a leader, catalyst and resource for philanthropy. Through innovative partnerships with donors and agencies, long-range planning and responsive grant making, we will continue to support and sustain a better life for the residents of Santa Barbara County.

If you are interested in learning more about the foundation please call 805-963-1873 or visit sbfoundation.org.

✦

*Above: Santa Barbara Foundation's
North County Headquarters, opening
October 2016.*

*Left: Major Max Fleischmann,
the founder of the Santa
Barbara Foundation.*

SANTA MARIA VALLEY YMCA

With a mission centered on community service, the Santa Maria Valley YMCA brings families together and empowers individuals of all ages. At the Y, we measure the success of our cause by how well we engage communities in our three areas of focus: Social Responsibility, Youth Development and Healthy Living. The 13,000 on and off site Y members are reflected by our diverse and long committed eighteen-member board. Y volunteers raise over $250,000 annually to provide financial assistance to our neighbors who need us the most.

The Santa Maria Valley YMCA began in the 1940s as the Y's Men's Club. In 1946 a thirteen-acre camp was deeded to the YMCA and Camp Ocean Pines was established. A board of directors was formed in 1961 and Carl DuBois was hired as the first CEO. Wayne Hesselbarth and Joe Gray were philanthropic founding fathers who saw the need for a Y and worked to build an organization that would benefit the community. Samuel L. Choller served as the first chairman of the board.

In 1962 a small building at 507 South McClelland Street was purchased and the Y Men's Club raised money to add a meeting room. In 1978, several local square dance groups joined to form the Independent Square Dance Society of Santa Maria. They joined forces with the Y and, in 1979, signed an agreement to raise $150,000 to fund a 3,000 square foot addition to the original facility. The premier programs in the early years were Y Indian Guides and Princesses for fathers and their little ones as well as Y-High, youth and government and swim teams for the high school ages.

The current Santa Maria YMCA facility at 3400 Skyway Drive was built in 1981 and includes a 38,000 square foot multipurpose facility, outdoor pool, racquetball courts, and two basketball half-courts. Renovations between 1992-2016 increased the facility to 45,000 square feet and included two fitness rooms, a skate park, soccer arena and family park.

Among the Y's most popular 'fun'-raising activities are the annual Y Golf Tournament, now in its thirty-eighth year, and Family Day in the Park, a joint venture with the Breakfast Rotary, which attracts more than 8,000 people annually.

The Santa Maria Valley YMCA employs 140 people, is helped by over 700 volunteers and partners with dozens of fellow community non-profits, four school districts, the city of Santa Maria and the County of Santa Barbara. The Y is a community staple and proud to be a part of the Santa Maria Valley.

❖

Above: The original Santa Maria Valley YMCA Office, located at 507 South McClelland Street in 1962.

Below: Today, in 2016, the Santa Maria Valley YMCA is located at 3400 Skyway Drive.

Senior housing in Santa Maria was sorely lacking in the mid-1970s when Teamsters Local 381 decided to sponsor, develop and construct the low income and elderly resident facility known today as Union Plaza. At the time, census records showed 4,676 seniors in need of housing, with only a high-rise and a handful of homes to meet the need. Union Plaza was envisioned as a senior citizen housing complex, multifamily apartments for medium income groups, a community center and medical offices.

The Teamsters obtained financing for the project through the federal Department of Housing and Urban Development. Union Plaza Corporation was incorporated on January 4, 1972.

At the dedication of the much-needed facility, Mayor George Hobbs said it "Would take an area dying on the vine and make it boom again." Councilman Dan Firth added that it was "A realistic approach that provides optimism and hope for the downtown situation." The facility was praised as "A fine step forward" by Councilman Tom Weldon, Jr.

Originally, the high-rise was proposed to be twelve stories but the fire department would not authorize a structure that tall because they did not have the equipment to reach that high. Union Plaza became a seven story structure with a total of 122 units, all of which are Section 8 assisted living units. The complex provides a safe and friendly environment for the elderly and low-income citizens of the area.

The first manager of the apartment complex was Harold Munn. The first couple to move in was Mr. and Mrs. John Moke. Directors and officers of Union Plaza are required to be members of the Local Teamsters Union. In 2012, after Local 381 merged with Teamsters 986, the dedication to the Plaza and its residents has continued.

The complex has continued to flourish under the leadership of Terry Krelle, presently the project superintendent. Hector Fuentes is the current project manager, handling the daily duties of general administration, maintenance and resident needs. The project manager is supported by a full-time service coordinator, office administrator and activity director, as well maintenance personnel.

♦

Above: Union Plaza, c. 1982.

Left: Union Plaza under construction in 1975.
PHOTO COURTESY OF THE SANTA MARIA TIMES.

Below: Project Superintendent Terry Krelle.

Bottom: Project Manager Hector Fuentes.

638—Beautiful Flower Seed Farms in California

Near Lompoc, Calif.

OB-H1492

✦

A flower seed farms in the
Santa Maria Valley, c. 1960.

THE MARKETPLACE

Santa Maria Valley's retail and

commercial establishments offer

an impressive variety of choices

ANDRE, MORRIS & BUTTERY

The history of the Andre, Morris & Buttery law firm stretches back more than sixty years in the Santa Maria Valley. And what a history it has been!

It began in 1948, when Peter and George Andre opened a law office in San Luis Obispo. The brothers' legal skills were soon discovered in Santa Maria, and the Andre brothers began drawing numerous farming and ranching families to their fledgling Andre & Andre law practice. Peter even took to wearing a cowboy hat with his business suits, earning him the moniker, "The Lawyer in a Stetson."

In those early days, the practice ranged from family law to criminal cases and focused on issues like property disputes, estate planning, and probate. As their client list grew, Peter and George added partners including Richard Wood, who in the 1960s tried cases in Northern Santa Barbara County Superior Court.

Over the years, the firm expanded and changed with the communities it served. Partner Michael Morris came on board in 1972 and Jim Buttery became a partner in 1977. The firm changed its name to Andre, Morris & Buttery and moved from general law to business practice, specializing in business and real estate transactions and litigation, while continuing the tradition of estates and trusts.

"We have a long history of advising agriculture and business," Michael said. "That includes the energy business, which has played a vital role in the economic development of the Santa Maria Valley." Michael noted that many Santa Maria community members depend on the oil industry for their livelihoods. The firm represented Unocal in significant cases in the 1990s.

Agriculture and oil remain mainstays of the Santa Maria Valley, but producers have changed with the times. Wine grapes and berries played a big role in expanding the economy of a valley once dominated by potatoes and sugar beets.

Above: Peter (pictured) and George Andre chose law over the grocery business, and in 1948 formed the Andre & Andre law partnership, which became Andre, Morris & Buttery in 1981, and quickly became the trusted advisors for Central Coast business leaders.

PHOTO SOURCE: MEMORIES OF A SMALL TOWN BOY, BY PETER ANDRE, COURTESY OF THE ANDRE MORRIS & BUTTERY LIBRARY.

Right: The Andre family's deep roots on the Central Coast were planted when they opened Andre Grocery Co. in downtown San Luis Obispo in 1902. Patriarch Jose Andre's compassion and generosity kept families on the Central Coast fed during the Great Depression by allowing many bills to go largely unpaid. The Andre Family's community spirit is carried on today through Andre, Morris & Buttery's many civic and philanthropic activities in both the City of Santa Maria and San Luis Obispo County.

PHOTO COURTESY OF THE HISTORY CENTER OF SAN LUIS OBISPO COUNTY.

Recognizing the economic expansion and opportunities in Santa Maria, in 2002, Andre, Morris & Buttery opened a Santa Maria office. Four partners, Jim Buttery, Kathy Eppright, Bill Douglass and Karen Gjerdrum Fothergill, and a full staff work from the third floor of the Community Bank building at 2739 Santa Maria Way.

"As our practice grew, it ultimately made sense for our firm to open an office here," Michael said. "The rest of the firm's attorneys are often working in this office as well, and our practice is the same in both locations."

For the past six decades, Andre, Morris & Buttery has assisted clients in achieving economic and personal goals and advised owners and operators on agricultural and business law and personnel management.

Andre, Morris & Buttery works hard to protect its clients' interests. Several years ago, Jim litigated a headline-making case in Santa Maria involving a mobile home park manager who attempted to swindle a woman's estate out of millions of dollars. An astute Santa Maria trust officer noticed just weeks before probate was scheduled to close that the estate's executor and beneficiary was a Santa Maria mobile home park manager he knew the deceased woman had not liked.

Probate was put on hold while Jim litigated the case. It took some sleuthing and the right connections to solve it, but, in the end, handwriting analysis determined the woman's signature had been forged. The woman's legitimate will was found and the park manager

went to jail. "That was one of the most meaningful cases for me," Jim said.

The firm's attorneys and staff have volunteered their time and talents to the Santa Maria community by serving on the boards of organizations such as SMOOTH, the Santa Maria Discovery Museum, and the YMCA; supporting its agencies and institutions such as the Farm Bureau, the Santa Maria Valley Economic Development Association, and Hancock College; and participating as members of organizations such as Rotary and the Women's Fund, to name two.

The attorneys at Andre, Morris & Buttery are proud to be a part of the history of the Santa Maria Valley and carry on the law firm's legacy, with or without a Stetson.

✦

Above: Photographed at the breathtaking Presqu'ile Winery and Tasting Room, Andre, Morris & Buttery attorneys (left to right) Bill Douglass, Karen Fothergill and Jim Buttery assisted the winery's owners in turning their vision for a winery into a reality in the Santa Maria Valley.
PHOTO BY JERED SCOTT

Below: Known as "the lawyer in the Stetson hat," Peter Andre (pictured right) and his firm attracted a clientele of farmers, dairymen and cattlemen throughout the region.
PHOTO COURTESY OF THE HISTORY CENTER OF SAN LUIS OBISPO COUNTY.

THE HISTORIC
SANTA MARIA INN

Top: The inn's elegant exterior welcomes guests with its signature fountain, shipped from location by owner Bob Hollingsead.

Above: The Santa Maria Inn combining the grace and style of a bygone era with modern hospitality and amenities.

Built in 1917, the venerable Santa Maria Inn boasts a unique blend of twenty-first century hospitality with the style and elegance of an English country inn.

The original inn, as conceived by entrepreneur Frank J. McCoy, had twenty-four rooms, twenty-four baths, a kitchen and a dining room. Due in large part to its unique first class accommodations, its location nearly midway between Los Angeles and San Francisco, and the burgeoning popularity of auto travel in the ensuing decades, the inn grew in popularity into the 1950s. The inn was refurbished and rejuvenated over the years, first in the 1940s and again in the 1980s, but its renaissance into the truly unique facility it is today began with its acquisition in 1999 and subsequent series of major renovations by the partnership of Hardy and Judy Hearn and Robert and Blanche Hollingsead.

A registered historic landmark and celebrity retreat, the Santa Maria Inn of today features 164 beautiful guestrooms and luxury suites, some with fireplaces and patios. Facilities including the Garden Room Restaurant, Wine Cellar and Martini Bar, and Old English Tap Room evoke an atmosphere of casual elegance. The grounds feature an abundance of palm trees, soothing fountains and rose gardens, and its spacious sitting room is filled with historic photos, period furnishings and original stained glass windows. The oversized guestrooms of its newer tower section and the cozy ambience of the original inn combine to provide the architectural grace and style of a bygone era with modern travel amenities.

Over the years, the Santa Maria Inn has welcomed an incredible array of celebrity guests. In the heyday of William Randolph Hearst's Hearst Castle, it was common practice for Hearst to host visitors on their way to the Castle at the inn the night before (some of the roses in the inn's rose garden actually came from Hearst Castle.) Such early entertainment luminaries as Douglas Fairbanks, Charlie Chaplin, and Rudolph Valentino were guests.

The inn was also a convenient and comfortable local headquarters during the making of some early (and not-so-early) Hollywood movies, including the entire cast for Cecil B. DeMille's *The Ten Commandments* in 1923, Douglas Fairbanks while filming *The Thief of Baghdad*, Adolph Menjou and Marlene Dietrich in 1930 while filming *Morocco*, Jimmy Stewart while filming *The Spirit of St. Louis*, and Walter Matthau and Jack Lemmon while filming *Out To Sea*. The list of well-known guests is long and many have had their visits memorialized with stars on guestroom doors. A few of the more intriguing visitors have been Marilyn Monroe (who actually lived in Santa Maria for a short period in her youth); William Randolph Hearst along with his long-time companion, Marion Davies; Herbert Hoover; Mary Pickford; Bing Crosby; Bob Hope; Joan Crawford; Lee Marvin; Mickey Rooney; Gary Cooper; Clark Gable; Cary Grant; Oliver Hardy; Gloria Swanson; Shirley Temple; John Wayne; and, yes, Michael Jackson.

With its rich and colorful history, it is no wonder that there are those who believe the inn may actually be haunted by some of its more "energetic" former residents. Rudolph Valentino reportedly likes to knock on room 221's door and even occasionally recline on the bed in that room. The ghost of a sea captain is rumored to appear inside the hotel and is associated in some forgotten way to room 210. Other whispered stories include a piano that plays by itself; mysterious footprints; unexplained perfume smells; spinning clock hands; opening and closing doors; music from disconnected speakers; and an elevator going to a certain floor on its own always at the same time of day. Stories and memories like these combine to make the inn an important link to the Santa Maria Valley's past.

For more information or to make reservations at the Santa Maria Inn, visit the website at www.santamariainn.com.

✦

Above: The owners of the Santa Maria Inn, left to right, Hardy and Judy Hearn and Blanche Hollingsead.

Below: One of the soothing fountains with giant Bird of Paradise plants.

DUDLEY-HOFFMAN MORTUARY

Founded in 1876, and now operated by the third generation of the same family, Dudley-Hoffman Mortuary has the distinction of being the oldest continually operated business in Santa Maria.

In the 1800s it was common for furniture companies that built caskets to offer funeral services as well, and Dudley-Hoffman began as T. A. Jones Undertaking and Furniture Co. The original location was 110 East Church Street in downtown Santa Maria.

From the introduction of motorized casket coaches in the early 1900s to the tranquil Memory Gardens and 'Tower of Light', Dudley-Hoffman has served the community well for 140 years. It is estimated that the mortuary has served more than 50,000 families during its long history.

The mortuary was purchased by the Dudley family in 1904 and they operated it until 1960, when it was sold to Asa and Janice Hoffman, parents and grandparents of the current owners, who had worked for the firm since 1945. Jeffrey Hoffman joined the mortuary in 1970 and his son, Michael, joined the family firm in 2006.

The Hoffman family is dedicated to providing trusted service and gentle guidance for families of all faiths and ethnic origins during their times of need. "We're a small town funeral home that takes care of everyone the best we can," says Jeffrey. "We try very hard to treat every person the way we would want our family to be treated during their time of need."

As Santa Maria has grown from a population of 6,000 to more than 100,000, Dudley-Hoffman Mortuary has grown with the times. The mortuary is located on a tranquil two and a half acre site at 1003 East Stowell Road. Families and friends may gather in one of three visitation rooms and memorial services may be conducted in a graceful chapel that seats 200.

The beautifully landscaped grounds include the Memory Gardens, which provide a cemetery

for cremated remains, twenty-four outdoor garden crypt banks, and two inside glass-front niche rooms. The restful and comforting 'Tower of Light', located within the walls of the Memory Garden, has twenty-seven levels designed to temporarily or permanently house cremated remains.

Dudley-Hoffman offers a full range of personalized services to meet the individual requirements of each family it serves. Among these services are traditional funerals, cremation services, multicultural or multi-faith services, and church, chapel and graveside services. The firm also provides personalized memorial markers and headstones and pre-planned services.

With more than a dozen employees, the Dudley-Hoffman staff includes several long-time employees. Two others retired recently after twenty-eight and thirty-three years of service. "We have a very competent staff and I can't say enough about them," comments Jeffrey. "We have a reputation for making sure things are done right. Whatever the faith or ethnic background, we treat everyone the same."

The goal of Dudley-Hoffman Mortuary is to help families quickly begin the process of healing after experiencing the loss of a loved one. The mortuary takes care of all the details and works within the client's budget to help choose the best type of service, selection of casket, urn or memorial marker, as well as handling permits and fees, and the transfer and disposition of remains.

"We try to keep our business family oriented and our plans for the future are to continue offering the same quality services we have been known for since 1876," says Jeffrey.

MICHAEL B. CLAYTON & ASSOCIATES

✦

Above: "Favorite picture" of Michael Clayton. He and his Grandmother, Edith Clayton, when she presented Michael with a Bible on his twentieth birthday.

Below: Michael, his wife, Lourdez, and sons, Christopher and Matthew.

Michael Clayton has become a well-known and respected attorney since coming to Santa Maria in 1989. However, Michael may be even more appreciated for his support of veterans and the Elks Rodeo, as well as an annual Christmas decorations display that has earned him the title 'King of Christmas'.

A native of Fort Smith, Arkansas, Michael earned his Bachelor's Degree in Business from the University of Arkansas and a Juris Doctor Degree from the school's law school. He then obtained a license to practice law in California after moving to Santa Maria, where he worked for a local law firm. On November 1, 1996, he started his own law firm across the street from the Santa Maria Courthouse at 400 East Orange Street.

Michael has always believed in giving back to his community and after watching the movie *Saving Private Ryan* with his wife, Lourdez, in 2000, he decided to concentrate on helping veterans. He explains that the idea of a barbeque appealed to him because he grew up in Arkansas, where barbeques are a frequent festive occasion.

The Claytons organized a Veteran's Day barbeque and began serving free meals to veterans each November 11. Last year, their fifteenth Veterans Day barbeque, they served 2,500 plates of food at the Veterans Memorial Building, where volunteers dished out tasty tri-tip, chicken and other delicious foods.

For his efforts, Michael was presented the Elks Lodge Citizen of the Year Award in 2011. He says he is very "humbled and very thankful" for the honor but insists the award with his name on it actually belongs to his family, office staff, and the many volunteers who help with the annual event.

Michael has also been deeply involved in the Annual Elks Rodeo and Parade. His entry in the parade was a Lady Justice float in 2007 that won the Mayor's Trophy for 'Best

Community Event' one of the five major awards presented to parade participants.

Michael's many contributions to the rodeo and parade were recognized in 2013 when he was selected to be the parade's Grand Marshall. Instead of riding his float well back in the parade lineup, Michael led the parade in his Corvette, with his popular Lady Justice float sailing along behind him.

Michael's spectacular Christmas display of lights and decorations has earned him the unofficial title of 'King of Christmas.' Michael put up 5,000 Christmas lights the first year he decorated his downtown office building in 1996. The following year, the number of lights exploded to 35,000 and the lights and other holiday decorations have grown each year since.

Last year, Michael had 50,000 lights on his business and the surrounding area. "We put all these up ourselves," Michael says. "PG&E is very happy with me."

Normally, Michael starts hanging lights in early November, outlining just about every part of his business—all his windows, the entire parking lot, trees, and signs. The trees and surrounding plants are also 'flocked' covered with a white, sticky substance that dries hard in the sun." Every year it gets more elaborate," he admits.

So famous are Michael's Christmas displays that children send their letters to Santa Claus to his law firm, and teachers sometimes bring their students by for a fun field trip to see the whimsical displays.

Michael was honored for his many contributions to the community when Mayor Larry Lavagnino proclaimed May 1, 2006, as Michael B. Clayton Day. The mayor presented the honor because of Michael's many services to Santa Maria, especially his support for veterans.

Michael is a dedicated family man with the loving support of his wife, Lourdez, and their two sons, Christopher and Matthew. Michael is very supportive of Santa Maria's youth population and the possibilities they provide for a stronger community and a more hopeful future.

✦

Above: Michael B. Clayton & Associates. Front row, Lily Rolon, Noemy Bautista, Sandra Alvarado, Elvira Sanchez and Mirella Ujano. Back row, Francisco Romero, Thomas Barnard, Michael B. and Lourdez Clayton and Marco Gonzalez.

Below: Grand Marshal, Michael B. and Lourdez Clayton, at the 2013 Elks Rodeo parade. Christopher and Matthew Clayton, ride at the front of the ship float following behind.

SANTA MARIA PUBLIC AIRPORT DISTRICT

The Santa Maria Public Airport District (SMX) provides a convenient, hassle-free flying experience for those flying to or from the California Central Coast. Boarding time and security checks are quick, simple and efficient. Patrons have the choice of two commercial airlines and parking is always free and only a few steps away. A Radisson Hotel is located on the airfield.

SMX also serves the general aviation and corporate communities and the airport is dedicated to make recreational or business aviation a pleasant and safe environment.

The history of SMX began during World War II when the Army Corps of Engineers constructed the Santa Maria Army Base to train crews for B-25 bombers. The facility later became a training field for P-38 pilots and ground crews.

At the war's end, the County of Santa Maria acquired the property in 1946 and the City of Santa Maria became a half-owner in 1949. This dual ownership/management proved difficult to administer and the Santa Maria Public Airport District was formed in 1964.

The Airport District encompasses 400 square miles and is governed by a five-member board of directors, which is elected at large. Since the district was organized, a number of projects have directly or indirectly benefitted each person in the valley. These projects include construction of Skyway Drive from Betteravia Road to the Orcutt Expressway, construction of an industrial park east of Skyway Drive, and construction of a new airport terminal building, fire/crash/rescue station, air traffic control tower, new hangars and other facilities. A 4,000 square foot baggage claim facility opened in 2007, making SMX the first airport on the Central Coast to use a state-of-the-art baggage carousel.

The airport is situated on 2,500 acres and includes two active runways. A runway expansion in 2012 extended the main runway to 8,004 feet. This improvement enabled the airport to transition to jet service by all current airlines and improved destinations. Additionally, the airport serves as a U.S. Forest Service tanker base protecting the Los Padres National Forest and beyond, handling up to the DC-10 air tanker on the extended runway. The airport provides facilities for SkyWest/United Express and Allegiant Airlines and serves as the home base for many commercial aviation businesses and more than 200 general aviation aircraft.

For more information about the Santa Maria Public Airport, please visit their website at www.santamariaairport.com.

The Radisson Hotel Santa Maria, one of the few California hotels located adjacent to a public airport, provides guests with direct access to their personal aircraft, easy access to the airport, the Santa Maria Airport Business Park, downtown Santa Maria, nearby Vandenberg Air Force Base, and Santa Barbara Wine Country with its plentiful boutique wineries and numerous scenic and challenging golf courses. The impressive lobby's aircraft-themed murals remind visitors of the hotel's connection to Santa Maria's historic Allan G. Hancock Airfield, today's Santa Maria Public Airport.

The hotel was built in 1984 in anticipation of rapid growth of the base's space launch programs. It was originally a Hilton franchise but with the eventual acquisition of the property in 2001 by current owners, Judy and Hardy Hearn and Blanche Hollingsead, who also own The Historic Santa Maria Inn, a rigorous investment in upgrades led to its resurgence as an award-winning Radisson Hotel.

One of the recent historical highlights was an extended musical show engagement featuring 1940s' screen legend Jane Russell of *Gentlemen Prefer Blondes* and *The Outlaw* fame, among many other memorable films. Since its opening, the hotel has had the honor of hosting many high profile guests. These guests include George W. Bush, Michael Jackson, John Travolta, Harrison Ford, Calista Flockhart and Betty White to name a few.

The hotel's large and flexible meeting rooms and spacious outdoor facilities have made it the venue of choice for a variety of community events including business meetings, nonprofit fundraising galas, conferences and seminars, and art and car shows, several of which have become annual events.

The Radisson Hotel Santa Maria offers 184 well-appointed guest rooms and suites, an outdoor swimming pool and whirlpool tub, a fitness center with sauna, business center, and two excellent dining options. The Atrium Bistro features an "All American" breakfast buffet served daily as well as cooked-to-order breakfast. The award-winning Vintner's Grill serves lunch and dinner and is renowned for its American style cuisine and exceptional wine list. On Sunday's, you can enjoy a fabulous brunch including bottomless champagne. Vintner's Bar is open daily for guests to relax and enjoy the scenic views of the airport runway and rolling hills that surround it.

✦

Top: Our guest rooms, lobby and restaurant overlook the airport runway.

Above: Our lobby, featuring custom painted wall murals, focuses on Santa Maria's rich aviation history.

Left: Dine in the award-winning Vintner's Grill with vistas of the airport runway and rolling hills.

VALLEY ART GALLERY

◆

Above: Digital photograph by Pat Stalter.

Below: Dancing Daisies by Hattie Stoddard.

The Valley Art Gallery is a group of varied artists local to the Santa Maria Valley. The Valley Art Gallery of today began as The Cultural Corner Gallery under the umbrella of the City of Santa Maria in 1983. Santa Maria has long fostered aspirations to elevate the standards of cultural and artistic presentation within the community. From Ethel May Dorsey's development of Santa Maria Valley Beautiful in 1963, Santa Maria has had a love affair with its cultural and artistic side.

The intention of the gallery both, old and new, is to provide a place where artists of many backgrounds from the Santa Maria Valley can exhibit their artistry for the enrichment of all.

Although having transitioned through many name changes and locations, that purpose has never altered. In June 2006, under the name Town Center Gallery, this guild of artists was incorporated as a nonprofit organization. Its mission remained unchanged as it continued under the supervision of a board of directors "to be a valuable asset to the community bringing local visual art to the public eye."

Today, a long shotgun style display space in the South East Oak Knolls Center is home to the Valley Art Gallery. It brims with variety. Art created by members of the valley's community is at last presented after nearly two years without a permanent address. The gallery is run by volunteers. Member artists show and sell their work. They also act as docents, and if required, interpreters for the range of visual art displayed before an admiring public. As an organization, the Gallery provides access to opportunities for artists to participate in community events and shows, scholarship funds for aspiring student artists, year-round art classes, and lectures and demonstrations for children and adults. Artists are encouraged to develop an awareness and interest in furthering their own creative endeavors.

Whether it be a city like Santa Maria with its insatiable thirst to be a cultural destination or an individual investor intent on support of a single artist, historically art has required great patronage to thrive. The Valley Art Gallery is an art organization with open arms. Learn more at www.valleygallery.org.

The Hitching Post in Casmalia, former cow-town of the Old West, where California-style barbecuing was brought to perfection by the pioneers, has kept this live-oak method of bringing choice, aged beef to the ultimate of gourmet flavor and tenderness. No wonder *Forbes* magazine named The Hitching Post one of the "10 Great BBQ Restaurants in the USA."

The Hitching Post traces its history to the Casmalia Hotel, founded in 1920 by Paul Veglia. The restaurant, which is now a historic landmark, was opened in 1946. In 1952 the business was purchased by Frank and Victor Ostini and their nephew, Jerry Ransom. The brothers bought out Ransom two years later. Frank did all the cooking behind the barbecue grill, while Vic bartended and worked in the kitchen.

There were no menus in the early days because the restaurant offered only one dinner option—an eighteen-ounce steak. The chef decided if you were served a T-Bone, Filet Mignon, Top Sirloin or New York Strip.

In 1957, Julio Zaragoza bought Vic's share of the business. Frank and Julio took turns cooking. In 1967, Frank bought Julio's portion of the restaurant and it has been solely owned by the Ostini family since.

When Frank, Sr., passed away in 1977, his oldest sons, Bill and Frank, Jr., took over the daily operation of the business and soon after purchased the restaurant from their mother, Natalie. Younger siblings Terri, Mike, Bob and Annette all worked (some still working) at the restaurant over the years. The brothers opened a second location in Buellton in 1986, which has seen great success for nearly thirty years. The HP is proud of their loyal staff, many of whom have worked for the family for more than three decades.

You will not find better steaks anywhere. On the menu it says "We endeavor to keep alive the traditions of the old romantic West. The weather-beaten walls of our 120 year old building are crammed with memories that induce an atmosphere of Western nostalgia to romantically inclined people who can relax and trade the pressures of the fast, modern world for an evening of Old West hospitality." This truly describes what you will experience at this destination landmark restaurant.

To learn more about The Hitching Post in Casmalia, click on their website at www.hitchingpost1.com.

✦

Left: Bill Ostini, 2014.

Below: Frank Ostini, Sr., c. early 1970s.

SANTA MARIA VALLEY CHAMBER OF COMMERCE

The Santa Maria Valley Chamber of Commerce is the largest business organization in northern Santa Barbara County. Its members include small businesses, corporations, associations, and individual professionals. Since its inception in 1902, the chamber has worked diligently to better the area's business climate, forge a stronger community, and improve the quality of life. The chamber works with local government, education, private industry and a host of other partners to improve the business environment and promote Santa Maria as a premier community in which to vacation, live, work, and do business.

The Santa Maria Valley Chamber of Commerce brings leadership to the process of creating a community where business thrives. Partnering with employers and community partners, we work to create a "culture of commerce."

Chamber programs are built around the core principles of:

• Creating a strong local economy;
• Promoting the community;
• Providing networking opportunities; and
• Representing the interests of business with government.

Santa Maria's business base (and chamber membership) has become increasingly diversified over the last several decades. Building on the foundation of agriculture and energy production, today companies of all types, from manufacturing to financial services to telecommunications to defense-related firms

successfully conduct their business in our region. Santa Maria based manufacturers produce a wide array of products ranging from medical testing supplies to aircraft interiors and baby care products to fire hoses.

The chamber organizes and directs the efforts of those who share the desire to improve the conditions under which business is conducted. Through participation in the chamber, members are able to accomplish collectively what they could not do individually.

Businesses that join the chamber receive a multitude of benefits and advantages ranging from networking, marketing and advertising opportunities, to legislative advocacy, educational forums to benefit business, and economic opportunities.

Through its Visitor & Convention Bureau and Economic Development Commission programs, the Chamber of Commerce plays a leading role in promoting tourism, attracting new businesses, and assisting existing businesses to grow and succeed.

Investment in the chamber is an investment in your business—and in the prosperity of the Santa Maria Valley!

Albert Hernandez loves cars. His business, City Motors Collision Center, is a reflection of his twenty-five years of hard work, determination, and inspiration. City Motors Autobody Shop was begun by the Musch family in 1959 and Albert has based his business on the reputation and ethics he learned from them.

Dedicating himself to doing business right and focusing on the work he is good at, Albert took inspiration early on when John Wannabe encouraged his talent in painting. As a young man of eighteen, he began his education at Airport Auto Center, sweeping floors and studying the business that surrounded his love of cars. A fast learner with a good eye, Albert was promoted quickly and began prepping cars for paint. The transformation process was so immensely rewarding to Albert that he became an avid learner in those early days as a young apprentice.

By 2012, Albert had moved on to work in San Luis Obispo, perfecting his skills and getting more hands-on experience with knowledgeable professionals. With more vehicles on the road than ever before, the demand for talented paint and collision technicians was growing and technology was transforming the industry. Over the next ten years, Albert built his reputation in the business; trading hard work for knowledge of autobody collision repair expertise.

Realizing accidents happen to everyone and there was going to continue to be a high demand for experienced collision repair and paint technicians, Albert challenged himself to take that next step and began working out of his own garage. Business took off and with success as a motivator, he purchased his own establishment. Albert brought his mix of on-the-job training as an experienced auto body painter and collision repair expert to Santa Maria, making City Motors Collision Center in the image the Musch family business while elevating it with his own skills and capabilities and a burning desire to own a business known for customer satisfaction and fairness.

Albert's promise at City Motors Collision Center is that you will get over fifty-five years of experience with eco-friendly innovations. First and foremost, "I'm a car lover and I take real joy in making vehicles look beautiful. I never get tired of seeing my customers' reactions when their cars are returned looking brand new."

✦

Top, left: Sign install July 1973.

Top, right: Sidewalk install August 1973.

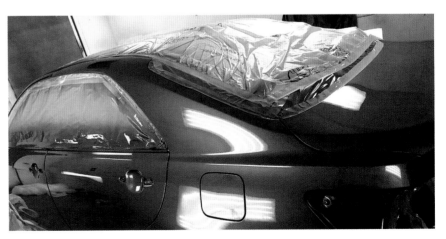

EDGEWATER INN & SUITES/ BEST WESTERN BIG AMERICA/ SANTA MARIA INN

A long and successful career in the hospitality industry began nearly fifty years ago when Hardy P. Hearn purchased a thirty-unit motel in Pismo Beach. A year later, he married Judy Hearn and together they have built a thriving travel and tourism business that includes Edgewater Inn and Suites, Best Western Big America, and the Santa Maria Inn.

Hardy was the manager of a meat market at a local grocery before enlisting in the Air Force during the Korean War. Before going into service, he invested his savings in Bank of America and Tennessee Gas Transmission stocks. By the end of the war, his investments had yielded enough to purchase half interest in his parent's business, Shell Beach Grocery and Meat Market. In 1967, Hardy purchased Edgewater Inn and Suites, a beachfront motel in Pismo Beach, which he operated while continuing to manage the grocery.

Hardy and Judy married in 1970 and a year later the grocery was sold so they could devote more time and resources to the expansion of the motel. In the ensuing years, five additional parcels were purchased. The motel was remodeled and expanded to its existing configuration of ninety-nine units, twenty of which are suites.

In 1989, Hardy and Judy purchased Best Western Big America in Santa Maria, which is rated three diamonds by AAA and three stars by Mobile.

The Hearn's, in partnership with Bob Hollingsead, purchased the historic Santa Maria Inn, which has been renovated to its previous splendor, the place where movie stars stayed on the way to Hearst Castle.

Meanwhile, other Edgewater development projects range from the development of sub-divisions, to the construction and remodeling of commercial and residential buildings.

Promoting tourism to the local area has been an important part of the Hearn's success in the hotel business. These activities have included involvement with the Pismo Beach Chamber of Commerce, Business Improvement Group, and Friends of Hearst Castle. Judy has been a member of the board of the Pismo Beach Chamber of Commerce for eighteen years and has served on the Friends of Hearst Castle Board since 1987. Hardy is a past president of the Pismo Beach City Council and the Planning Commission, and served on the board of directors of the California Lodging Industry Association.

Overland was founded by Bruno J. Zemaitis. Bruno built a business that was to become a staple of the Central Coast; married, raised a family and left his mark on our city.

Bruno came to California seeking employment during the Great Depression. In 1947, Bruno was selling Mac Tools during the day and as a relief patrolman for the Merchant's Patrol Service in Santa Maria. In that same year, he married Mary Elizabeth Harding and later, raised a family.

That year, he was offered the ownership of the business and went to Bank of America for a $1,000 loan from bank manager, Frank Shields. Shields was famous for making "handshake" loans to local citizens. In doing so, he earned the deep respect and loyalty of many in the valley.

In 1948, Bruno changed the name to Overland Investigation Bureau and his service area grew to include the four cities: Nipomo, Mesa, Lompoc, and Guadalupe. Service offerings included investigation, uniformed security services, mobile patrol and in 1961, became one of the few polygraph or lie detector examiners on the Central Coast.

In 2005, Bruno's son, Edward, continued operations in providing safety and security to citizens, business and agricultural concerns. Service offerings, training and technology have improved to reflect the needs of the times. Edward, is active in the community and looks forward to future challenges and an opportunity to serve our city. In doing so, in 2017, Overland Security Services will celebrate our seventieth anniversary serving the people of the Santa Maria Valley.

OVERLAND SECURITY SERVICES

◆

Above: Bruno J. Zemaitis.

Left: Bruno and Beth Zemaitis.

◆

Deane Laughlin, Santa Maria's fire
chief from 1911-1920, was a race car
driver, and winner of the National 40
held on July 4, 1912.

BUILDING A GREATER SANTA MARIA VALLEY

Santa Maria Valley's real estate developers,

construction companies, heavy industries,

and manufacturers provide the

economic foundation of the valley

SPECIAL THANKS TO

Ken Fargen

DIANI
COMPANIES

From the dairy to dirt to deep space. The Santa Maria Valley is the only community the Diani family knows. Lorenzo Diani emigrated from Switzerland in the 1920s, entering the United States through New York's Ellis Island. After establishing himself in San Francisco he sent for his bride, Mary Dolinda Balzani. They were married and had two children, Americo and Madeline. In 1928, they moved to the Santa Maria Valley to operate a dairy in partnership with Union Sugar Company and lived in the town of Betteravia. In 1939, Lorenzo bought out Union Sugar's share and moved the dairy to a family owned site off Stowell Road just west of town.

Americo, known as A. J., spent three and a half years in the Pacific theater during World War II as a Navy Seabee (Construction Battalion). A. J. met his future wife, Margaret Bowden, while on leave in New Zealand. After the war, A. J. and Margaret were married in Auckland, New Zealand, then returned to Santa Maria and raised five children.

The Diani Companies seeds were sown when A. J. began doing grading jobs for some of the local farmers and started A. J. Diani Construction Company in 1949 and incorporated in 1958. Today the legacy includes three second generation principals and six third generation family members.

The company grew as it helped build post-war public works projects in the area and was primarily engaged in grading, paving and highway construction. With the second

generation joining the company in the 1970s, the company expanded its capabilities in 1978 by creating a Building Division and began performing general building construction. In 1990 the company again expanded by adding an environmental remediation and restoration division thus offering a diverse and comprehensive line of general engineering construction, general building construction and environmental remediation services.

In 2005 the company reorganized to provide construction services through a family of corporations know as the Diani Companies under the leadership of sons, Jim and Mike Diani and brother-in-law Don Ward. The reorganization retained A. J. Diani Construction Co., Inc. and in addition created Diani Ward Diani, LLC, Ward & Associates, GP, Central Coast Remedial Resources, Inc., Diani Building Corp. and

Coulter Equipment Co., Inc. Then in 2006, after fifty-seven years in the highway construction business, the family sold its highway and civil construction division to a large national heavy civil contractor and construction material provider while retaining A. J. Diani Construction Co., Inc.'s environmental services division. The sale also resulted in the decommissioning of Coulter Equipment Company. The Diani Companies currently perform general building construction, pre-engineered metal building construction, construction management, design build, environmental remediation and restoration services and NHIS landfill operation services.

Over the years A. J. Diani Construction Co., Inc., through its highway and civil construction division, performed many notable private and public works contracts in the area. The company has a long history at Vandenberg Air Force Base and performed a great deal of highway work for Caltrans. The company, prior to its divesture, was the largest dirt moving contractor on the central coast. The company prided itself on always seeking a better way to "move dirt" in an effort to achieve greater efficiencies and production. This philosophy has carried over to the "hog and haul" operations that the company performs today through its remediation operations as well as the operation of the City of Santa Maria's Non-Hazardous Hydrocarbon Impacted Soil (NHIS) program at the Santa Maria Regional Landfill through its affiliate Central Coast Remedial Resources, Inc. In addition, the company focuses on emergency fire debris and recovery services under CalRecycle's protocol program. In 2007 the company was part of the initial implementation of the program established by the State of California for fire debris and recovery services with the company being selected as the prime contractor to remove the debris from 257 homes tragically destroyed by the Angora fire in South Lake Tahoe, California.

Diani Building Corp. (formerly A. J. Diani Construction Co., Inc.'s Building Division) has an extensive portfolio of military, public works and commercial building projects. Its accomplishments include the construction of the Hearst Castle Visitor Center, a phased twelve year renovation of the Santa Barbara Bowl, the Historic Repair and Seismic Upgrade-City Hall Renovation for the City of Atascadero and the structural

♦

Above: Office at 295 North Blosser Road, 1950s-1960s.

Below: Santa Barbara Bowl.
PHOTO BY A. ARTHUR FISHER.

concrete for the restoration project of Santa Barbara's Granada Theatre. The company also built the Santa Barbara County Juvenile Hall in Santa Maria and is currently building the new Juvenile Hall for San Luis Obispo County. The company is also constructing the National Search Dog Foundation's twenty-five acre National Training Center (NTC) in Santa Paula. It is the first facility of its kind in the nation where selected rescued dogs learn to be rescuers and Search Teams train through disaster simulations.

With its long history in military construction at Vandenberg Air Force Base, its expertise has taken it to Florida, Alaska, and the Kwajalein Islands among the most notable locations. The company has—and continues—to build launch, radar and satellite infrastructure for the government and government contractors. The company design-built the first privately owned launch complex in the country for Spaceport Systems International at Vandenberg Air Force Base known as SLC 8 and

has refurbished missile silos at Vandenberg under the Ground Base Midcourse Missile Defense system and constructed new silo systems in Alaska under the same program. The company also constructed the SLC 6 Horizontal Integration Facility at Vandenberg and as a result was awarded a "Golden Trowel" at the World of Concrete in Las Vegas for the construction of the flattest and most level floor slab placed in the world in the previous year. The company has performed over twelve design-build installations under the Space Launch Range System Contract and is currently performing an Antenna Rail Replacement project for a radar system in the Kwajalein Islands.

One of the company's most intriguing accomplishments was the renovation of NASA's seventy meter (230 foot) antenna located at the Deep Space Network Site in Goldstone, California, operated by the Jet Propulsion Laboratory for NASA. Officially known as Deep Space Station 14, it is informally known as the Mars Antenna after receiving the first signal from Mariner 4's mission to Mars in 1966. The structure is twenty-four stories high and weighs 7.2 million kilograms (16 million pounds). Despite its size, with its complex electronic equipment and unique mechanical systems, it is a precise instrument capable of communicating with spacecraft at the edge of the solar system. The antenna had operated almost continuously, 24/7, for over forty-four years and required a bearing replacement that enables the antenna to rotate horizontally and track up and down the horizon.

The work required lifting the antenna base weighing 3.2 million kilograms to remove and replace the steel bearing plates. The company redesigned the governments' original operation plan to save two months of scheduled down time and $500,000. This project team effort was also recognized by *National Geographic* and was featured on an episode of NatGeo's *"World's Toughest Fixes."*

Today the company continues to evolve to meet the dynamics of the market place and has just begun a multiyear remodel and renovation project for the Santa Barbara Museum of Art and

is a team member with Mustang Power to construct Santa Barbara County's Tajiguas Landfill Resource Recovery Project to turn waste into energy through an anaerobic digestion process.

The Diani family dedicates this profile to A. J. Diani (1922-2002) and all the employees, business associates and friends who have provided the foundation for the success we have been blessed with as we continue to strive to reflect our Core Values and our "Commitment to Jesus Christ: 'For we are taking pains to do what is right, not only in the eyes of the Lord but also in the eyes of men.' 2 Corinthians 8:21."

◆

Above: Atascadero City Hall Main Rotunda.

Below: Ground Base Midcourse Missile Defense Systems—Silo Modifications (Vandenberg AFB, California, and Fort Greely, Alaska).

DAN BLOUGH CONSTRUCTION, INC.

✦

Above: Tim Seifert.

Below: A two-story beauty at 900 East Main Street.

Opposite, top to bottom:

Santa Maria Car Wash, 2301 South Broadway, Santa Maria.

Rancho Harvest.

Central Coast Kidney Disease Center.

In only a few short years, Dan Blough Construction, Inc., dealing primarily in commercial and high-end residential construction, has become one of the most respected and successful construction companies in the Santa Maria Valley.

Dan Blough Construction was established in 1979, but partners Dan Blough and Tim Seifert had already crafted long and successful careers in real estate, development and construction before combining their talents. Dan literally grew up in the business, and Tim began working construction while still in high school.

Dan's father, Harry Blough, was a licensed general contractor in Sacramento. From the age of seven, Dan accompanied Harry on weekends and during the summer as he worked on his projects. His first job was sweeping, clean up, and stacking lumber.

After moving to Santa Maria in 1974, Dan worked a short time for Sawyer Building Materials and MHC Trucking until 1977 when he became the real estate broker for the tract known as Country Club Gardens. When that tract was completed, Terry Flatley and Dan began building spec houses in Morro Estates. They ended up building a number of homes throughout Santa Maria Valley, including two large subdivisions, before dissolving the partnership.

Harry moved to Santa Maria in 1988 to work as his son's construction superintendent and became a partner in Dan Blough Construction, Inc. In 2001, Tim became superintendent and soon became a partner in the company.

Dan, a licensed Real Estate Broker, obtained his license in 1971. He then became a certified commercial investment member (CCIM) in 1980 and consulted with many commercial clients.

In 1985, Dan and his wife, Peggy, joined Coldwell Banker Real Estate and became a franchisee, eventually growing the company to more than 240 agents and employees with eight offices in Fresno, Clovis, Oakhurst and the Central Coast of California. The firm was headquartered in Santa Maria. At its peak, the Colwell Banker franchise was grossing in excess of $20 million per year, serving residential clients as buyers and sellers as well as providing mortgage and property management services.

In 2006, Dan and Peggy sold Coldwell Banker Dan Blough and Associates to their partner, George Murphy, who still owns and operates the business today as Coldwell Banker Premier Real Estate. After selling the real estate business, Dan concentrated on construction and development.

In 2008, Dan was asked by Supervisor Joe Centeno to become the 5th District Planning Commissioner, a position he still holds.

Tim was born in Los Angeles and raised in the San Fernando Valley. He began working in construction during high school, becoming a jobsite laborer with Eastern Pacific Corporation at the age of fifteen. The company specialized in building custom homes on odd-shaped lots in the valley. Tim learned the many aspects of the residential construction business during this time.

Tim moved to Santa Maria in 1977 and soon became assistant superintendent of The Bower, a 161-home subdivision. In 1979, Tim ran a seventy-five lot subdivision in Santa Ynez as construction superintendent. He began framing for Famco Development in 1982 and by 1987 had obtained his contracting license and started his own business, Seifert Construction. For the next fourteen years, he specialized as a framing contractor on both commercial and residential projects as he greatly expanded his knowledge of the construction industry.

Tim married his wife, Shannon, in 1988 and built their own home where they raised their daughters, Katie and Rachel. After an industrial accident in 1995, Tim moved into residential remodeling. He became a partner with Dan Blough Construction in 2001.

◆

Opposite, top to bottom:

Sims Physical Therapy.

Wayne's Tire Shop.

Dr. Lane, DDS, Pacific Smile Center.

Left: Coldwell Banker Real Estate.

Below: Peggy and Dan Blough.
PHOTOGRAPH BY LUIS ESCOBAR,
REFLECTIONS PHOTOGRAPHY STUDIO.

*Bottom: Professional building at
2400 Professional Parkway.*

Together, Dan and Tim developed a reputation as the premier builders in the valley and soon built a number of multimillion dollar projects. Included were such varied projects as a 70,000 square foot beverage distribution center, gas station, car wash and lube center, Walmart shopping strip mall, and professional offices for architects and doctors. The firm also constructed a senior living development, a kidney dialysis office and treatment center, as well as countless other buildings and tenant improvements. The two even found time to construct a few high-end residential projects along the way.

In addition to Tim and Dan, Dan Blough Construction employs two superintendents, an office manager, a cabinet maker and finish carpenter and one assistant.

Starting in 2016, the company opened A Street Cabinets, a division of Dan Blough Construction, Inc., which builds custom cabinets for commercial and residential customers.

Having chosen Santa Maria as the place to raise his family, Tim's roots are deeply tied to the community. He volunteers yearly for the Santa Maria Valley YMCA, is past president and an active member of the Santa Maria Breakfast Rotary Club, and currently serves the City of Santa Maria as a planning commissioner.

He also serves on the community block grants advisory committee and is a member of the board of appeals.

Dan and Peggy are also deeply involved in the community with such organizations as the Santa Maria Valley YMCA, Santa Maria Valley Humane Society, Boy's and Girl's Club, Marian Regional Medical Center, Allan Hancock College, CALM and Santa Maria Breakfast Rotary. He has also served as a county planning commissioner.

The business plan for Dan Blough Construction, Inc., is to continue to grow and seek opportunities to provide construction and development services.

PACIFIC COAST ENERGY COMPANY

ORCUTT HILL

◆

Above: Orcutt Oil Field overlooking the Santa Maria Valley, 1911.

Below: CEO and Chairman of the Board, Randall H. Breintenbach and President, Member Board of Directors, Halbert S. Washburn.

Pacific Coast Energy Company (PCEC) traces its roots to 1988, when Hal Washburn and Randy Breitenbach—two Stanford petroleum engineers who had a dream of starting their own oil company—bought their first two wells in California. Today, PCEC is one of the largest onshore oil and gas producers in Santa Barbara County. Through its strategy of using innovative technology to organically develop and grow its oil and gas reserves, PCEC provides Californians with affordable energy through professional, safe, and environmentally friendly operations.

Orcutt Hill, which covers about 6,000 acres near Santa Maria in Santa Barbara County, is PCEC's largest operation. PCEC also produces oil from the West Pico, East Coyote and Sawtelle fields in the Los Angeles Basin. The oil produced is transported by pipelines to California refineries where it is converted mainly to gasoline, diesel and jet fuel. The natural gas that is produced in the Los Angeles Basin is sold into the local network, Orcutt Hill gas is used internally for field operations.

Orcutt Hill has played a vital role in Santa Barbara County's history since it began production more than a century ago. The field is named for William Warren Orcutt—incidentally another Stanford-educated engineer. Orcutt oversaw development of the field in the early 1900s, which ultimately led to the creation of four local oil towns: Bicknell, Graciosa, Orcutt and Orcutt Hill. Today, the only surviving community is Orcutt.

Hal and Randy acquired the Orcutt Hill Oil Field in October 2004. They assembled a team of top-notch engineers to develop Orcutt Hill's shallow diatomite formation, which was known to contain large quantities of heavy viscous oil at depths ranging from 700 to 1,100 feet, but which had not been successfully produced. After testing their cyclic steaming ideas—a process that injects steam in a pattern, or cycle, to facilitate the movement of heavy oil—with an initial three-well program, the team launched a commercial scale pilot project in 2007. Over the next four years, the pilot program was expanded and became a central component of PCEC's drilling activities at Orcutt Hill. PCEC's cyclic

steaming wells are more efficient, create less noise and have a smaller footprint than traditional pump jack wells. PCEC also incorporated linear rod pumps into its steaming process, a unique feature that has boosted production.

PCEC's employees closely monitor Orcutt Hill operations 24/7 from a centrally located control room equipped with state-of-the-art digital technology. This careful monitoring helps ensure that operations remain safe and environmentally friendly at all times.

Since being acquired by Hal and Randy, Orcutt Hill production has almost doubled with the addition of ninety-six new cyclic steaming diatomite wells. Today, the wells produce an average of twenty-three barrels of oil per day with a very efficient steam-oil-ratio of 2.5 due primarily to the innovations that the PCEC team has implemented over the years. These results place PCEC operations in the top quartile of all diatomite cyclic projects in California.

PCEC is a major contributor to the economy of Santa Barbara County. At last count, PCEC had approximately fifty full-time employees at Orcutt Hill. The company also works with approximately 200 contractors and suppliers at Orcutt Hill, and in 2014 spent approximately $38.5 million on goods and services, including $3 million on local contract labor and professional workers. Currently, PCEC is the fourth largest property tax payer in Santa Barbara County.

Since 2006, the Breitburn/PCEC Community Sponsorship program has invested approximately $250,000 dollars in local organizations focused on youth, scholarships, education and the arts. In addition to its charitable contributions, PCEC makes available its storied picnic grounds and old schoolhouse for community use.

Looking to the future, PCEC plans to continue the vision set by its founders, Hal and Randy, nearly thirty years ago when they bought their first two wells in California. Plans are to grow production at home by applying technological advancements and following their entrepreneurial spirit.

✦

Above: CEO Randy Breintenbach, employees and contractors at the December 2012 dedication of PCEC's first ninety-six cyclic steaming diatomite wells.

Below: Cyclic steaming diatomite well POD on Orcutt Hill.

ENGEL & GRAY, INC.

Since its beginning seventy years ago, Engel & Gray, Inc., has grown from a trucking and construction company serving the local oil and ag industries into a regional recycling resource for the central coast.

The company was founded in 1946 by Carl Engel, who was born in Bakersfield and moved to Orcutt in 1928 with his parents, Karl and Ada Parrish Engel. After graduating from Santa Maria Junior College, Carl went to work for Union Oil Company. Carl met his future bride, Rosemary Croake, a Wisconsin transplant who was working as social worker, in Los Angeles. They were wed in 1940 while Carl was working for Unocal in Bakersfield. He was soon transferred to Santa Maria where he served as foreman of the transportation unit.

When Union Oil discontinued its trucking operations in 1946, Carl sought out Joe Gray. They joined forces, bought a truck, and established Engel & Gray Trucking. Soon cranes and construction crews were added as the company expanded along with the growth of Central Coast oilfields and agriculture. Carl and Rosemary raised four children: Mary Ellen, Eileen, Carl, Jr., and Robert. Joe and Norma Gray raised two daughters, Joni and Dorothy. Carl and Joe's partnership lasted for over fifty years

The company transitioned to the next generation in 1986 when Carl, Jr., and Robert purchased the company.

Carl, Jr., graduated from Cal Poly San Luis Obispo with a degree in economics and has worked for the family business for fifty years. He serves as president of Engel & Gray and is in charge of operations.

Robert graduated from Santa Clara University with a degree in business administration. He serves as vice president and is in charge of administration and compost production and marketing.

Like their father, who was active in civic affairs and served on Santa Maria City Council, Carl, Jr., and Robert are deeply involved in local civic affairs, community, and industry organizations.

Sensing a change in the oil service business, the brothers drove the company forward, targeting the environmental construction industry, both within and outside the oil industry. Starting with removal of underground storage tanks, Engel & Gray began to work with soil bioremediation to clean up environmental problems naturally.

By 1992 the company had developed cost effective methods for composting organic materials and this evolved into the development of Engel & Gray Regional Compost Facility, which transforms a variety of organic feedstock from different waste streams into environmentally friendly Harvest Blend Compost products. This is the only facility of its kind on the Central Coast.

Traditionally most organic waste would be considered as nothing more than a disposal problem, but Engel & Gray has been able to transform green waste, ag waste, manures, bio solids and other types of organic materials into a valuable resource.

These organic materials, are fundamental ingredients in its compost production business. Engel & Gray's completes the cycle of recycling

❖

Bottom, left: Engel & Gray, Inc., offices with 1948 postwar Buick and Ford sporting Betteravia Road, which is in the forefront at a more quiet time in its history.

Bottom, right: Carl Engel and Joe Gray posing with drilling rig draw works ready to be hauled to a new drill site in the Santa Maria Valley, c. 1949. Inset is Carl and Joe (on the left) at Engel & Gray, Inc.'s forty-fifth anniversary celebration 1991.

by helping customers keep organic material out of the landfill, while also manufacturing useful, soil enriching compost back to growers, landscapers and homeowners. Harvest Blend Compost products are sold throughout the Central Coast either direct by company trucks or by landscape supply centers.

Throughout the seventy-year history quality employee team members have contributed to the organization and community providing customers with reliable, trustworthy, efficient service.

Today, Engel & Gray, Inc., is a diverse construction, transportation and waste recycling firm, working with both large and small customers. The company intends to continue meeting the challenges of the business world and society with a strategy that is able to shift focus to expand and develop new services for customers and provide opportunity for employees. With its seventy-year history, Engel & Gray has demonstrated its innovation and stability as a privately held family company.

✦

Above: The Engel & Gray, Inc., Regional Compost Facility recycling organics for healthy soil, 2010.

Below: Carl Engel, Jr., (on the right) and Bob Engel, owners of Engel & Gray, Inc., for the last thirty years, 2015.

SANTA MARIA VALLEY RAILROAD

The Santa Maria Valley Railroad provides an efficient, cost effective, and environmentally friendly method of transporting products in the Santa Maria Valley. Each day, the railroad transports frozen vegetables and strawberries, fertilizer, tractors, lumber, drywall, steel, aluminum and dozens of other commodities. Truck-to-rail and rail-to-truck facilities provide access to Central Coast customers who need rail service but are not on a rail line.

The colorful history of the Santa Maria Valley Railroad began in 1911 when Santa Maria city officials persuaded an English syndicate to build a fourteen-mile short line railroad to service Roadamite, at that time the largest asphalt plant in the world, and to serve the Union Pacific Sugar Plant in Betteravia.

The railroad struggled in its early years because of competition from the Pacific Coast Railway and the closing of the sugar plant. The railroad was purchased in 1925 by Captain G. Allan Hancock who improved the railroad by purchasing locomotives and rebuilding the main line, investing in engine and blacksmith shops, and building a new corporate office. Hancock developed vegetable packing plants and the La Brea Ice Plant to feed into the railroad.

By the 1930s, the railroad was profitable and for years it was one of the most profitable short line railroads in the west. Hancock developed new row crop agriculture in the valley, including sugar beets for the Union Sugar refinery, fresh vegetables destined for the eastern market, outbound crude oil, and inbound merchandising traffic. The railroad was very busy from the 1930s to the 1970s as Santa Maria grew from a sleepy agricultural town to an economic powerhouse.

Captain Hancock passed away in 1965 and two Hancock trusts—the Marian Mullin Trust and the Rosemary Trust—took control of the railroad. Marian Hancock became president of the railroad and Sue Sword was general manager. At the time, SMVRR was the only railroad—and probably the first in the nation—to be controlled by women.

The railroad continued to be successful under the leadership of the two women but trouble was on the horizon. As large trucking companies entered the competition for general merchandise traffic, large retailers such as Sears and Montgomery Ward stopped receiving product by rail. By the late 1960s, most fresh vegetables were shipped by truck, rather than train, and the railroad's crude oil business went away as pipelines were constructed. By the 1980s, the Union Sugar plant represented over seventy-five percent of the car loadings. Holly Sugar's decision to close its Betteravia facility in 1993 was a major blow to the railroad.

In 2000 the Rosemary Trust bought out the Marian Mullin Trust in an effort to save the railroad, but those efforts failed. After many years of neglected maintenance and little marketing, the family decided to sell the railroad to someone who could save Hancock's legacy.

The railroad was sold to Coast Belle Rail Corp. in 2006. The new owners and management

embarked on a turnaround campaign that included marketing to potential customers, improving customer service by offering seven days a week service, catching up on maintenance projects, and running excursions and sponsoring special events to raise public awareness about the railroad. Railroad operations were moved to the former Union Sugar Plant in Betteravia in 2008.

Rafael Sanchez and Sergio Silva were hired by Coast Belle and were instrumental in the railroad's turnaround. General Manager Al Sheff, formerly with Union Pacific, was hired in 2011

and began to lure customers by providing seven days a week service, staffing extra trains, and cross-training the entire staff including office workers so everyone was qualified to run trains. Business has quadrupled the past four years and SMVRR recently moved into a new facility at 1599 A Street.

Future plans for the Santa Maria Valley Railroad include renovating the main line with heavier rail to accommodate growing traffic, double-tracking the main line, and extending sidings. It appears that Captain Hancock's heritage is secure.

CHRIS' COUNTRY PROPERTIES, LLC

♦

Top, right: A view from the front yard featuring the historic Santa Maria Inn.

Above: Christine Aleto, owner and real estate broker.

Below: The 1918 Craftsman Building, home to Chris' Country Properties, located at 824 South Broadway.

A beautifully restored Craftsman-style house built in 1918 is now home to Chris' Country Properties, a well respected California real estate brokerage firm. The home/office is located at 824 South Broadway, directly across from the historic Santa Maria Inn and just south of the famous Landmark Building.

The home, built for the Maurice Zanetti family, was designed by Louis N. Crawford, Santa Maria's first architect. He also designed the Santa Maria City Hall as well as many schools and homes up-and-down the Central Coast. The Zanetti family lived in the home for fifty-eight years, but as downtown Santa Maria developed, the property was rezoned for commercial/mixed use. Although the home will soon be century old, only four owners have experienced the beauty, grace and elegance of this beautiful example of Craftsman-style architecture.

The home was lovingly restored by Christine Morton Aleto, owner of Chris' Country Properties, and her husband, Jack Aleto.

The firm was established by Christine in 1988 after a successful career as a real estate salesperson that included experience with Century 21 and Realty World. The first location for Chris' Country Properties was in Lakeport, where Christine and five sales associates sold a high volume of residential, commercial and industrial properties.

A second Chris' Country Properties office was opened in downtown Las Vegas, Nevada, in 1993 and a third location was opened in downtown San Diego, where Christine and Jack purchased and restored an 1893 Victorian mixed-use building.

Christine and Jack returned to California in 2013 and, together, they renovated the beautiful home on South Broadway as their new office. The project took ten months of hard labor, with Christine and Jack doing all the work themselves.

"My husband and I feel especially grateful to have had the opportunity to lovingly restore and save this amazing building and the grounds on which it sits, as it is an important part of Santa Maria's history," Christine says. "Best of all, I am now living and working in the beautiful city of Santa Maria, and I am here to stay."

Few developments have had as much impact on Santa Maria as The Crossroads, the premier mixed-use development serving the Central Coast. The 150 acre development includes shopping centers, an auto mall, self-storage, residential housing, office buildings and active recreational venues. The centerpiece of the development is The Crossroads Shopping Center, a forty-eight acre, 470,000 square foot power center that includes such major retailers as Walmart, Home Depot, PetSmart, TJ Maxx, and Best Buy.

Westar Associates, the developer of The Crossroads, began the development in 1995. Westar purchased 150 acres of open land that had been an oil field with ten capped oil wells remaining. The developers worked closely with the City of Santa Maria to provide a proper mix of uses that would benefit residents and provide significant tax revenue to the city. The Westar team, planning consultant Harrell Fletcher, and numerous city officials and staff were involved in the project. They included Mayors Roger Bunch, Joe Centeno, Abel Maldonado, and Larry Lavagnino; City Manager Tim Ness, Director of Community Development Bill Orndoff; and numerous planning commissioners and staff.

After three years of planning, construction began in 1998 with the Home Depot building in The Crossroads Shopping Center, and was completed ten years later with College Square, a 55,000 square foot retail center which includes Panera Bread, Starbucks, Jamba Juice, Verizon Wireless and many other well know retailers.

Many public improvements were made during the course of construction, including traffic improvements along Betteravia Road, College Drive, Bradley Road, Southside Parkway, and at the intersection of Bradley and Betteravia. Underground improvements included new water, sewer and storm drainage systems.

The $150 million-plus Crossroads Commercial Development has provided many benefits to the City of Santa Maria, including more than $1.2 million in traffic improvement fees, and the creation of more than 1,900 construction jobs and over 1,500 permanent jobs. The commercial development area is consistently the city's largest sales tax producer.

Deeply committed to the community, Westar is active in the Chamber of Commerce and has made charitable donations to local law enforcement, Marian Medical Center and other causes.

♦

Above: The 150 acre Crossroads Development consisting of shopping centers, auto mall, self-storage, residential housing, office building, and active recreational venues.

Below: Construction for the project began in 1998 starting with The Crossroads Shopping Center. Home Depot was the first building to be developed.

SANTA MARIA TOOL, INC.

Santa Maria Tool, Inc., is a full service machine shop catering to the oil field industry as well as transportation, farming, mining, fishing, manufacturing, waste management and food processing businesses.

Santa Maria Tool was founded in 1937 by Robert and Ruby Weber, who were attracted to Santa Maria after hearing of the opportunities in the new central coast oil fields. Robert was born in Switzerland and immigrated to the U.S. in 1916. He settled in Little Rock, Arkansas, where he met and married Ruby M. Wood. Robert and his bride moved to Artesia, California, when Robert found a job with an oil field machine shop in Long Beach.

Robert's dream was to own and operate his own business, so the Weber family: Robert, Ruby, and son, Robert Jefferson Weber, relocated to the Santa Maria Valley, purchased a building on South Broadway, and established Santa Maria Tool. The company was located on Broadway, just south of Betteravia Road, near the famous Beacon Outpost. After thirty years at that location, the company purchased two lots at the corner of Oakley and McCoy Streets and erected the building that still houses the company today.

Robert's 1937 Individual Tax Return revealed that his net income from his first year in business was $4,292. About this time, the Los Flores oil pool was discovered, re-igniting the oil boom in the Santa Maria Valley. Business at Santa Maria Tool soared as Robert built a key business relationship with Union Oil Company of California.

Today, Santa Maria Tool is the region's 'go-to' machine shop with broad-spectrum capabilities that include portable machine work and the ability to handle large jobs, down to finely CNC machined parts.

Santa Maria Tool is now owned and operated by the grandson of Robert and Ruby, Brian R. Weber. As the third generation head of the business, Brian has led the firm into the twenty-first century through machinery upgrades and expansion into untapped markets. The simple oil field related business of nearly eighty years ago now has the technology to tool and build complicated pieces used in the medical industry as well as maintaining the ability to handle large off-shore drilling repair work.

JOHN'S PLUMBING COMPANY

John's Plumbing Company is owned and operated by John Childers, who was born and raised in Indianapolis, Indiana. After graduating from high school, he joined the United States Navy and served on the USS *Horne* CG30; built at the San Francisco Naval Shipyards—Hunter's Point. The *Horne* was a cruiser in the Belknap class and at the time of its construction it was classified as a Guided Missile Frigate.

After discharge from the Navy, John, who loved working with his hands and enjoyed challenging work, found employment in the oil fields in Long Beach, California. He later transferred to Santa Maria and has made it his home ever since.

John worked as a maintenance engineer for the Historic Santa Maria Inn, which eventually led to his employment with Ray Zierman. The Zierman family has been in the plumbing business since 1950. John received quality experience and is still grateful for the education and know-how he gained while working for Ray Zierman Plumbing.

Discovering that he had an interest in a special niche in plumbing, John opened his own business, John's Plumbing Company. His work is highly specialized as he works with commercial medical buildings—doctor's offices, surgery centers, hospitals, and digital medical imaging facilities.

Like many entrepreneurs, John is community minded. He serves on the City of Santa Maria Board of Appeals and as a volunteer for the Court Appointed Special Advocates (CASA). All of this would not be possible without the support of his family; his wife, Carla, and sons Thomas, Scott, and Austin.

John's Plumbing Co. is located at 325 North Palisade Drive in Santa Maria.

PACIFICA COMMERCIAL REALTY

◆

*Above: Left to right, Pat Palangi,
Jerry Schmidt and Mike Kelly.*

*Below: Left to right, Brian LaCabe
and Chris Garner.*

Pacifica Commercial Realty is the Central Coast's largest, full-service commercial, industrial, and investment real estate company. The firm's tradition of excellence is built upon expert market knowledge, integrity and dedication to client satisfaction.

Pacifica, originally known as Beaver-Free Corporation, was founded in Santa Barbara in 1968 by Jerry Beaver and his original partner, Jim Free. Free left the firm in the early years and Beaver has guided nearly fifty years of prolific development and deal making.

Beaver-Free Corporation opened an office in Santa Maria in 1989 to serve the growing North County community. The firm's first significant projects in Santa Maria were the acquisition and positioning of two of the city's largest industrial parks—Skyway Business Park next to the Santa Maria Airport and Thompson Industrial Park. Jerry Schmidt was hired to head the Santa Maria office in 1989 and Pat Palangi joined the firm in 1990.

Jerry and Pat worked together and brokered the majority of industrial and large office transactions in the North Santa Barbara marketplace from 1990 to the present. In 2006, Pat and Jerry were joined by Chris Garner and Brian LaCabe to purchase Pacifica Commercial Realty's Santa Maria office from Pacifica Real Estate Group. Both Chris and Brian had worked with Prime Commercial Real Estate for years and have impressive resumes in the sales and leasing of retail and shopping center properties.

In January 1995 the firm was renamed Pacifica Real Estate Group when Beaver-Free Corporation merged with Invest West Companies

of Santa Barbara, a leading hotel development and management company.

Pacifica Commercial Realty moved to its present location on Professional Parkway four years ago. Currently, the company has six agents and brokers in its Santa Maria office as well as a vice president of property management and three support staff. In addition to the ten team members in Santa Maria, Pacifica is still affiliated with its sister office in Santa Barbara and another office in Paso Robles.

Pacifica represents and consistently closes the majority of all office, retail and industrial real estate transactions in its marketplace, and is striving to reach one million square feet of managed properties in the near future.

The goal of Pacifica Commercial Realty is to remain the dominant source of trusted, professional commercial real estate service into the future. In keeping with their company statement, Pacifica Commercial Realty is, "Your Central Coast Commercial Real Estate Solution."

THE TOWBES GROUP, INC.

The remarkable career of Michael Towbes in Santa Maria began nearly sixty years ago when he and a partner built their first apartments and single-family homes. Today, Towbes is one of California's most successful entrepreneurs, philanthropists, and community leaders. Although now based in Santa Barbara, Towbes has fond memories of the early beginnings of his business career in Santa Maria.

Towbes, who grew up in Washington, D.C., graduated Summa Cum Laude and Phi Beta Kappa from Princeton University with a degree in civil engineering. After a semester in graduate school at MIT, he joined the U.S. Navy during the Korean War, and it was because of his assignment to Point Mugu that he first visited Southern California's beautiful Pacific Coast. He describes the event as ushering "a whole new world" into his life.

After marrying Gail Aronson in 1954, Towbes settled in California after three years in the Navy and began working as a project engineer for the George A. Fuller Company. Meanwhile, Eli Luria, a graduate of UCLA, had become a successful builder in Washington, D.C., but wanted to return to California. After a fortuitous meeting, the two men became friends and decided to go into business for themselves. A partnership was formed in 1956 and the men started building in West Los Angeles. Although only one house was built their first year, they soon expanded with small apartments in Redondo Beach and Palos Verdes Estates.

In 1957 the partners heard the exciting news that Camp Cooke, a former U.S. Army training center, was to be converted to a space and ballistic missile test facility known as Vandenberg Air Force Base. "We knew there was going to be a housing boom in that area, so we bought land in Lompoc and Santa Maria," Towbes explains.

Towbes moved to Santa Maria in 1959 to supervise the Luria-Towbes construction projects. There was so little office space available that he rented the kitchen of a home at 609 South Broadway, which had been converted to a real estate office. "We were very busy in Santa Maria for several years," Towbes recalls. "We built four apartment buildings and forty-eight homes in the Virginia Park Subdivision."

It was the start of a career that would eventually make The Towbes Group, Inc., one of the most successful firms in the state. But Towbes still remembers that much of it started in a kitchen in Santa Maria.

✦

Above: Knollwood Terrace, 1982.

Below: Woodside Park, 1977.

ART CRAFT PAINT, INC.

♦

Teresa Arredondo.

With a fierce determination, dedication, and a fighting spirit inherited from her mother, Teresa Arredondo has become one of the most successful business women in the valley.

Teresa's humble origins began in Michoacan, Mexico. Her father was murdered when she was five and her mother, Maria Luisa Torres Arredondo, was left with ten children to raise. Drawing on the examples of the many strong women in her family, Maria Luisa moved to the U.S. to forge a better life for her children. Teresa and her siblings were left in the care of her aunts. Maria Luisa worked diligently for ten years and was able to obtain residency for her children. Teresa was fifteen years old when she immigrated to the U.S.

Teresa began her career as a harvest worker in the strawberry fields. Driven by a strong entrepreneurial spirit, she had leased two parcels of her own and become a strawberry grower by the age of nineteen. Realizing the need for more education, she studied electrical engineering and mathematics at the Center of Employment Training in Santa Maria.

A newspaper ad for an upholsterer led her to the aviation business. The company, Aeroflair, turned her away, saying the position was "a man's job." However, her ex-husband got the job and Teresa was hired as his assistant. A year later she was running the upholstery division of the business and she seized the opportunity to buy the firm. The company, however, was saddled with unmanageable debt and Aeroflair was forced into bankruptcy.

Undeterred, she started over and started a new business as Art Craft Paint, Inc. For more than twenty years, Art Craft has built a reputation for providing the highest quality aircraft painting and interior refurbishment, using skilled craftsmen and artisans. The company has been ranked as one the Top Five aircraft paint facilities in the nation. Her success has brought Teresa many awards, including Business Woman of the Year by Women's Economic Venture.

Teresa's eldest daughter, Esmeralda Arredondo-Mendoza is a company executive. Her sons both serve in the military, Arturo Arredondo in the Marines and Alejandro Arredondo in the Army. Teresa's entrepreneurial spirit and admiration for aviation continues in the next generation of her family as her grandchildren, Angela, April, and Arik are active members of the aviation community and soon will welcome an additional grandchild, Annabella.

"I believe I was born a fighter," asserts Teresa. "I fight for what I believe. I fight against injustice. I fight for what I want, and sometimes I fight just because it's part of who I am."

The Mayer tract c. 1950. The site is the present location of Peppertree Plaza..

◆

Fred Wickenden and his six sons at the Wickenden Home, Rancho Tinaquaic, c. the 1890s. Shown are (from left to right) James, Ernest, Richard, Albert, Fred Wickenden, Robert, Fred, and a friend A. Leslie.

FAMILY PORTRAITS

Families and individuals whose

legacies continue to shape the

future of Santa Maria Valley

OLIVERA FAMILY

By Jerry Olivera

As the story passed down in the Olivera family is told, a young man only twenty-one years of age would begin his dream of coming to America by stowing away on a Portuguese ship leaving the island of Pico in the Azore Islands chain. The year was 1885, some seven years before the opening of Ellis Island in New York. His name was Manuel Ygnacio Oliveira, born in the small Portuguese village of Bandieras, Pico. Where Manuel landed in America and how his journey brought him to the Santa Maria Valley remains a secret of history. Manuel began working as a farm laborer in Oso Flaco, near Guadalupe. In 1893, Manuel would take a wife, Mary Perry.

Mary would never again see her father, Antone Perry, alive as he drowned in the ocean after being knocked off the Point Sal wharf by a wave in a storm in November 1877. The original Portuguese spelling of our family name was "Oliveira" but when so many people left out the second "i", Manuel changed it to "Olivera" to end the confusion, as the name Olivera was a common Spanish name in California.

After years of hard work, Manuel was able to purchase two small ranches in the Santa Maria Valley, one being the family home on North Suey Road and the other on Bull Canyon Road. Manuel and Mary would have thirteen children: Manuel, Joseph, Irma, Alfred, John, Frank, Mary, Henry, Antone, Lena, Minnie,

Mabel and Fred. Of the thirteen children, three would die in their childhood years. Tragedy also struck the family when the elder Manuel died of stomach cancer in 1921. Manuel and Joseph would continue on farming the two ranches, but two years of drought and failed crops would leave the family financially broke and both ranches were lost to the bank in foreclosure.

Joseph would leave the life of farming, after losing the ranches and marrying Martha Dorothy Sousa in 1918 and begin his own family. Joseph and Martha would have five children: Wilfred, Joseph, Jr., Elizabeth, Edmund and Eugene.

Joseph Anthony Olivera, Jr., my father, who was only a small child when the family lost their ranching livelyhood, would later promise the family that they would someday own another ranch. Joseph "Joe", Jr., was born in 1922 in Santa Maria in the front bedroom of his grandmother's house. In the 1930s,

♦

Left: The Olivera family.
Back row, left to right, Manuel Enos,
Manuel I., Mary Perry and Irma.
Center row, left to right, Joe, Sr.,
Frank and Tony. Front row, left to
right, Henry and Mary.

Right: Wedding of Joe, Sr., and
Martha Sousa Olivera, 1918.

Maria High campus. The Southern Counties Gas Company then hired Joe as a meter reader.

Enter the historic events of Pearl Harbor on December 7, 1941, and the entry of America into World War II. Joe tried to join in the fight to defend his county by trying to enlist in the Air Force and the Navy, only to be rejected on the basis of his color blindness. But Uncle Sam had other plans and Joe was drafted to the U. S. Army in November 1942, only a week after his marriage to his high school sweetheart, the

✦

Above: Joe Olivera, Sr., at his Richfield Gas Station at Orange and Broadway, Santa Maria, c. 1940.

Left: Joe Olivera, Sr., on Suey Road ranch, c. 1920.

Below: Joe Olivera, Jr., photo taken upon his winning Santa Maria Times subscription sales contest at age fifteen in 1937.

Joe was a paperboy for the *Santa Maria Times* and gave much of his earnings to the family, as his father was stricken with TB and in the hospital in Santa Barbara for a time. Joe graduated from Santa Maria High School in 1940 and attended one year at Hancock College, which was then located on the Santa

former Jean Shoup. His unit was initially assigned to defend the Hawaiian Island chain from further attack. In mid-1944, Joe was deployed to the Marianna Islands and participated in the Invasion of Saipan in June 1944. After several weeks of trench warfare against the Japanese Imperial Army on Saipan, Joe was seriously wounded on July 7, 1944, when a mortar shell landed in his trench. This was during the final battle on Saipan when the Emperor of Japan ordered his forces to conduct a "gysus-ki" more commonly known as a "banzai attack" in which all Japanese soldiers were ordered to fight to the death and kill as many of the American forces as possible in a final suicide mission. For Joe, the war was over and he would lose his lower right leg to that mortar shell. After a year of rehabilitation in an Army hospital in Provo, Utah, Joe was fitted with an artificial leg and returned to Santa Maria. With only about $2,000 in combat pay to his name and his 1936 Ford Coupe, his total net worth, Joe formed Olivera Investment Company in 1946 and began his business career. Joe also returned to his job at the gas company. Joe would retire from the gas company in 1985 after forty-three years of service at the position of distribution division supervisor. Joe's first property purchase in 1946 was a ten-house court in the 400 block of South Lincoln. The houses rented for thirty-five dollars per month and the property was

heavily mortgaged to the local Bank. Joe's next business venture in 1951 was the purchase of a corner parcel at Main and McClelland Streets. This property had four commercial rental units including the site of the old Gaity Theater, which he remodeled and would later become the home of Fullers Stationary for many years. In the corner store, Joe and his brother Gene opened

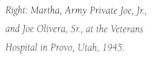

◆

Right: Martha, Army Private Joe, Jr., and Joe Olivera, Sr., at the Veterans Hospital in Provo, Utah, 1945.

Below: In 2006, Joe Olivera built and opened the La Brea Plaza Shopping Center at 700-722 East Main Street, Santa Maria.

Olivera's Liquor and Sporting Goods, followed in the rear building with Olivera Boat Shop. The fate of that property succumbed to the wrecking ball in the early 1970s when the property was purchased by the City of Santa Maria Redevelopment Agency and later became part of the Town Center East redevelopment project.

In 1962, Joe purchased the original shopping center development known as Stowell Center Plaza in the 1500 block of South Broadway. He would later purchase several of the remaining vacant lots in the center and would open the Kleanerette Dry Cleaners and Laundry.

early 1900s. After purchasing a total of eight parcels over a period of fifty years, Joe now had enough land to build his first, from the ground up, shopping center. Construction then began on the La Brea Plaza Shopping Center in 2004 and the first building was completed in 2006, followed by the second larger building in 2007.

In the middle of all of Joe's business activity, Jean managed to raise their four children; Joan, 1946; Jerry, 1948; Jim, 1954; and Jason, 1957. Joe and Jean have been blessed with seven grandchildren and fourteen great grandchildren.

✦

Olivera family photo taken in 1982. Back row, left to right, Jason, Joe and Jim. Front row, left to right, Joan, Jean and Jerry.

Joe was finally able to make good on his determination to one day have a local family ranch with the purchase of the Alamo Ranch in May 1976. The Alamo Ranch, which covers 1,683 acres, is located north of Highway 166 in Alamo Creek and was once part of the Cary Calvin Oakley Ranch originally purchased by Oakley in 1880.

In 1988, Joe along with several local businessmen formed Hacienda National Bank, where Joe served on the board of directors. Hacienda National Bank would later merge into Heritage Oaks Bank.

Beginning in 1954, Joe also began purchasing parcels in the 700 block of East Main Street, several with homes on them dating back to the

Joe, in his spare time, was able to sit on the City of Santa Maria Planning Commission for many years, leaving as the chairman, and sit on the boards for the Santa Barbara Foundation and Marian Medical Center. The Santa Maria Elks Club honored Joe in 2015 for his seventy years of membership in the organization.

Now in their nineties and still residing in the home they built back in 1959 in the Carriage District of Santa Maria, Joe and Jean have placed all of their property holdings into an LLC (Limited Liability Company) and named it Olivera Properties, LLC. Joe and Jean have since handed over the reins of their lifetime accomplishments to their children.

POWELL-ILIFF FAMILIES

Few families have had as much influence on the development of California's Santa Maria Valley as the Powells and the Iliffs. Their impact began in the early 1880s with two larger-than-life men Colonel William V. Powell and Horace Greeley Iliff—and their many descendants have continued to enlarge and enhance their legacy.

Colonel Powell's name first appears in the annals of Santa Maria Valley history in 1881 when he took up an eighty-acre homestead south of the Santa Maria River, located on the main state highway leading north. Colonel Powell was fifty-five years old at the time and had already led an exciting and productive life.

The Powell's trace their ancestry to England. Colonel Powell's great-grandfather, Thomas W. Powell, was educated in London before sailing to America at the age of seventeen as a lieutenant in the King's Light Horse Cavalry. During the Revolutionary War, Thomas deserted the British and offered his services to General George Washington and the fight for American freedom. Thomas later fought under General Andrew Jackson at the Battle of New Orleans, where he was wounded in the left hand. He died in Boone County, Indiana, in 1835, regretting that he could not live long enough, "To lick 'em again."

William was born on May 22, 1826, in Brown County, Ohio, which was still considered part of the nation's frontier at the time. His education was received in the subscription schools of the day and he learned the arts of farming at an early age. He lived in Indianapolis, Indiana, from 1830 to 1835 and then moved to Shawnee Prairie, Tippecanoe County, where he remained until 1847. His next move took him to Miami County, Indiana.

Colonel Powell first visited California in 1850 as a member of a train of ox teams and prairie schooners that made the long and hazardous journey. It is believed that he came to California hoping to make his fortune in the gold mines, but after three years, he returned to Indiana.

On September 11, 1853, William married Mary A. Smith, the youngest daughter of John Smith, a direct descendant of the Pilgrims. Among the distinguished members of the Smith family was an uncle, Caleb B. Smith, who became a member of President Abraham Lincoln's Cabinet; and a great-aunt, Abigail Adams, the wife of President John Adams. The Smith family had lived in Virginia during the Revolutionary War and some members of the family married into the distinguished Randolph family, one of the celebrated 'First Families of Virginia.'

Colonel Powell was farming near Xenia (now Converse), Indiana, when the Civil War broke out. He put aside his plow, turned his horses out to pasture, and enlisted in the federal army, helping to organize Company I, 99th Indiana Volunteers. He was elected captain of the unit and served during the war under General William Tecumseh Sherman. In 1865, Powell was promoted to major. At the close of the war, he was commissioned a lieutenant colonel.

Colonel Powell returned home after the war and reestablished his farming operations near Remington, Jasper County, Indiana. He returned to California in 1871 with his wife and two sons, Addison M. and William G., and a daughter, Eldora. He settled in Mendocino County where he engaged in farming and raising stock. He is credited with introducing the first Poland-China hogs into that part of the state. It was while living in Mendocino County that William and Mary became parents of a daughter, Ida, born in 1874.

In 1881, Colonel Powell moved to the northern part of Santa Barbara County, took up his original eighty-acre homestead and lived there until his death in 1903. After his wife, Mary, died in 1885, Colonel Powell made his home with his daughter, Ida. Eldora became the wife of James Means of Hollister, California, and they had one son, Walter. Ida married H. G. Iliff and lived on the old homestead with their three daughters and a son.

Addison M. Powell, a son of William and Mary, became a scout and guide for the United States Military Expedition that explored the Copper River country in Alaska during 1899-1900. He wrote *Trailing and Camping in Alaska, Echoes from the Frontier,* and other stories.

During his eventful life in the Santa Maria Valley, Colonel Powell played a major role in the development of the region. He was an advocate of good roads, good schools, churches, transportation improvements, and the establishment of good markets. With other pioneers, Colonel Powell laid the foundation for the Valley's prosperous future.

The Iliff family came to the United States from England about the time of the Revolutionary War. Two cousins—both named John Iliff—descended from the progenitor of the family. They came west from Ohio and one of the John Iliffs settled in Colorado, where he became well-known as the 'Cattle King of Colorado.' The other John Iliff, born in Ohio in 1824, settled in Nebraska and became the father of Horace Greeley Iliff.

Horace Greeley Iliff was born in Richardson County, Nebraska, on March 5, 1871, the son of John Wesley and Nancy Carroll Iliff, who lived in Missouri for a time before purchasing farm land in Richardson County. John and Nancy raised a family of nine children, including Horace. Until the age of fifteen, Horace worked on the family farm in Nebraska and attended the public schools. By the age of twelve, he could handle a team of horses and a plow and was soon capable of doing a man's work. Horace and a brother, John W., eventually migrated to California.

Following the death of his parents, Horace made his home near Lincoln, Nebraska. He came to California in 1894 to visit his brother John, who was living in Santa Barbara County. Horace intended to stay only a few months, but became so enamored of the climate and the possibilities available in the state that he decided to remain. He acquired a ranch where he did nearly all the work by himself. In 1916 he harvested 500 sacks of beans and a thousand sacks of potatoes.

In 1895, Horace married Ida M. Powell, a daughter of Colonel Powell, one of the pioneers of the Santa Maria Valley. Horace and Ida had five children: Eva Mabel, Florence Fern, Lelia Tresssa, Claudie Wesley (who died at the age of nine), and Addison Powell.

The Iliffs made their home on a ranch one-and-a-half miles north of Santa Maria. The land was inherited by Ida from her father, Colonel Powell. The Iliffs erected a modern residence on the land and lived there for many years in peace and contentment.

Colonel Powell and Horace Greeley Iliff have many descendants, many of whom have made significant contributions to the growth and development of the Santa Maria Valley.

✦

Above: Horace Greeley and Ida May Powell Iliff.

Below: Standing, left to right, Addison "Babe", Ida, and Horace Greeley Iliff.

◆

Above: H. G. Iliff and Son Sand and Gravel Plant.

Below: Iliff Ranch.

Addison Powell was the son of Horace Greeley Iliff and was in the rock and sand business, H. G. Iliff and Son. They hauled rock and sand for many of the buildings in Santa Maria. Addison, fondly known as 'Babe' married Mary Britanick. In 1941, they had their only child,

Dale Ronald Iliff. Dale graduated from Santa Maria High School and had many football scholarship offers for his athletic ability. He chose to attend Allan Hancock College and played football under Coach John Madden during an undefeated season in 1960. Dale worked

for Santa Maria Glass and when his father-in-law, Phil Baciu, retired, Dale and his partner, Jack Frazier bought the business in 1974.

Dale married Karen Baciu in 1958. They have two sons, Lance Ronald and Christopher Philip. Later, Dale bought out his partner and the firm is now owned by Dale and his two sons. Lance has three girls, Leah, Lynnae, and Lauren. Leah graduated from Cal Poly, San Luis Obispo with a teaching degree. Lynnae is a design student at Allan Hancock College. Lauren is in high school.

Chris has two sons, Camden Christopher and Cole Wesley. Camden has two sons, Addison and Ashton. Cam is co-owner of Eagle Software and is the director of Student Systems Development. Cole has a master's degree from Johns Hopkins. Dale, Lance and Chris still live on the old homestead north of Santa Maria.

◆

Above: Left to right, Chris, Dale and Lance Iliff at Santa Maria Glass.

Below: Dale Iliff.

TEIXEIRA FARMS, INC.

Teixeira Farms, Inc., was established in 1971 but the company roots go much deeper.

The legacy of Teixeira Farms began with the marriage of Joseph and Elsie Teixeira in 1937. Joseph and Elsie farmed row crops while their five boys were growing up and passed on their passion for farming to their sons. Joseph and Elsie provided the initial 300 acres of land to start the farming operation and the two oldest sons—Norman and Allan—began the farming operation known as Teixeira Farms. Marvin

Teixeira joined the operation when he returned from the Navy and his brothers—Glenn and Dean—followed shortly thereafter.

The brothers are fourth generation farmers in the Santa Maria Valley. When researching the history of a ranch they purchased in Oso Flaco, they discovered their great-grandfather had once owned the land.

"In the early days, we did everything from moving sprinklers to cleaning bathrooms," recalls Allan. "It was continual work, but very gratifying because we felt we were building a legacy."

At first the brothers grew seed beans, carrots, broccoli and iceberg lettuce. They tried different marketing strategies to sell their crops, learning from experience which approaches worked, and which ones did not.

Getting the operation going was not always easy. Allan remembers that one year there was so much unexpected—and early—rain in September that seed beans sprouted in their pods in the windrows, resulting in a total crop loss for the year. Another year there was not a good market for broccoli and the brothers discovered it was costing more to harvest the crop than it could be sold for. To meet the challenge, the older brothers and their wives went into the fields and harvested the

♦

Top: Harvesting lettuce during the
1980s (from left to right) Glenn,
Marvin, Elsie, JC, Norman, Dean,
and Allan.

Middle: A board meeting in the mid-
1990s (from left to right) Norman,
Dean, Allan, JC, Glenn, and Marvin.

Bottom: One of the semis used to
haul lettuce south on the 101 to
McDonald's processing plants in
Los Angeles.

broccoli for a local freezer company so their families would have money to celebrate Christmas.

"We didn't make very much money and our backs gave out, but it gave us a new appreciation for farm workers," Allan says.

There were also memorable stories that continue to generate much laughter today in family circles, but were not quite as funny when they happened. There were confrontations with union bullies and driving trucks through picket lines, as well as staying up all night trying to capture tractor thieves in the act.

As the company grew, the brothers divided responsibilities for the operation, capitalizing on each brother's strengths. "We didn't want our employees to have too many bosses and receive conflicting job orders, so Norman handled the shop and cooler management and I was in charge of the office and crop production," Allan explains. "Marvin oversaw land preparation and cultivation, Glenn managed the sales department, and Dean took care of harvesting."

the spokes of the wheel. This structure has enabled the company to maintain a high standard of quality and control in the farming of broccoli, lettuce, cauliflower, cabbage and celery.

The original 300 acres their father and Uncle Ernie Novo had farmed eventually grew to 4,500 acres in the Santa Maria Valley as well as more than 2,500 acres in the Imperial Valley. Along the way, the brothers started Teixeira Desert, Highline Cooling, Frontier Cooling, Pioneer Supply, Teixeira Veggies, and Wilderness Carton. Teixeira Farms was a pioneer in bulk vegetable sales to processors. In the late 1970s and early 1980s, the farms supplied McDonald's restaurants with all the lettuce consumed at their locations in eleven western states.

Teixeira Farms, Inc., along with its supporting entities, reached its peak with over 1,200 employees, $50 million in sales, and a customer base that extended to such foreign countries as Japan, Taiwan, Canada and Mexico, to name only a few.

"Our workers have always been more important than just employees," says Allan. "Their personal lives mattered to us as much as their jobs did. We know we could not have had any measure of success without the hard, backbreaking work of our loyal employees."

Allan is hesitant to mention specific employees by name, fearing someone important

Teixeira Farms built its own cooler in 1980 and organized its own sales company to cool and market the vegetables.

Teixeira Farms now has an integrated business structure that was developed early on with the creation of various entities that support the farming operation. The structure is best described as a wagon wheel in which the farming operation—Teixeira Farms—is the hub and the various entities such as transplant, supply, cooler, sales, and labor contractor companies are

would be left off the list, but he does single out Grace Motez, who joined her mother on the hoeing crew as a teenager. She worked her way up from the hoeing crew to the management position she held until just before her death in 2014. Grace's tenacity and loyalty are legend in the company's history.

The Teixeira brothers are also grateful for their Uncle Edwen, their dad's younger brother. "Uncle Edwen was a key part of our success," says Allan. "When we had difficulty or an idea we could brainstorm with him, he always came up with practical and functional solutions. With Uncle Edwen's help, we created equipment to enhance the development of harvesting equipment and drip irrigation in the valley."

As the five Teixeira brothers approached retirement age, it was found that most of the next generation did not want to continue in crop production and left the company to pursue their own interests. With the growth in popularity and demand for strawberries on the central coast, Teixeira Farms has recently begun subleasing its land to strawberry growers while maintaining the cooler for the strawberries.

Over the years, Teixeira Farms has supported and been personally involved with various community and charitable organizations. Among these are COLAB, FFA, Boy's and Girl's

Clubs, Bonita School, California Women for Agriculture, YMCA, Food Bank of Santa Barbara County, Santa Barbara County Fair, Growers and Shippers, Western Growers, United Agribusiness League and Trust, as well as personal charitable organizations.

Teixeira Farms commitment to food safety and quality of customer service is second to none. Excellence in the finished product must begin with excellence in the raw product, which is achieved through generations of total commitment.

Above: An aerial view of the Teixeira Farms/Frontier Cooling facility in 2001.

Below: As of 2006 these were the members of two generations of the Teixeria family working at Teixeira Farms:Back row (from left to right) Dean, Glenn, Marvin, Allan, and Norman. Front row (from left to right) Norman's daughter Pam Teixeira Lind; Norman's son Mark; Allan's son-in-law Vince Ferrante; Allan's son Steven; Norman's son Gary; and Allan's son John.

Ca' Del Grevino Estate & Vineyard

Greka Integrated, Inc.

After phenomenal success in the oil business, Randeep Singh Grewal is now developing a different sort of liquid gold—wine—under the name Ca' Del Grevino, which means "House of Grewal Family Wines." The fine wines produced on the estate are steeped in Italian tradition with a distinctive California style and are winning awards in every competition they attend.

Grewal has been in California since 1983 when he went to Northrop University in Los Angeles to attain his mechanical/aerospace engineering degree. The Zambian (southern Africa) raised, Indian heritage engineer quickly fell in love with Santa Barbara County, which reminded him of Cape Town. He has not left California since and continues to continually expand his varying operations concentrated in Santa Maria.

Grewal, the owner of Greka Integrated, Inc., purchased the 110-acre Addamo Estate Vineyards in Orcutt, located directly across the street from Grewal's Oil Company in 2012. The Addamo Vineyard had been established in 2000 by David Addamo, who produced popular and critically acclaimed Pinot Noir, Chardonnay, Syrah, Dolcetto, and Grenache for more than a decade.

Grewal says he purchased the property because it is one of the few estates in the Santa Maria Valley with Italian heritage, influence and winemaking techniques. He fell in love with the estate and surrounding atmosphere and immediately initiated the highest standards of farming practices. The estate's fifty acres of grapes are planted methodically and meticulously, with special attention paid to varietals best suited to the estate's terroir.

In order to achieve a high standard of quality, properly grown, cropped, evenly ripened, hand-picked and hand-sorted grapes are used. The vineyard managers firmly believe that winemaking starts in the vineyard and growing well-balanced grapes results in a well-balanced wine. The vineyard is sustainably farmed and uses only 100 percent French oak barrels in the winemaking process with the reserves in new barrels.

✦

Right: Coming soon.

Located only ten miles east of the Pacific Ocean, the vineyard benefits from cool, maritime influences and its sandy loam soil and micro-climate make it the perfect location for producing Pinot Noir, Chardonnay, Grenache, Dolcetto, Riesling and Syrah wines.

Addamo has continued as the estate's wine-maker since its acquisition by Grewal and plans to continue developing award-winning wines. Currently, wines are produced under the labels Ca' Del Grevino, Grevino, Element, Red Carpet and Giovanni.

The Grevino Riesling 2013 won Double Gold at the 2016 San Francisco *Chronicle* wine competition. Ca' Del Grevino Dolcetto won Best of Class in the *Chronicle*'s 2015 wine competi-tion, and Ca' Del Grevino Pinot Noir Reserve 2011 won Double Gold in the *Chronicle*'s 2014 awards. The wines have also received a number of awards in Hong Kong, Singapore and China.

The vineyard is the latest venture of Grewal in California. He also founded Greka Integrated, Inc., a consolidation of several companies from 1997 to 2002. The year 1997 was a cornerstone when Greka Integrated strategically acquired a 200-acre oil and gas lease in the Cat Canyon Field in Santa Maria, adjacent to an oil and gas lease operated by Saba Petroleum. Being on the oil lease boundary, Greka's strategy was to demonstrate its successful well drilling tech-niques as an available service to Saba Petroleum. This strategy, initiated by Grewal, developed into communications between the companies' management about possible business opportu-nities that could be shared. These discussions eventually led in 1999 to Greka acquiring Saba Petroleum, which owned assets in the energy sector, including California oil and gas leasehold interests with an abundance of remaining reserves concentrated in the Santa Maria Valley, and an asphalt refinery to process up to 10,000 barrels per day of heavy crude in Santa Maria, assets in Texas, Louisiana, Michigan, Canada, Columbia, and Indonesia. Later in 1999, these California assets were transferred to Greka as part of the vertically integrated operation that exists today and all non-California assets sold.

In 2003, Greka, which was previously part of a public company, was privatized by Grewal. Since then, Greka has engaged in various strategic transactions for the acquisition and divestiture of interests, concentrating in Santa Maria.

Greka is headquartered in New York, but its principal office is located in Santa Maria where the assets are concentrated. Greka Integrated employs more than 100 people throughout California, most of whom are located in the Santa Maria Valley. The company's interests in the oil and gas fields span approximately 13,000 mineral acres.

Grewal's vision for Ca' Del Grevino is to develop an estate perfectly suited for the creation of a high quality wine that reflects this unique place. Ca' Del Grevino has passion, harmony and balance throughout the estate, the vineyard and the micro-climate, and thus the wine.

Ca' Del Grevino currently produces 10,000 cases of wine annually, but after completion of a new 35,000 square foot winery and tasting room in 2017, production will grow to 50,000 cases.

The new winery is designed to suit the unique characteristics of the vineyard. One new feature will be a production facility, which flows into a hillside, thus utilizing the natural cooling of the earth and caves to cultivate the harvest. Inside the winery will be stainless steel fermenters with gravity flow designs, French oak barrels, and basket presses tailored to match the diverse blocks in the vineyard.

In addition to producing fine wines, Ca' Del Grevino Estate & Vineyard hosts corporate retreats, weddings, concerts and other events. Spectacular, unobstructed panoramic views, amphitheater, regal estate buildings and a

European-style courtyard provide several unique venues from which to choose. From formal meals seated at tables in marquee tents to California-style barbeques out in the open, the estate can accommodate fifty to 500 guests.

Also located only a few miles from the estate is Ca' Del Grevino Café & Wine Bar, a quaint café offering the suite of the estate's wine, great food and personalized service. The café and wine bar serves lunch and dinner and offers wine tastings Tuesday through Sunday. Each Wednesday and Saturday evening, the café provides live music to provide a special ambience for diners. Special events, such as winemaker dinners, wine and food pairings, nightly specials and holiday menus add creativity to the weekly program and menu offerings.

The café menu is focused on local in-season, farm-fresh produce, meats and cheeses. The vast majority of the menu items are made from original and fresh ingredients, including dressings, soups, pasta dishes, pizzas, ciabatta bread and desserts. Daily specials feature special ingredients from farmer's markets and local farms. The café

proudly features Ca' Del Grevino and estate wines, as well as other fine wines and beers.

Ca' Del Grevino Café & Wine Bar is located at 400 East Clark Avenue, Old Town, in Orcutt.

Greka Integrated and Ca' Del Grevino are major supporters of the Boys & Girls Club of Santa Maria Valley. This support includes sponsorships, donations and volunteer time. The group keenly supports the Boys & Girls Keystone Club and enjoys celebrating Christmas with Santa delivering gifts to the Club's children from their wish lists.

As a supporter of youth in the community, the organization has also been a proud sponsor of such other local events as the Santa Barbara County Fair, Court Appointed Special Advocates (CASA), the Santa Maria Christmas Parade of Lights, the Santa Maria Valley Chamber of Commerce, the Elks Rodeo, the Santa Maria City Firefighters Benevolent Foundation, the Rotary Club and various youth sporting teams.

To learn more about the beautiful Ca' Del Grevino Estate and Vineyard, check their website at www.grevino.com and Greka Integrated at www.greka.com.

DOUD/PORTER FAMILY

Maria Rosa Sparks Porter and grandchildren

❖

Right: Maria Rosa Sparks Porter and her grandchildren.

Below: William Arza "Bunny" Porter.

Bottom: Josephine Adam Porter, wife of William Porter.

The annals of California history are filled with the exploits of rugged, larger-than-life individuals whose bold determination created the dynamic spirit still ingrained in the state's unique personality. Few families have had a greater impact on weaving the rich tapestry of California than Isaac Sparks and his descendants, and none have been more colorful.

The family patriarch, Isaac James Sparks, was one of the 'Yankee dons' who moved west in the nineteenth century in search of excitement and riches. Sparks, a native of Maine, left St. Louis in 1831 with a group of fearless pioneers led by Jedediah Smith, who had earned the title 'pathfinder' for becoming the first man to find a way across the Sierra Nevada into California. Eighty-three men, including Sparks, traveled in a caravan of twenty-one mule-drawn wagons and dozens of horses.

Soon after reaching Santa Fe, Sparks was thrown into jail by Mexican officials for lack of a proper passport. Sparks, however, managed to escape from jail and make his way to San Pedro. It was here that Sparks shot his first otter from shore and swam out to secure the animal. At the time, a sea otter pelt was worth about forty dollars so he soon had enough money to buy a boat and hire a 'swimmer' to retrieve the otters he shot. Eventually, Sparks had four boats and a number of employees. From 1832 to 1848, he

maintained a working interest in the business, which made him a wealthy man.

In 1843 the Mexican Governor granted Sparks 22,000 acres in the Huasna, where he established a successful ranching operation. Much of this original land grant remains in the family today. The early days on the Huasna were never monotonous. There were numerous run-ins with the Tulare Indians, who crossed the valley to raid herds of horses. Wild animals abounded and one vaquero reported seeing fifteen grizzly bears in just a short ride on the Huasna Rancho.

Legend has it that Sparks acquired the vast El Pismo Rancho in 1846 by winning a card game.

Sparks married Maria Eayrs of Bodega Bay, California in 1842 and they had three daughters: Flora, born in 1846; Maria Rosa in 1851; and Sallie in 1854. The family lived in the first brick house built in Santa Barbara. Sparks' heart was in Santa Barbara, where he had numerous business interests. He built the first two-story hotel with bricks brought from Hawaii. He also operated a trading post, general store and the town's first post office.

All the Sparks daughters lived colorful and eventful lives, none more so than the middle child, Maria Rosa, who married Arza Porter in 1870.

Porter, whose grandfather had fought with revolutionary forces during the War for Independence, was born in 1838 in Livingston County, New York. When Porter was sixteen, his father's health forced the family to move to Grundy County, Illinois, where they acquired a farm.

Porter helped with the chores on the farm for a few years but was intrigued by the tales of adventure told by those who had moved out West to seek their fortunes. His opportunity to explore the unknown territories came in 1858 when a wagon train of immigrants bound for California were massacred at a place called Mountain Meadow in Utah. President James Buchanan suspected the deed had been perpetrated by Mormons acting under orders from Brigham Young. The president placed Utah Territory under martial law and sent a wagon train of supplies for the troops. Young Arza was hired to help get those supplies to their destination.

After an adventurous trip, the wagons reached Salt Lake City at the onset of winter and bad weather closed the trails back to Illinois, where Arza had planned to return. To avoid spending the winter in Utah, Arza and some companions packed supplies and headed off for California, arriving in the Los Angeles area three months later. He found a job as a stagecoach driver on the route from Los Angeles to Santa Barbara.

In 1863, Arza moved to Santa Barbara to manage the stagecoach stop and soon became active in politics. He was elected sheriff in 1865 and in 1869, he married the saucy Rosa Sparks. The union produced ten children, three of whom died in infancy.

Rosa, a strong-willed young woman, felt her husband's duties as sheriff were too dangerous for a family man and begged him to bow out of a race for reelection in 1871. But Arza's challenger had defeated him in an election four years earlier by only three votes and he was determined to win the election for sheriff.

Unable to persuade Arza to withdraw from the race, the twenty-year-old Rosa hitched a horse to a buggy and drove around Santa Barbara campaigning for her husband's opponent. Arza lost the election by sixteen votes. Rosa viewed the results with great

satisfaction while Arza kept his opinion to himself.

Taking his defeat with good grace, Arza concentrated on business but kept his hand in politics as well. In 1873, he was elected to the Santa Barbara City Council (without opposition from Rosa) and, after moving to San Luis Obispo County, he was elected to the state assembly in 1884.

Rosa and her two sisters inherited Isaac Spark's 22,153-acre Mexican land grant and Rosa came into her share of those Huasna lands after her marriage to Arza about 1870. The Porter's leased the acreage until 1879. When Arza decided to move to the Huasna

◆

Above: Children of Josephine and Bunny Porter. Left to right, Isaac Joseph Porter, Anastasia Porter Paulsey, Rosemary Porter Doud and Charles Robert Porter.

Below: Rosemary Porter Doud and husband Joseph E. Doud.

Rancho, Rosa objected to moving 'way out in the sticks' wanting to remain near friends in Santa Barbara. Arza moved to the rancho alone, although he visited Santa Barbara from time to time.

Rosa relented in 1886 and decided to take the children for a summer on the ranch. The 'visit' stretched to twelve years until Arza became ill and the couple returned to Santa Barbara to seek medical care. Arza died in 1899 and Rosa lived as a widow until 1933.

The descendants of these colorful pioneers have continued to play a prominent role in the Santa Maria Valley in modern times. Today, the Porter Ranch spreads over more than 6,800 acres of rolling hills dotted with oaks and chaparral. Over the years, the Porters have cultivated about seventy acres of wine grapes

and 200 acres of farmland, which is leased to farmers who grow squash, peppers and other crops. The Porters also raise beef cattle.

William A. 'Bunny' Porter (Rosemary Doud's father) married Josephine Ponchetta during the 1930s and moved to the ranch where their children Anastasia, Charlie, Isaac (Ike), and Rosemary were born. Charlie moved back to the ranch in the 1980s; his brother, Ike, has lived there his entire life.

Charlie studied animal science at Cal Poly and worked on the ranch for his father for several years before taking over ranch operations with Ike.

Rosemary married Joseph Eugene Doud, II and had two children, Joseph Eugene Doud, III and Derek Porter Doud. Joseph married Lisa Fulford and their children are Kendall and Joseph Eugene Doud, IV. Derek married Carolyn Rust and their children include Shey, Devon and Chase.

Kendall is currently attending Cal Poly University in San Luis Obispo and is on the college riding team, traveling to rodeos as a barrel racing and roping star. She carries on the ranch's long history of accomplished riders.

Family members fondly recall growing up on the ranch or gathering there frequently for celebrations, holidays and reunions. The family continues to celebrate Thanksgiving and Christmas in their grandparent's former home, which is still used for ceremonial occasions.

✦

Opposite, top: Sons and grandchildren of Rosemary and Joseph Doud.

Opposite, bottom and above: Porter Ranch is still a working cattle ranch.

THE PAUL & SUSAN RIGHETTI FAMILY

FAR WESTERN TAVERN

SUSIE Q'S BRAND

This is a story of three longtime local families—Righetti, Minetti and Maretti—who all originated from the Swiss-Italian region of Ticino and put down roots in the Santa Maria Valley and went on to become pillars in the valley's ranching and culinary communities.

Elvezio Righetti immigrated from Someo, Switzerland to the United States at the age of seventeen and bought what would become known as the Righetti Ranch in 1907. He and his wife, Lillie Pezzoni, raised seven children, including a son, Paul A. Righetti.

Paul's son, Paul T. Righetti, grew up on the ranch in the 1950s and 1960s, and was driving equipment by the time he was eight years old. His teenage years involved working with the ranch's cattle and horses. His leisure time was spent enjoying the outdoors, riding, and hunting.

In keeping with local ranching tradition, neighbors pitched in to help each other during the spring branding season. One of the helpful neighbors was the Minetti family. Paul got to know Susan Minetti then and afterward while attending Righetti High School. Ultimately, Paul and Susan married in 1970.

Paul and Susan chose to make their home on the Righetti Ranch and still live there today in the original Doane-built 1917 Craftsman home along with Paul's sister, Paula Righetti Pyche. Other historic houses on the property are home to their daughter and son-in-law, Renee and Mark Fowler and granddaughter Regan; son Tim Righetti and grandchildren Ryan and Alexis.

Today, the Righetti Ranch remains a family operation and maintains its history of cattle ranching, breeding horses and farming. It is also the foundation of Susie Q's Brand, a specialty food purveyor founded by Susan in 1981 with ranch grown pinquito beans. Paul and Susan's children, Renee and Tim, perpetuate the family's traditions. Both are actively involved and continue to move forward the ranching and culinary operations.

Rosalie Maretti was born in Guadalupe, California, in 1919. Rosalie was raised on her family's Corralitos Ranch in Oso Flaco by her parents, Charles and Adeline Acquistapace Maretti. She attended elementary school in Guadalupe and graduated from Santa Maria

High School in 1937. Rosalie went on to study business at Woodbury College in Los Angeles.

Rosalie married Clarence Minetti on August 10, 1940. Clarence was born in Cayucos, California, in 1918. Clarence moved with his parents to Guadalupe in 1925 and graduated from Santa Maria High School in 1935. As a young cowboy living in Guadalupe, he said he got the biggest break of his life when he met and married Rosalie.

In 1941, Clarence and Rosalie moved to Corralitos Ranch and made their lifetime home there. Here, Clarence learned the cattle business from her father, Charles. When Charles passed away in 1947, Clarence and Rosalie took the helm of the family cattle ranching and dry farming operation. They formed the Maretti-Minetti Ranch Company in partnership with her brother, Ralph Maretti, and his wife, Wilma. They built up an exceptional cattle herd over the years, which today the ranch company is in its third generation of family ownership.

Clarence and Rosalie had three children—Susan (who married Paul Righetti), Marie, and Tyke.

In 1958, Rosalie and Clarence co-founded the Far Western Tavern along with Rosalie's cousin, Richard Maretti and his wife, Jean.

Originally located in the historic Palace Hotel building in the town of Guadalupe (and now located in Old Town Orcutt), the Far Western Tavern quickly became a hometown favorite, attracting locals and visitors alike with its legendary fare and welcoming hospitality. Today, the restaurant remains a landmark of Santa Maria Valley hospitality and the regional culinary tradition of Santa Maria Style Barbecue.

Since those early days, the Far Western Tavern has outlasted countless culinary trends, remaining true to its original style while keeping pace with contemporary tastes. As Clarence was fond of saying, "To last in this business, you have to like people and you have to serve great food. It's that simple."

While working at her family's Far Western Tavern while growing up, Susan Righetti (née Minetti) saw travelers discover the delights of Santa Maria Style Barbecue—and often heard them express interest in preparing it for themselves.

Later, Susan began considering the possibility of sharing the classic ingredients of Santa Maria Style Barbecue in the form of retail products. In 1981, at the urging of her husband Paul, she established Susie Q's Brand. Her first product was the Righetti Ranch grown pinquito beans, sold at one retail outlet—the Far Western Tavern.

In 1982, Susan developed her inaugural mail order catalog. Then, in the fall of 1983, her little company was suddenly thrust into one of the brightest spotlights of the time—the food section of *USA Today*, which showcased Susie Q's Brand's pinquito beans in its "Fine Living" column.

"That really put us on the map," Susan recalls. "I came into the office and the message machine was full, and the phone was ringing with people requesting our catalog. I had no idea what was going on until someone told me that *USA Today* had recommended our beans."

Today, Susie Q's Brand is regarded as the original purveyor of artisan Santa Maria Style Barbecue foods, including a signature seasoning,

the original pinquito beans and several other products rooted in this local culinary tradition.

The Righetti Ranch continues to be operated by Paul and his son, Tim. Susie Q's Brand remains a family affair led by Susan and her daughter, Renee.

Susan and Paul, along with Susan's sister, Marie, and her husband, Steve Will, continue to operate the Far Western Tavern along with the family's next generation.

Marie and Steve are also co-owners of Riverbench Vineyard, an estate winery specializing in artisan Chardonnay and Pinot Noir from an iconic local vineyard.

Susan's brother, Tyke, manages the Maretti-Minetti Ranch Company's cattle herd at Corralitos Ranch.

Collectively, these interests belong to both a longtime multi-family tradition of hospitality and a legacy of local flavor rooted in the Santa Maria Valley, where famous barbecue, world-class wine, abundant agriculture and traditional ranching are woven into the fabric of the community.

THE BATTLES/ BARCA PIONEERS

Among the first settlers in the Santa Maria Valley were the ancestors of Glenn and Janice Barca Battles. Glenn is the fourth generation of one of the pioneer homesteaders in the valley, and Janice represents the third generation of her family to settle in the area.

Glenn's great-grandfather, George Washington Battles and his wife, Rachel Kinsey, came from Pennsylvania to the Santa Maria Valley in 1868 and homesteaded 160 acres.

"Conditions were tough for the early pioneers," Glenn says. "They contended with wild horses, grasshoppers and wild fires destroying their crops."

Despite the hardships, George played an important role in the development of the area. He framed a petition to have the first school built in the valley and a local elementary school bears his name today.

George's son, Ulysses Grant Battles, married Ella F. Hourihane, an immigrant from Ireland, in 1899. Ulysses continued farming, was a bean and grain broker, and the parents of James G. and Mary T. Battles.

James G. Battles continued farming and raised hogs. He married Thelma L. Chamberlain of Santa Barbara, and they became the parents of James, Glenn, Myron and Barbara.

Glenn currently manages the Battles Ranch, which is under lease for growing strawberries and row crops.

Janice's grandfather, Bartolomeo Barca, emigrated from Switzerland to California in 1878. After working on several ranches, he returned to Switzerland in 1901 and married Virginia Grossini. Upon their return they purchased the Todos Santos Ranch in 1904. He operated a dairy, farmed and raised cattle, and were the parents of Peter, Albino, Adelina, Mary, Walter and Zilda.

Janice's father, Albino, married Evelyn Bonde of Paso Robles, and were the parents of Virginia, Carol, Janice, Gerald and Charles.

Peter and Albino operated the home ranch as Barca Brothers until their deaths. It was then divided between the two families.

The ranch is currently co-managed by Janice and is under lease for cattle grazing and irrigated crops.

When old enough, both the Battles and Barca children were expected to help with the harvesting; baling hay and hoeing bean fields during summertime. It was through their devotion and perseverance that both properties remain in their families today.

Glenn and Janice were educated in the local school districts. They were married in 1960 and are the parents of Lori, Kari and Julie.

Both Glenn and Janice have been active in supporting a number of worthy organizations and Janice has a deep interest in genealogy and preserving the memories of the early settlers for future generations.

✦

Top left: Glenn Battles.

Top right: Janice Barca Battles.

OSR ENTERPRISES, INC.

For more than 150 years, the Rice family has farmed the rich soil of the Santa Maria Valley, establishing a fourth-generation agricultural enterprise that is among the largest in the region.

The Rice family first moved to the Santa Maria area in the 1860s and the founder of the family enterprise, Owen T. Rice, was born in 1880. The family moved to a ranch east of Santa Maria in 1882 and, in 1906, Owen T. started farming on his own. The first piece of land he farmed was just across the street from where the family had moved twenty-four years earlier. In 1910, Owen T. married Viola Cook, a teacher in a one-room schoolhouse, and the young couple built a home on the property. That house now serves as the company's corporate office.

World War II as sugar beets became more attractive and potatoes were added to the mix. The Rices even grew cabbage to make sauerkraut for the war effort.

Following the war, the family began focusing on four main crops: sugar beets, potatoes, dry beans and chili peppers. In 1950 the Rices built the company's first dehydrator, which allowed them to process their chili peppers on-site, rather than shipping to a dehydration facility in Los Angeles.

Owen T. Rice & Son was incorporated in 1952 and, a year later, a second family corporation was formed, Santa Maria Chili Products. The company purchased a used grinder and blender and began manufacturing its own brand of ground chili powder. As demand for its product grew, the company was forced to add other spices such as paprika chilies, garlic, onion flakes, cumin, oregano, coriander, and black pepper, to name a few. These products were either ingredients in chili powder blends or sold on their own.

◆

Left: Owen T. and Owen S. surveying land to be leveled.

Right: Inventory of processed chili powder being readied for shipment.

Owen T. and Viola's son, Owen S. Rice, was born in 1912 and learned the family business early, working alongside his father. He attended local schools and earned a football scholarship to San Diego State College. After graduation, Owen S. returned home and started farming on his own, working out a relationship where he used his father's equipment on his farm in exchange for doing all of Owen T.'s tractor work.

Father and son worked so well together that they established a partnership, Owen T. Rice & Son, in 1939. Up until this time, the farm's crops had consisted mostly of dry beans and sugar beets. The crops began to change during

The third generation of the Rice family, James, graduated from San Diego State in 1968 and, after six months on active duty with the National Guard, joined the family business.

Owen T. passed away in 1970 and management of the business passed to Owen S. and

James. Crop acreage was increased through purchases and leases and the products slowly changed from row crops to vegetable crops. Meanwhile, Santa Maria Chili continued to increase its market share to the point that raw product had to be purchased from outside growers. Some of these chilies were imported from far away locations such as Spain, Mexico, Turkey, India, Pakistan, and Japan, as well as other local growers to provide the proper tastes in the many chili powder blends being produced for customers.

OSR Enterprises, Inc. was formed in 1983 to become the parent company of Owen T. Rice & Son, Inc. and Santa Maria Chili, Inc.

In a strategic move, Santa Maria Chili purchased Valley Chili Co. of Vinton, Texas, in 1986. The purchase allowed production of chili peppers from another region and also brought in a new line of jalapeño products, which included brined jalapeños for salsas and cheeses, jalapeños sliced as wheels for nachos, as well as dehydrated jalapeños.

The chili company continued to grow and was sold to a competitor, Cal Compact Foods, in 1991. At this point, Owen T. Rice & Son began operating as OSR Enterprises, Inc., the name still used today.

Without the chili products, the family began concentrating solely on its traditional crops. Additional land was acquired and the company began to emphasize vegetable production, distribution and cooling. The company no longer grew sugar beets or chili peppers and potatoes and dry beans became minor crops. In 1998 the company purchased and began operating its own vegetable cooling facility called Central City Cooling.

In 1999, OSR Enterprises began marketing its vegetables through Pacific International Marketing (PIM) of Salinas. At the time, vegetable buyers were demanding that suppliers become year-round shippers and supply products from more than one area. Pacific International filled this need for OSR Enterprises by shipping in season from Salinas, Cochella, Yuma, and Mexico.

Since the affiliation with PIM, OSR Enterprises has continued to concentrate on its fresh vegetable business and has completely phased out dry beans and potatoes. The farm's current crops include broccoli, cauliflower,

♦

Above: The original home of Owen T. and Viola, now the corporate office.

Below: The original logo and brand for Owen T. Rice & Son.

Bottom: Potatoes being dug for shipping to fresh market outlets.

Above: Three generations of the Rice family, left to right, Owen S., James and Andrew.

Right: A state-of-the-art vegetable cooling facility built in 2010.

celery, cilantro, spinach and mixed lettuce. In partnership with PIM, the company built a new state-of-the-art vegetable cooling facility in 2010.

James credits his father, Owen S., with guiding the company's success and establishing it as a major producer. "Dad was the one who really got the business going," he explains. "He put every dime we made back into the business. He was also very big on education, insisting that we all go to college. He served on the local school board for more than thirty years."

Owen S., considered the company patriarch, passed away in 2010 at the age of ninety-eight.

James feels the company has been successful for more than a century because of the owners 'hands-on' approach, a close relationship with its employees, innovative equipment, and a willingness to change with the times.

OSR Enterprises now farms more than 3,000 acres in the Santa Maria Valley. The company employs about 150 persons, as well as several hundred seasonal workers. Employee turnover is very low and a number of people

have worked for the company more than thirty years. One employee, Salvidor Peinado, recently marked his fifty-first year with the company.

The fourth generation of the Rice family, James' son, Andrew, graduated from Arizona State University and received a graduate degree in business administration from Cal Poly, San Luis Obispo and joined the family business in 2011. Under the leadership of James and Andrew, OSR Enterprises is poised for many years of success and prosperity in the future.

The Sheehy family, who first settled in the Santa Maria Valley in 1944, is largely responsible for the development of strawberries as one of the region's major crops.

The Sheehy family traces its ancestry to County Cork in Ireland, and all are descendants of John Sheehy and Mary Donovan. Their children began immigrating to California in the 1840s and eventually settled in Watsonville. One of John's grandsons, Patrick 'P. H.' Sheehy, married Isabel "Belle' Adam, daughter of William Laird Adam, a well-known Santa Maria pioneer. Their sons were Kenneth and Rod.

While Kenneth's sons, Bob and Terry, fought overseas during World War II, he and his brother, Rod, began talking with Ned Driscoll, founder of Driscoll Strawberry Associates. The three men felt there would be a big demand for fresh strawberries when the war ended.

In 1944, Kenneth and Rod, along with their wives, Byra and June, moved to Santa Maria and began their first test plots of strawberries. Prior to this, strawberries had not been grown commercially in Santa Maria and no one was really sure which varieties would do well.

The Sheehy's first farm in Santa Maria, located on Donovan Road, was called the Gardena Ranch since they almost chose Gardena, California, to plant strawberries. At war's end, Kenneth's sons were persuaded to return to Santa Maria and help develop the strawberry business with their father.

The Sheehys were instrumental in bringing Japanese-Americans, many of whom were forced into internment camps during the war, to the valley to grow strawberries. Many Japanese-Americans who worked for the Sheehys—including the Furakawas, Kagawas and Matsumotos—went on to form their own berry farms.

The Sheehys, who have always taken pride in their fair treatment of employees, have been responsible for many innovations in the Santa Maria Valley, including the first air shipments of berries in 1947, first drip irrigated berries in 1968, first use of predatory mites in 1988, and the first bug vacuum in 1989.

Ken died in 1953, followed by Rod in 1956, but Bob and Terry continued farming together and eventually formed their own companies. Their sons, Rob, Patrick and Brian, continue to be involved in Santa Maria Valley's strawberry production today.

NEWHALL/
WOODS FAMILY

H. M. Newhall, who established a family legacy, was born in Saugus, Massachusetts, in 1825, the fifth of nine children. Born with a bold and adventurous spirit, he rebelled at working on the family farm and sailed from Boston as a ship's cabin boy at the age of thirteen, bound for the Philippines. After a fall from the ship's rigging, Newhall broke both his legs, he returned to Saugus to recuperate. He left home again at age fifteen and learned the trade of auctioneering, quickly becoming a partner in an auctioneering business in Nashville, Tennessee.

Newly married in 1849, Newhall left his wife behind and sailed for California, hoping to earn his fortune in the gold rush. As it turned out, his path to riches came not from the gold mines but from his auctioneering skills. By 1852, he was very well established in San Francisco from buying the cargos of abandoned ships in the port and selling them through his auction house. His wife, Sarah Ann White, joined him and they began a family as he moved into acquiring properties in the San Francisco area.

At the age of forty, Newhall was involved in building the San Francisco-San Jose railroad. That enterprise was sold to the new Southern Pacific railway system and he used his profits to greatly expand his land holdings. By 1875, Newhall had acquired more than 143,000 acres in six cattle ranches located from Monterey County to Los Angeles County. One of the ranches was the 48,834-acre Rancho Suey, located east of Santa Maria, purchased sight unseen at auction in 1875.

Newhall was seriously injured in a horse accident and died at the age of fifty-six. His widow and five sons formed the Newhall Land and Farming Company to continue the legacy he had established.

The family's modern-day saga began in 1938 when Edwin 'Bob' Newhall Woods, a great-grandson of H. M. Newhall, graduated from Stanford. He briefly considered a career as a teacher and fencing coach but soon decided that fifty cents an hour was not enough to live on.

◆

Above: Bob Woods and Pat, 1939.

Below: Harvesting grain on the Suey, 1929.

Instead, he became a cowboy on the Suey Ranch for $80 a month, plus $20 for keeping the books after hours.

Bob lived in the bunkhouse with the other single employees and on his rare days off he drove round-trip to San Francisco to go ice skating. On one of those trips, he met Jeanne Portnoff and they were married in 1945 at the Stanford Chapel.

Bob served in the Navy during World War II. When he returned home, the young couple worked at the Newhall Ranch for several years before moving up to the remodeled bunkhouse at the Suey Ranch in 1947. Bob managed the Suey Ranch until he retired in 1973. Jeanne was the ranch bookkeeper and was also very involved in a number of activities, including 4-H, Cub Scouts and the Camp Fire Girls as she raised her three children.

Bob served on the Newhall Board of Directors for forty years and was also a founding member of the H. M. Newhall Foundation Board of Directors. During these decades the way the land was utilized on the Suey Ranch changed dramatically. From being a cow-calf operation, along with some dry-land grain, the operation evolved to include cultivation of carrots, lima beans and sugar beets. Bob began experimenting with small plantings of lemons, walnuts and avocado trees and eventually a number of acres were planted in lemons.

In addition, several hundred acres were planted in various wine varieties.

During their decades of living in the valley, Bob and Jeanne became very involved in contributing to many nonprofit organizations throughout the area. In 2004, they created the Edwin and Jeanne Woods Family Foundation to continue their philanthropy. Although both Bob and Jeanne passed away in 2011, the foundation continues with family members continuing to assist a wide variety of organizations. They were honored posthumously in 2011 by Celebrate Philanthropy! for their endeavors to help others.

◆

Above: Bob Woods and Buster, 1939.

Below: Bob and Jeanne Woods.

BABÉ FARMS

Babé Farms, which began in 1986 as a producer of delicate spring mixes, has grown to become one of the country's major suppliers of more than seventy different varieties of gourmet vegetables, including a wide variety of colorful root vegetables, baby cauliflower, baby lettuces, specialty greens and organic kales.

The fourth generation business has always been a family enterprise and its roots run deep in the farming and ranching of California's Central Coast. The grandparents of company founder Judy Lundberg-Wafer, Joseph and Anna Machado, emigrated from Pico Island in the Azores in the early 1900s and settled in the Santa Rita Hills, east of Lompoc.

In the 1940s, Judy's father and mother, Ed and Margaret Cardoza, settled west of Lompoc in the rich, fertile fields of the Lompoc Valley. Judy worked in the fields with her family, hoeing beans, driving tractor and moving sprinkler pipe.

Boster Farms. Frank began moving his equipment to the Souza farm as manager of production and Judy continued to manage the books.

The family moved to the Santa Maria Valley in the early 1960s and Judy graduated from Santa Maria High School. The family was now growing lettuce, broccoli and celery and the entire family was involved in the operation. Judy married Frank Lundberg and they began farming with Judy's father. The couple took over the farm when her father retired and Frank managed the operation while Judy kept the books and raised three children, Jeff, Brad and Kim.

In the early 1980s, Frank and Judy were approached by Will Souza to manage Souza and

Babé Farms was established by Frank and Judy in 1986, along with partners, Souza and Greg Pedigo. At first, the small company specialized in just Mesclun greens and baby carrots. On the cusp of a food revolution in the 1980s, Babé Farms was inspired to expand their gourmet vegetable product line. Judy, a 4 foot 11-inch dynamo of energy, developed Babé Farms initial marketing campaign and traveled the nation promoting and introducing the company to the produce industry. With their quality baby vegetables, Babé Farms grew quickly with the motto of 'Only Tomorrow's Harvest is Fresher.'

In 2004, Judy's husband of thirty-nine years died of cancer. Knowing the farm was worth fighting for; Judy decided to buy out the remaining partners in July 2005. "Obviously, I would have rather had my husband here and running the company, but when he passed away my son, Jeff, and I had to step up because you don't sell a company like this. It was something we had to keep going because a lot of people depended on us," Judy explained.

Judy's management style blends a pragmatic business sense with a passion for possibilities. She helped guide Babé Farms from a small holding in 1986 to become one of the Santa Maria Valley's premium specialty vegetable growers, with customers throughout the U.S. and Canada.

The torch was passed to the fourth generation in 2015 Jeff took on the role of president and CEO. Judy continues to play an active role as chairman of the board. Jeff grew up working at Babé Farms and, like his mother, learned a little bit of everything over the years, from planting to harvesting, to operating a tractor and laying pipe. Like his father, Jeff studied Agriculture at Cal Poly San Luis Obispo.

From working the fields, managing a farm and serving as CEO of the successful firm Babé Farms has become, Judy has seen it all. "Hard work is the secret to success, along with surrounding yourself with great employees," she says. Babé Farms has more than 200 employees who Judy sees as family members.

Although it has become a large operation, Babé Farms still has the heart of a small family farm operation and reflects the way Judy was raised. She is very community oriented and

makes a difference in the lives of those with whom she comes in contact.

Remaining active in her retirement, Judy and husband, Jim Wafer, enjoy traveling and spending time with Judy's grandchildren, Eddie and Karli.

Innovative, creative, collaborative and blessed with an ideal growing climate, Babé Farms continues to expand on its colorful profusion of high quality gourmet vegetables that are packed and shipped across the U.S. and Canada.

◆

Left: Judy Lundberg, owner and chairman of the board of Babé Farms.

Below: Clockwise, starting from the top, left, Kelli and Jeff (daughter-in-law and son, fourth generation); Judy (third generation) and Karli and Eddie (grandchildren, fifth generation.)

FOXEN FAMILIES

There has been a Foxen presence in the Santa Maria Valley since 1837 when William Benjamin Foxen bought almost 9,000 acres and started his Rancho Tinaquaic. He came to California as an English seaman and married Eduarda Osuna at the Santa Barbara Mission in 1831. They had eleven children. The ranch has always been a working ranch, today growing more grapes than anything else.

Juan Santiago Alejandro Foxen, born in 1845, married Adelaida Botiller in 1872 and they had a son, Alejandro Albertino Foxen II, born in 1873, and an infant female who died at birth. Juan Santiago Alejandro Foxen died in 1877, and his widow, Adelaida, married his brother, Francisco Thomas Foxen in 1878. Thomas raised Alejandro, along with the seven children he and Adelaida produced. The combined family considered themselves "double cousins."

Thomas was a rancher in Foxen Canyon, but the children did not always want to stay as ranchers; some took a different direction. Alejandro married Bertha Boll, of German descent, and settled in Los Angeles. They had two sons, Raymond Victor and Reginald Herbert. Since Thomas considered these children almost his own grandchildren, he treated them very well. Herb (Reginald Herbert) remembered always how he enjoyed coming to Los Alamos on the train from Los Angeles to spend the summer with the Los Alamos Foxens. He must have been quite young to be traveling on his own, but he loved the area and settled in Los Alamos after he retired from North American Aviation in 1978. He and his wife, Consuelo Holman Foxen, built a house on Wickenden Lane, which has sub-sequently been torn down to build condominiums. They had no children. Connie died in 1986 and Herb in 2004. They are buried in the Los Alamos Cemetery.

Raymond settled in Los Angeles and worked for American Telephone Company all his life. He married Thelma Brodie in 1926 and they had two children, Barbara Jean Foxen Orozco and Donald Raymond Foxen. Raymond died in 1962 from lung cancer. Thelma died in 1973 from emphysema. Barbara and Manuel Orozco and their family of six children live in the Torrance area of Los Angeles.

❖

Top, left: William Benjamin Foxen, 1796-1874.

Top, right: Eduarda Osuna Foxen, 1812-1894.

Below: Left to right, Raymond Victor and Reginald Herbert.

Donald and Patricia Hamilton Foxen raised six children in the Los Angeles area while Donald was a captain in the Los Angeles County Sheriff's Department. Upon retiring, they moved to Santa Ynez, California, accompanied by their son, David Russell Foxen and his wife, Bertha Nava Foxen. David and Bertha have daughters Ashley Marie Foxen McKillop and Samantha Kelley Foxen.

and Bertha's daughter, Samantha, is working in the wine and hospitality industry after getting her degree in hospitality business management.

Jim and Wendy have worked in the Valley for the past thirty years. Wendy is in banking and currently with Community Bank of Santa Maria, and Jim worked for MTC trucking in the valley. Their daughter Jamie is currently a student at Cal Poly.

Also accompanying Donald and Patricia to Santa Ynez was their son, James Raymond Foxen. Jim married Wendy Hamilton, and they have a daughter Jamie Rae Foxen. The other children of Don and Pat Foxen settled in various areas of southern California.

David and Bertha have worked in the Santa Ynez/Santa Maria Valleys for the past thirty-four years; Bertha is a banker in the valley, and David in the construction industry currently with Westside Building Material in Santa Maria. Their daughter Ashley, now Ashley Foxen McKillop, received her nursing degree from Santa Barbara City College and worked for a while at Lompoc Community Hospital before moving out of state. Ashley and her family are currently in Arizona. She is now studying to become a nurse practitioner. David

For more than 175 years, descendants of William Benjamin Foxen, through his son Alejandro Foxen, have continued the Foxen presence in the Santa Maria Valley. Hopefully they will continue that presence far into the future from the many children of William Benjamin Foxen.

✦

Above: Left to right, top row, Gabriella, Cristine, Kent Stalwick, Michael, Wendy, Carrie Manning Wiley, Casey Manning Litwin, Gary Manning, Ashley and Bertha. Center row, Michael, Diane Foxen Stalwick, Jim, Patricia, Don, Kathryn, Donna Foxen Manning and David. Bottom row, Jake Stalwick, Kyle Stalwick, Isabella, Jamie, Patrick and Brad Stalwick and Samantha. All last names are Foxen except as indicated.

Left: Foxen branding iron.

DB
SPECIALTY FARMS

DBA
DARENSBERRIES

✦

Above: Daren Gee.

When you love what you do, it shows, and Daren Gee's love for what he does is obvious when you see the meticulously maintained 700 acres that make up his strawberry business, DB Specialty Farms, known more commonly as Darensberries.

Daren's love of agriculture began in the little town of Moorpark in Ventura County. His first job was harvesting apricots with his brother and mother. Later, he and his brother, David, worked on poultry units and harvested lemons.

Daren attended the University of Fresno on a football scholarship and was studying to become a forest ranger. However, after participating in a cotton growing project his senior year, he decided he was much more interested in agriculture. Daren graduated in 1973 and got a job selling agriculture chemicals.

Eventually, Daren decided to follow his dream and become a farmer. He quit his sales job, took a pay cut, and became an apprentice farmer in Oxnard with Chas Nikama. Later, he worked for Saticoy Berry Farms, where he met some of the people who work for his company today.

Daren took the big step of starting his own strawberry growing business in 1990 with 132 acres, partnering with Babe' Farms and San Ysidro Farms in Santa Maria. "I'm very grateful for the wonderful suppliers and bankers who had the confidence to invest in this business and watch it grow," Daren says. "It's just amazing to

me what we have been able to accomplish in the last twenty-five years."

Daren also says, "It's impossible to express how thankful I am to the wonderful people who took a chance and followed me up to Santa Maria from Oxnard. Without their commitment and tireless work, this project could never have been accomplished."

The farm produced about 350,000 boxes of strawberries the first year, a figure that has grown to more than 5 million boxes per year.

There are more than 600 varieties of strawberries but Daren concentrates on five of the most succulent and flavorful varieties: Albion, San Andreas, Monterey, Fronteras and Portola. "Our most popular variety is the Albion strawberry," Daren explains. "It has that beautiful red color and is one of the prettiest berries on the market. We can also ship Albion berries at full color, something that had eluded us for years."

Daren's strawberries are marketed under Daren's trade name of Darensberries and under the Foxy label. Darensberries and Foxy are consistently rated the top quality in the entire industry.

Daren's two brothers, Dawayne (Chip) and Dale also work in the business. Chip owned his own welding and repair shop in Simi Valley but, in 1955, Daren convinced Chip that his skill was sorely needed at the farm. Dale moved up from Palmdale in 2008 and jumped in and

helped on a wide array of projects. Most recently, in 2013, Daren's wife, Ottsy, and his oldest son, Kevin, have joined the company.

Along with his family members, Daren has about 250 full-time loyal employees, including a number of long-time and second-generation workers.

"We consider ourselves a community of workers," says Daren. "We believe people are everything. If you have the best people, then you're going to have the best farm. It's not just the idea of growing strawberries; you have to have people who will help you execute your plan. I never dreamed we would become this successful, but the success story is about our people. We feel we're a community, not just a farm."

Daren explains that he has learned three very important principles during his twenty-five years in business. First, develop good people. Train them and give them freedom and responsibility. Ask them to pass on what they have learned to their fellow employees.

Second, utilize technology to keep current. "You have to dominate in research and development if you want to be the front runner in any industry," Daren believes.

Finally, and most importantly, Daren feels it is vital to be a good person because honesty, hard work and respect will pay off in the long run more than anything else. Daren says his ultimate goal is, "To be a good family man, wholesome, hard working and love what I'm doing.

"The best part is when someone tells me, 'These are the best strawberries I've ever eaten.' Now that's the real thrill!"

TOMOOKA FAMILY

For more than a century, the Tomooka family that immigrated from Japan survived racial prejudice and economic upheaval to establish one of the most successful farming operations in the Santa Maria Valley.

The Tomooka family's story, worthy of a Hollywood movie, began in 1903 when Toyokichi Tomooka immigrated from a small farming village in Japan. He was followed by \his brother, Toyokuma, in 1906. The brothers moved to the Santa Maria Valley where they worked in the sugar beet fields for Union Sugar in Guadalupe. Although they earned only ten dollars per week, they managed to save enough money to lease 300 acres in Oso Flaco.

The two brothers raised sugar beets and potatoes at Oso Flaco until about 1924, when seventeen of Tomookas personally trained horses were killed in a stable fire. It is believed that the fire was racially motivated and set intentionally. At the time, the Tomookas were under intense pressure to replace their work horses with tractors but refused because the horses were so well trained by Toyokuma.

Meanwhile, immigrants were no longer allowed to lease land because of the Alien Land Law. This forced the Tomookas to relocate and find employment locally.

In 1930, undaunted by the injustice of the Alien Land Law, Toyokichi and Toyokuma decided to form a new produce company, Santa Maria Produce. Because of the law, the farm leases were put under the name of a second

generation natural born Japanese friend. Land below the Nipomo bluff on Riverside Road was leased from the Donovan and Souza families. There they grew cauliflower, lettuce and celery. Toyokuma later moved to a 140-acre parcel next to Oso Flaco Lake owned by the Enos family. The land was overgrown and wild with willow, weeds, and junk but Toyokuma transformed the acreage into prime farm land. Toyokuma bought his first tractor in 1937 and farmed the leased land until 1941.

Despite the Great Depression of the 1930s, the vegetables grown by the Tomooka family were grown, harvested, packed and loaded onto railroad cars for shipment across the nation. At times the Tomookas did not have the money to pay the rent but, most of the time, landlords were understanding because they knew the farmers were doing their best. Santa Maria Produce went heavily into debt during the Depression, similar to what other companies were going through.

About this time, the Tomookas began to experiment with a crop none of the other farmers in California had even heard of. General Manager Ted Akahoshi brought some seeds from Chicago for Italian Sprouting Broccoli and started growing about four or five acres on a trial basis. Akahoshi believed broccoli was going to be the 'next big thing' and felt he could find a market among the Italian community in Chicago if he could not sell it in California. When it came time to harvest, the Tomookas sent ten crates to the

Los Angeles market to see if it would sell. Back came a telegram saying they would pay five dollars for it. Toyokichi, who had a bit of a temper, said, "Forget it. Disc it all up!" Later it was learned that the price quoted was five dollars per crate, a good price for that day. That is how broccoli became a major crop in Santa Maria Valley and California.

Things began to take a turn for the better in 1938 and, by the end of 1940, sales started to pick up and the company was able to get out from under some of its debt.

Unfortunately, the good fortune did not last long. The bombing of Pearl Harbor in 1941 sent the Japanese-American community into turmoil and upheaval. Without warning, the FBI conducted a midnight raid at both Tomooka homes. They took Toyokuma and Toyokichi from their homes and separated them from their families.

Toyokichi's oldest son, Masataka, and Toyokuma's eldest son, Massey, took over the farming operations on their respective ranches, although they were only in their early twenties.

Conditions worsened with President Roosevelt's infamous proclamation 9066, which evacuated all Japanese from the coasts to the interior. Puritan Ice Co. agreed to act as trustees for the family's farms and operate them during the war. At the time, the family farmed about 1,500 acres.

In April 1942 all the Japanese on the Central Coast were sent to the Tulare County Fairgrounds in the San Joaquin Valley. From there, the Tomookas and others tried to keep their businesses going. However, they were not allowed to leave an assembly center, or use a telephone.

When Puritan Ice offered to buy the farming companies, the Tomookas decided the best they could do was grab what they could and then do the best they could. And so, Santa Maria Produce was sold.

Toyokuma Tomooka was released from detention in January 1946. With the $150 provided by the government as compensation, he boarded a train for Arizona where Toyokichi was already farming, having been released from Gila River detention camp a bit earlier.

Toyokuma's family ended up living in what was little more than a shack where the roof leaked so badly the ceiling fell down. With hard work and perseverance, they were able to purchase forty acres where they grew lettuce and cantaloupe. The family worked day and night to buy a tractor.

Toyokuma and his family returned to Santa Maria in 1952, while the Toyokichi Tomooka family stayed in Arizona. Toyokuma and Massey got a new start in farming through the generosity of H. Y. Minami, who asked them to farm ninety acres on Riverside Road in Nipomo. Yoshito and Isamu joined them to form Tomooka Brothers and they were soon able to expand their farming operations to 450 acres.

The farm operations eventually expanded to about 1,000 acres where the family grew lettuce and broccoli, which remained their major crops.

Toyokuma received two honors for his contributions to agriculture from the Japanese Government. He worked on the farm until he suffered a stroke at the age of seventy-eight. He died in 1972. His wife, Kane, passed away in 1994 at the age of ninety-four.

The Buddhist Church played a large part in Toyokuma's and Kane's lives and they gave generously to the church. Toyokuma was also a strong contributor to Marian Hospital, now Marian Medical Center. Tomooka Farms supported many local nonprofit organizations.

Yoshito and Isamu retired in 1991. Masayoshi became partners with Betteravia Farms in 1993. The business was sold to Betteravia Farms in 1995. Massey was honored as Farmer of the Year in 1997 at the Santa Barbara County Fair.

♦

Toyokichi Tomooka married Yone Matsuoka and together they had eight children—Tsuyako, Masataka, Ayako, Chikayoshi, James, Ruth, Lillie, and Fred.

TILDON MCGILL FAMILY

In the spring of 1859, Elizabeth McGill wrote from Red River County, Texas, to one of her sons, who lived in Franklin County, Alabama. She was urging her son to move to Texas and made some very persuasive arguments. "Land can be had here from $3 to $5 per acre, which will produce from 30 to 50 bushels of corn, 15 to 20 of wheat, oats in proportion, and from 1,000 to 1,500 lbs. of cotton to the acre," she wrote. She did add one negative—labor was expensive, with workers earning seventy-five cents per day.

This 1859 letter from Elizabeth is evidence of the restless spirit that has inspired the McGill family through the ages. Helen McGill Campbell, a first cousin of Tildon McGill, taught genealogy at the college level for more than fifteen years, and has authenticated the family's relationship with a number of influential ancestors.

The McGills are related to John Knox, the Scottish clergyman who led the Protestant Reformation and established the Presbyterian denomination. They are also related to the mother of James Knox Polk (eleventh President of the United States) who was a descendant of the brother of the religious reformer. Another direct descendant was Reverend John Knox Witherspoon, a native of Scotland who was a leader in the American Revolution and a signer of the Declaration of Independence.

In more recent times, William and Mary McGill Humphries are credited with founding the town of Bogota, Texas. Mary was the daughter of John McGill, Tildon McGill's 3X great-grandfather.

Tildon's life started in humble circumstances, but through hard work and perseverance, he carved out a successful business career and became a prominent Mason.

Tildon was born in DeKalb, Texas, in 1935, the low point of the Great Depression. His parents, John and Iva McGill, and two older brothers, Norman and Clarence, all worked on the farm to scratch out a living during those severe economic times. The days were filled with hard work and Tildon remembers his father plowing behind two mules while his mother cooked on a wood-burning stove. There was no electricity in the area so the family used Kerosene lamps for illumination. Times were tough, but families were very close. The McGill family tended a huge garden and grew almost everything they ate.

The McGill family moved to Santa Maria in 1946 and Tildon attended local schools. While in high school he played football, both offense and defense, and was a member of the track team. He also made many lifelong friends during high school.

Tildon and his first wife, Patsy Roberson, had three sons—Tim, Randy and Norman. While growing up, the boys enjoyed fishing and playing water sports at Righetti. Their father was their Scout Leader.

Tildon's professional career included positions with Union Oil Company, working as an investigator for the Retail Credit Bureau, serving as supervisor for two divisions of IBC, and acting as a consultant for Federated. He spent eight years in the U.S. Navy Reserve and was on the board of trustees that started Valley Christian Academy.

Tildon became interested in Masonry because of his father, who told of how he and his siblings were helped as little children by an uncle, 'who was a good Mason'. Tildon became a Mason in 1977 and served as president of the Santa Maria Shrine Club and Master of Guadalupe Lodge #237, two positions of honor of which he is extremely proud. He is also a thirty-second degree Scottish Rite Mason, York Rite Mason, member of the Royal Order of Scotland, a Knight of the Red Cross of

Constantine, Past Worthy Patron of Eastern Star, and a member of Elks Lodge #1538.

He married Susan Junod after the death of his first wife. Susan's son, David, became Tildon's fourth son. In their retirement, Tildon and Susan have enjoyed traveling to many countries.

BONIPAK PRODUCE

BETTERAVIA FARMS

ALCO PACKING

BONITA PACKING CO.

✦

Above: Bonipak Produce partners.

From humble beginnings in 1932, Bonipak Produce has grown to meet its customers' needs while maintaining a dedication and passion for the community, its people and the land.

Now a third-generation family business, the company began with the leadership of Milo Ferini and Dominick Ardantz, who formed a partnership to operate a small sugar beet farm in Guadalupe. Their partnership was based on the shared values of hard work, devotion and loyalty. They chose to locate their enterprise in the Santa Maria Valley because of its rich, fertile soil and mild year-round climate. These optional growing conditions allowed the partners to produce premium quality produce throughout the year.

The company has been through the tough days of the Great Depression. Henri Ardantz and Patrick Ferini remember packing beans in Henri's garage with the help of their wives. "We began packaging in the garage since we had nowhere else to go and had a need for it. It was challenging, but also fun," Henri adds.

Throughout the 1940s and 1950s the business continued to grow as crops expanded from sugar beets to include additional vegetable crops like lettuce, cauliflower and celery. During this period agriculture changed dramatically through the use of modern mechanization and advanced farming practices.

In 1962, Founders Milo Ferini and Dominick Ardantz had the opportunity to buy property

known as the lake-bottom. It was the family's second generation—Patrick Ferini, Henri Ardantz and Milo Ferini—that purchased the land and the organization became Betteravia Farms. "Our dads gave us the opportunity, for which we were grateful. But, it was also stressful," recalls Henri. "We had big shoes to fill. We also had our own way of doing things and all of a sudden we had to put all our heads together and figure out what we were going to do. Things worked out well, obviously. The company continued to grow throughout the next twenty years never leaving its core values behind."

The tradition continued in the 1990s with the addition of the third generation. Mitch Ardantz, Craig Reade, Rob Ferini, Tom Minetti and Alan Pincot joined ownership team. It was during this time the company opened a new cooling and office facility on Stowell Road. The company continued to expand and grow within the Santa Maria Valley. Bonipak stays deeply involved in the community by supporting a large number of charitable organizations including college scholarships for young men and women.

Today, Bonipak remains a family owned, multi-generational agriculture company that believes in their people, their families and the hard work put in each and every day. Never compromising their commitment to the environment and responsible growing practices, Bonipak will leave the land for future generations as bountiful as today. The owners, as well as the rest of the Bonipak family, are devoted to planting and investing for a brighter future.

G. ALLAN HANCOCK FAMILY

◆

Clockwise, starting from the top:

George Allan Hancock in his private railcar around 1926.

George Allan Hancock's daughter Rosemary Hancock, 1906-1977, with her daughter Patricia Zeiser Brennan around 1929. Patricia or "Patsy" was born in April 1928.

Genevieve Deane Mullen Hancock, 1879-1936. She married George Allan Hancock in 1901.

George Allan Hancock was an extraordinary man. After becoming a leading businessman and one of most distinguished citizens of Los Angeles, Hancock turned his attention to Santa Maria, which was becoming an important oil producing region in the 1920s.

Hancock was born in San Francisco in 1875 to Major Henry Hancock and Ida Haraszthy. Ida's father, Count Agoston Haraszthy, was known as the father of California viticulture. Henry, along with brothers Samuel and John were early explorers in the California gold fields.

Henry's abilities as a lawyer and surveyor kept him in demand following his gold mining days, but money was tight so he was paid for much of his work in acreage. He gradually sold his land for cash and by 1860 turned his attention to the acquisition of a dusty, dry patch of 4,444 acres known as Rancho La Brea. The pueblo's residents often dug brea (tar) from the ranch to waterproof their roofs. After seventeen years of legal disputes, Henry gained control of the land.

Henry and Ida lived in a shack on Rancho La Brea, now known as the La Brea Tar Pits. They had three children, including twin boys—Allan and Harry—and Bertram. Harry died in infancy and Bertram died of typhoid at the age of sixteen, leaving Allan as the surviving sibling.

Henry died when Allan was only eight years old, leaving Ida with a big mortgage. Her only income was from dry land farming leases and the transportation of brea to the docks for shipment to San Francisco.

Thanks to a successful oil lease in 1900, oil wells started producing on the Hancock land and in a twenty-year period, 350 wells operated on the property. This oil strike led Allan to success as a businessman and developer and enabling him to become a major benefactor of many educational and cultural institutions. Many knew Allan as the 'captain' because he held a master's license to command any vessel of any tonnage in any ocean.

After surveying the economic potential of the valley and purchasing a short line railroad, the Santa Maria Valley Railroad, a farm he later named after his daughter, cattle ranches and oil property in Cat Canyon, Allan moved to Santa Maria in 1925. His wife, Genevieve, and daughter, Rosemary joined him. His son, Bertram, died in the Santa Barbara earthquake earlier that year. His many contributions continue to echo throughout the Santa Maria Valley.

In 1928, Allan purchased and outfitted a bi-plane, the *Southern Cross*, with the best technology of the day. The *Southern Cross* in which two underfunded Australian aviators became the first to fly the Pacific from the United States to Australia. This sparked an interest in aviation and Allan purchased eighty acres, which became The Hancock College of Aeronautics, now known as the Santa Maria Airport. The college

trained nearly 9,000 cadets for the Air Force during World War II and is now know as Allan Hancock Community College.

In addition to his business skills, Hancock was a talented musician who played cello in the Los Angeles Symphony and organized a community orchestra in Santa Maria. He also had a dairy, a zoo and prize thoroughbreds.

♦

Left: George Allan Hancock, a true renaissance man, 1885-1965.

Below: Water is a vital part of farming and living. When George Allan Hancock needed water on his La Brea Ranch near the Tepesquet Adobe, he "water witched" it himself.

Allan was a strong believer in giving back to his community and was involved in numerous civic and charitable activities. This strong belief in community service is still practiced today by Hancock family descendants, who include Jane Brennan and daughters, Brenna and Sydney McGovern, who live in San Luis Obispo; Sheila Brennan lives in Paris, France; and Steve Brennan lives in Denver.

"We are continuing our great-grandfather's legacy," says Jane. "We are developing our vacant lands and updating our buildings into something the city and Papa (George Allan Hancock) can be proud of. GAH Properties is still the largest property owner downtown and is erecting a new apartment building, Hancock Terrace, in the area. Also, we still own property in Cat Canyon. We always strive to be good neighbors and community minded, as Papa was."

Gold Coast Packing, Inc.

Gold Coast Farms, Tri-Valley Harvesting, Fresh Venture Foods

✦

Left to right, Bob Espinola and Ron Burk at GCP Depot Street office in 1988.

The year was 1974 and Ron Burk and Bob Espinola were looking for a change. At the time, they were partners in an agricultural pest control business but were looking for an opportunity to own their own farming business. For their first venture, the partners decided to establish Gold Coast Greenhouses to grow hothouse tomatoes that were marketed in a local chain grocery store.

The success of the greenhouse venture led to several other opportunities that appeared almost simultaneously. Ron and Bob were willing to take a risk to start to realize their dream and buy out a local grower who was retiring; and a collaboration with another local grower allowed them to start a packing and sales company. Gold Coast Packing and Gold Coast Farms were founded in December 1978. Ron's father-in-law, Edward Pryor, a produce broker, helped support

the start-up of the sales aspect of the company. The partner's wives—Mary Burk and Sandi Espinola—were a huge support in the beginning and have continued to be an important influence on the company's growth.

Initially, Gold Coast packed for its own farms and one other grower, but the company eventually grew into packing and harvesting for other customers. In the 1980s, Gold Coast opened its own harvesting company called Tri-Valley Harvesting. In 1984 the company became partners with other growers in Coastal Valley Packing and Cooling, which processed shed-packed broccoli. Gold Coast, along with others in the industry, moved into packing the product in the field by 1988.

A major event in the growth of Gold Coast came in the early 1990s, when the company entered the value-added, fresh-cut produce industry. Gold Coast began packing cilantro for food service firms and acquired a large national restaurant chain, Taco Bell, as a customer, a relationship that continues today. In the early days, Gold Coast ran the cilantro on another grower's line. As the company continued to grow in the value-added industry, a plant, which had formerly been Knudsen's production facility, was leased on Boone Street.

Gold Coast then began producing broccoli florets for a large clubhouse store and, although more machinery was added, the business began to outgrow the Boone Street facility.

The growth continued in 2000 when Gold Coast and a group of Santa Maria and Salinas growers formed Fresh Kist, a sales organization founded to market commodity products in order to have more clout in the marketplace. Today, Fresh Kist includes Gold Coast Farms and several farming companies in the Santa Maria Valley and uses Guadalupe Cooler to cool and ship their commodity products.

Along the way, two long-time employees, John Schaefer and Mark LeClaire, became partners in Gold Coast Packing and have been instrumental to the company's growth and success.

In December 2012, Gold Coast and another local grower—Babè Farms—built a new state-of-the-art produce processing facility called Fresh Venture Foods. The new building, at 1205 West Craig Drive in Santa Maria, houses sales teams for both Gold Coast and Babè Farms

and the plant processes packaged produce products for both companies. Gold Coast Packing's headquarters are located at 1259 Furukawa Way in Santa Maria.

Through its various companies, Gold Coast has provided a great number and variety of jobs for the community. Current employment is approximately 500. Gold Coast's customer base includes retail, club stores, industrial, national chains, and world export.

Gold Coast is deeply committed to giving back to the Santa Maria Community that has played a large part in the company's success. The company supports a number of local charities, including the Foodbank, YMCA, Boys and Girls Club, Dignity Health and others.

Recently Ron and Bob were honored as Farmers of the Year for 2015 by Santa Barbara County for all of their various accomplishments throughout their careers. One of the admirable and unique points of the Gold Coast story is that it is a start-up company, just two entrepreneurial partners, willing to work hard and do whatever it took to keep moving forward and growing. Their vision and respect for each other, their employees, customers and all aspects of the business has been key to their success. These qualities and intentions have been passed-on to the next generation as their children have become involved in Gold Coast.

Gold Coast Packing continues to grow all aspects of its business and the future appears bright. Sales is focusing on continuing as a leader in the value-added industry by providing customers with top-quality products and developing new products to stay current with the changing marketplace. Fresh Venture Foods and Gold Coast Packing continue to use new and innovative technology to maintain high standards of operation.

✦

Above: Left to right, Mark LeClaire, John Schaefer, Ron Burk and Bob Espinola, owners of Gold Coast Packing, 2016.

Below: Left to right, Farmers of the Year, Ron Burk and Bob Espinola, Santa Barbara County, 2015.

JOHN BRANQUINHO FAMILY

The ancestors of John and Brandy Branquinho were among the very early settlers of the Santa Maria Valley and helped build and develop a rich ranching and farming heritage. They also passed on to their children a deep love of the land and the excitement of rodeos. All three of John and Brandy's sons are rodeo champions and Luke Branquinho has become a superstar on the rodeo circuit.

"The entire family has worked on the family ranch and we all rodeo in one way or another," explains Brandy. "The grandchildren are now following in the family footsteps. We are all hunters and enjoy the outdoor way of life."

John's grandparents came to the Santa Maria Valley in the mid-1800s. They had eleven children; John's father, also named John, being one of the younger ones. He was raised in the valley and married Ellinore Potter, whose family had also moved to the valley in the early 1900s.

Brandy's family goes back to the Santa Barbara Mission days of the early 1800s. Her great grandparents were John Bell and Katherine Den Bell. Katherine was the daughter of Roza Ortega Den and Nicholas Den. Their daughter, Caroline Bell, married Dr. George Luton and they had a son, William Franklin (Bill) Luton. Bill married Nancy Dickinson of Santa Barbara in 1936 and moved to Los Alamos. One-half of the land on which the city of Los Alamos was built was donated by her ancestors.

"John and Ellinore Branquinho and Bill and Nancy Luton were all key to the lives of the immediate family. Without their love, support and physical help, their knowledge and life experiences, our lives would have been very different," Brandy says.

John and Brandy have three sons: Tony, Casey and Luke. They were raised on Rancho San Juan on Alisos Canyon Road, in Los Alamos,

a 14,000-acre ranch that had been in Brandy's family since the 1800s.

Tony, like his brothers, grew up on the family ranch and became involved in rodeo at an early age. He was a high school and college star and became a professional rodeo contestant. He married Sharla Jackson and they have two children: Cersten, nineteen, and Kylee, eight. Tony is a rodeo coach at Fresno State and also works All American Trailers North.

Casey, who is currently single, has two children; Blake, nine, and Betty, eight. Casey was also a star high school, college and professional rodeo contestant and now trains horses and gives lessons on the family ranch.

Luke married Lindsay Favour and they have three children: Cade, eight, Jameson, six, and Bear Luke, nine months.

Luke competed in rodeo events in high school and college and is now a superstar on the rodeo circuit where he competes in the steer wrestling. He has won five world titles and his career earnings total $2.4 million. Luke has been diagnosed with Type I diabetes and uses an insulin pump in order to keep his blood glucose levels under control.

At the 2003 Redding Rodeo, both Luke and older brother Casey won event titles.

The Branquinhos now reside and headquarter their ranching operation on eighty-seven acres they purchased in 2004. This property is one mile west of Los Alamos on Highway 135. It also belonged to Brandy's great-grandparents at one time.

"Our sons were raised in the ranching tradition and all have passed these values on to their children," Brandy says. "We would love for our grandchildren to be raised with the same lifestyle."

Above: Brandy, Johnnie and Bear Branquinho, December 2015.

Below: Back row, left to right, Taylor Scott, Kylee, Betty and Jameson Branquinho and Trinity Scott. Front row, Cade, Cersten and Blake Branquinho, December 2015.

CARRARI RANCHO ALAMO

Joe Carrari is considered by all as one of the most colorful characters in California's often volatile viticulture business. Joe's career has ranged from California to Argentina and back and he has worked for some of the biggest names in the industry—Paul Masson and Rene DiRosa's Winery Lake Vineyards to name just a couple. He has also consulted with Jekel, J. Lohr and other grape growers and wineries in the Paso Robles area. He has been a consultant for grape growers in New Zealand, and delivered grapes to Mexican wineries in the Guadalupe Valley. When he was farming in Cucamonga, he delivered grapes to the only winery in Santa Barbara County at the time.

He has planted 6,000 acres of grapes and installed more than 400 Ford industrial engines on good pumps through his company, Videco. His stake driving count is in the hundreds of thousands.

The gregarious eighty-two-year-old grape grower, who claims to have picked his first wine grapes when he was five, loves to share the exciting stories of his dramatic career and is not bashful about revealing his failures as well as the successes.

Joe inherited his indomitable spirit from his father, Mike, who was born in Argentina, but raised in Italy. Mike came to the U.S. in 1929, just in time for the depression years. He moved to California in the early 1930s, got a job in the vineyards and managed to save ninety-six dollars. He used twenty dollars of his stake to buy an old, broken-down truck and started his own farming operations.

Joe was born in Alta Loma in 1934 and learned the business by following his father around. Among his other ventures, Mike managed some of the vineyards for Secundo Guasti, who founded the Italian Vineyard Company and built it into a major enterprise.

Joe and Mike later farmed together and, eventually, their vineyards reached 1,400 acres. One of their vineyards was planted in 1906 and was farmed continuously until 1984. One year the Carrari family shipped 4,500 tons of grapes to home vintners.

During a depressed period in the wine industry, Joe decided to join a brother in Argentina and try his hand at farming there. He moved to Argentina at the age of thirty and helped his brother plant 3,000 acres of corn. The crop grew well and everything looked good until it was time to harvest, then disease killed the corn on the cobs. "I came back north in 1964 with nothing," Joe recalls.

Left: Joe pruning a grapevine, 1943.

Right: Joe hand harvesting grapes, 1963.

Fortunately, Joe's viticulture skills helped him land jobs with some of the companies that pioneered the 1970s evolution of the wine industry. He was working for Masson when the Central Coast wine grape planting boom of the 1970s began. He was involved in both the success and the failure of that venture. But the failure opened the door for him to start his own vineyard management and consulting business and plant his own coastal vineyard.

In the 1990s, Joe was losing money but refused to sell his Santa Barbara County premium red wine grapes at prices lower than it cost him to produce. This stubbornness left him floating in 326,000 gallons of bulk wine. "I refused to take what wineries were offering and lose money," Joe explains. "I worked too hard to do that. Production credit was taking wine as collateral on loans back then so I decided to crush the grapes myself."

Joe blended the varietals he had in storage and produced a passable red wine. He then had an artist create an art deco black-and-white checkerboard label and called his new wine Dago Red. The wine sold retail for $1.99 a bottle and soon became a phenomenon. "I was way ahead of Two Buck Chuck," Joe says. "It made a helluva wine. I liked it and nine out

of ten people who tasted it liked it. Everyone liked it, especially the price. We sold it by the case in Los Alamos for $1 per bottle."

Joe sold his vineyards a few years ago and the wine country legend now spends his time at Rancho Alamo, his 3,600-acre ranch at Los Alamos. He leases out 400 acres for vegetable production and grazes cattle in the foothills. Joe loves to sit on the porch of his remodeled 1918 ranch house and tell stories of his six decades in the business.

Above: Joe exposing fruit for machine harvesting, 1968.

Below: Joe and Phyllis enjoying a bottle of Dago Red.

Brooke Bradley's family story begins with her grandparents, Dick and Jaye Armstrong, who owned Garden Dairy at 219 East Main Street in the heart of downtown Santa Maria. Dairy was a twenty-four-hour business. They eventually moved into the real estate business for many years until retirement.

Brooke's mother, Roxanne Armstrong Ventriglia, was the 1969 Dairy Princess. Sponsored by Santa Maria Valley Dairymen's Association, the honor provided money toward a college scholarship. She and Brooke's father, James J. Ventriglia, have been proud and successful real estate business owners in Santa Maria for more than thirty years. James has been involved in the Santa Maria Breakfast Rotary Club and the Santa Maria Elks Lodge for over thirty-five years.

Her mother's diary princess legacy inspired Brooke to pursue the crown as an Elks' Rodeo Queen. After many community events and fundraisers, she was crowned the fifty-first Elk's Rodeo Queen in 1994. She was sponsored by Your Orcutt Youth Organization. She was also the very last rodeo queen crowned in the Clarence Minetti Rodeo Arena, which provided a scholarship opportunity that sent Brooke off to CSU, Chico.

"The advantages of participating in community programs are endless," Brooke feels. "The life tools you develop build your character and extend your vision toward other goals. After college, I was the youngest sales person ever hired for Hershey Chocolate."

Brooke soon met her husband, Ken Bradley, who also attended Chico State. He is a senior project manager at Atlas CopCo Mafi-Trench in Santa Maria and is also involved with the Santa Maria Breakfast Rotary and Elks Lodge. He is an active mountain bike rider who loves the Central Coast.

Ken and Brooke have three children, Tate Joseph (12), Ava Joan (11) and Parker James (5). "We have a great family," Brooke says. "I currently own and operate a local family business named All American Screen Printing on Oak Street."

Brooke is the sitting president of the historical society for the 2016-2018 term. She is also a board member and vice chairman of the board for the SMV YMCA and has headed their major gifts campaign for the past ten years. In conjunction with that, Brooke volunteers throughout the community. "I hope to share my love of community and grow my family in this valley, encouraging my daughter and sons to participate in their community," she declares.

✦

Top: Roxanne Armstrong Ventriglia.

Above: Brooke Bradley.

Right: Standing, left to right, James Ventriglia, Ken and Brooke Bradley. Seated, left to right, Roxanne Ventriglia, Ava Bradley, Jaye and Dick Armstrong, Tate Bradley, and Britt Ventriglia Meyer.

At Manzanita Berry Farms, the goal is to produce the finest strawberries possible, while being a true steward of the soils, and to promote an ethical and productive environment for all its employees.

Manzanita was established in 1995 when David Peck and his wife, Diana, learned of the potential for new strawberry enterprises in Santa Maria. The Pecks had farmed raspberries and strawberries in Oxnard for eight years and decided to take advantage of the opportunity. At the time, Santa Maria Valley had only about 2,500 acres of strawberries. Today, that number has grown to 8,500 acres and strawberries are the number one grossing farm product in Santa Barbara County.

"My wife and I had the good fortune at the beginning to employ very talented farming employees: Fidel Ferreira, Gilberto and Paquin Varela, Antonio Esquivias and Eliseo Montejano. Together we forged a very stable, profitable and long-lived farm company," David explains.

Diana has been office manager and human relations director from the beginning, and all five of the Peck children have worked for the company, both in the office and in the field. Currently, two daughters work in the office and a son is head mechanic. More than two dozen full-time employees have been with the company since it was founded.

Manzanita produces strawberries from patented varieties under exclusive contract for Well-Pict, Inc. "Our enduring relationship from the beginning with Well-Pict has provided us with exceptional strawberry varieties, competitive sales, and enormous farming resources,"

David notes. "And, it can't be overemphasized how important Betteravia Farms was to us in the early days by leasing us superior farm ground and cooling our produce at their new facility on Stowell Road."

Since 1995, Manzanita has grown from harvesting 135 acres with around 200 peak-season employees; to more than 400 acres, including 150 acres planted in organic berries. The company employs more than 500 people during the harvest season.

Manzanita is a consistent supporter of community fundraisers and the California Strawberry Commission's annual scholarship drive for dependants of California strawberry workers.

As market demand for strawberries continues to grow steadily, Manzanita Berry Farms expects to continue providing the healthiest, tastiest berries it can well into the future.

More information is available on the Internet at www.berryfarmer.com.

MANZANITA BERRY FARMS

◆

Above: David and Diana Peck.

Left: Farmer of the Year award belt buckle.

Below: The original staff, left to right, Fidel Ferreira, Paquin Varela, Eliseo Montejano, Antonio Esquivias and Gilberto Varela.

NEWLOVE FAMILY

By Jean Martin

John Newlove was born in Lincolnshire, England. At fourteen, he crossed the ocean and settled in the area of Toronto, Canada. He thirsted for knowledge but was able to secure only limited schooling. However, he was a great reader and improved his time when he was not engaged in work in reading good books.

He found employment on a farm and worked for wages until he married Maria Beynon. Canadian winters were long and severe, so they came to California by ship through Panama. In California, he took up his residence in the Santa Maria Valley. He bought a large tract of land south of Santa Maria including Mount Solomon; he owned over 3,000 acres. He improved it, raising cattle and crops. People began to purchase land in greater numbers, values rose, and villages developed into cities. John felt that his early predictions were fulfilled, the West was coming into its heritage.

Union Oil bought Newlove property about 1904. They paid one million dollars. As time passed and John passed on, the discovery of oil on their land gave the family the opportunity to build the beautiful Maria Beynon Newlove Mansion.

In 1982 it was to be moved by the Roger Ikola family to south of Santa Maria to become part of the Santa Maria Valley Historical Park. Government regulations stopped this dream, but in time the beautiful Newlove Home was noticed by Adam Firestone and his parents, Brooks and Kate Firestone. They were so moved by its historical significance that they pursued a vision of making it beautiful again. The house was moved to Los Olivos where it became an architectural edifice of outstanding remark and note.

The Newlove family remained leaders in the community. In 1907, Maria's daughter, Henrietta Louise Newlove Martin, built the Martin townhouse at 800 South Broadway. It later became known as the Santa Maria Club. In 1982, A. J. Diani completely restored it. The original architect and builder was E. D. Bray (father of Pauline Marguerite Bray Martin.) Later this structure became the Landmark Square and was designated as a State of California Landmark to be preserved forever.

Jean Martin is the granddaughter of Henrietta Newlove Martin.

Top: John Newlove.

Above: Maria Beynon.

Top, right: Wedding picture of Henrietta and Frank Martin, Santa Maria, c. 1888.

Right: Newlove Mansion, built 1907 and located two miles south of Broadway and Main Streets on South Lincoln, c. 1913.

Dedicated to those who made me the man I became: My sister, Barbara Jean; my mother, Birdie; and my mother's brothers, Kenneth and Clarence Cooper, who gave their full measure on the USS *Arizona* December 7, 1941, and to Franklin Constance Firanzi, my step-grandfather who showed me that life could be fun.

All of these important people came from Casmalia, a little town best known today for its BBQ. During my time the town sported about 200 souls. At the turn of the century, it was more like 1,500 but nearly 1,300 were Chinese workers along the Southern Pacific Railroad living in tents. As early as the 1940s, the Southern Pacific Railroad provided a job for my step-grandfather, Franklin Constance Firanzi. He was a signal man and drove a speeder (putt-putt car), which he hand-loaded on the tracks between Surf and Guadalupe, including downtown Lompoc. He passed the house twice a day on his run. Grandpa was well known in Casmalia for furnishing fresh vegetables via the gunny sack to people in town. Eventually, he got caught with a sack of artichokes, went to jail and received a fine of $250. I still remember him as the most fun person to be with.

Casmalia is located just outside the borders of Vandenberg Air Force Base about five miles southwest of Santa Maria. As a young boy, I had the responsibility of 'plowing' three quarters of an acre twice a year using only a shovel. I did the work before and after school and during lunch. It was imperative that I get the work done for two reasons. The first, of course, because we needed it to sustain the family. More importantly to me was that once the job was done, my mother took me into the Casmalia Hills on adventures. We caught rattlesnakes, traipsed through high grass and forded little water ways as we explored the open area around us. The weather was generally warm, but not hot, with dry summers. Casmalia has a warm Mediterranean climate, and the time with my mom climbing every hill was wonderful.

I have a lot of pride in Casmalia. Besides my uncles who were lost on the *Arizona* in 1941, there have been some prominent figures rise out of this town. Joe Centeno, Santa Maria police chief for many years and then a Santa Barbara County supervisor for the fifth district.

Harold English, also a Santa Maria police chief, married a Casmalian, Frieda Muscio.

I grew up and left home like everyone else, but I never ceased to love the little town where nobody locked their doors and everyone felt like family.

✦

Above: The Cooper family.

Below: Railroad man Franklin C. Firanzi with dog.

JAMES FRANKLIN GOODWIN

A pioneer in the true sense of the word, James Franklin (Jimmy) Goodwin was born in Nebraska Territory in 1855. His trek to California began in the spring of 1856 in a wagon drawn by oxen and badgered by Indians. From 1869 to 1876, Goodwin spent his time on the family farm and at school. Late in 1876, he came to the town that would be Santa Maria.

In the spring of 1878, Goodwin opened a mercantile and butcher shop in the little town of Central City, population 50-100 persons. At this time there was one main store. It belonged to Thornburgh & Company. The rest of the town consisted of two blacksmiths shops, a hotel and salon, and a few residences.

The most significant event, in his own words was his marriage to Sarah Belle McGaugh on July 11, 1883. It was reported in local newspapers of the wedding "that there was music in the hearts that rejoiced in the union of the young couple." The bride and groom boarded at the home of T. A. Jones until their new home was completed in a grainfield on a lot in the Fesler Division, two blocks from the center of town. This cottage, an exact duplicate of the one built by Mr. Doane for Johnny Long, was where their three children were born, Bessie, Guy and Donald.

Goodwin's life in the valley was prosperous. He served as postmaster in Santa Maria from 1879 to 1885. By 1890, Goodwin sold out his interest in his merchandizing business. He worked with Paul Tietzen to incorporate the Bank of Santa Maria in 1890, and served as its cashier from 1891 until 1903.

Above: James Franklin Goodwin, c. 1878.

Right: Pinal Well #3, came in as the first gusher in the Santa Maria Oil Field in June 1903.

Below: Goodwin & Bryant Mercantile at the southwest corner of Main and Broadway, c. 1878.

During the beginning of the twentieth century oil was discovered across the hills of the southern slope of the Santa Maria Valley. Goodwin formed the Pinal Oil Company incorporating it October 7, 1901. The first well Pinal #1 was drilled in 1902. Goodwin realized oil was his next great adventure. May 1903, Pinal #3 flowed over the derrick, a gusher! It was described as the 'greatest strike of its time.' Equally great excitement overtook the attention of oil men from all over the state of California. Santa Maria was experiencing an oil boom and Goodwin was its leader; Santa Maria's first oil barron.

At his passing it was written in the *Santa Maria Daily Times*, July 16, 1932, "that of all the pioneers of Santa Maria none were as outstanding and prominent as James F. Goodwin." No other single person was so intimately connected throughout its history and development as that genial personality, who for fifty years had made his home in the Santa Maria Valley. He was described as energetic of spirit and one whom the Santa Maria Valley should apprize as one of its foremost pioneer and citizen.

A Thank You from the Publisher

As the project manager for this book, I wish to thank everyone for both the pleasure of working on this incredible book and for welcoming me into the community of Santa Maria, the place I now call home.

Santa Maria is one of the most beautiful places I've visited in the entire country. Just look at the cover of this book and you'll see why I fell in love with it here. The way in which the gorgeous rolling green hills in the winter and spring contrast so brilliantly with our golden summers, providing a perfectly temperate climate for a twelve month growing season. What's not to love?

◆

Left: Daphne Fletcher.
PHOTOGRAPH COURTESY OF LYRICA GLORY.

Bottom, left: Bill Wurth receiving the Elk of the Year Award.

Below: Bill Wurth in the 1940s.

Most of all, it's the people in this valley that make this place so special. It has been a true honor to include such eloquent stories from the earliest of California's history at the Porter Ranch to Walt Disney's friend Alan Hancock to Joe Carrari, pioneer of California wine.

One individual I believe should not be forgotten is Bill Wurth, an amazing man I met in the very beginning of the project who fosters a great love of history (he volunteers at the museum and historical society). He opened many doors for me and invited me to join the Elks Lodge BPO 1538, where I've met many friends. As a young man, Bill was a hero in WWII, and he continued his service to the community of Santa Maria. He was Elk of the Year not long ago and has been honored many times for being one of their biggest volunteers. By his own example, Bill shows us what it looks like to lead a rich and fulfilling life. Thank you Bill for all of your help on this book.

Last but certainly not least, I would like to thank all of the sponsors for sharing in the vision of this project and seeing it through to fruition.

–Daphne Fletcher

SPONSORS

About the Author

LUCINDA K. RANSICK

Lucinda K. Ransick grew up in the south among people who could name their family tree back to the American Revolutionary War. History and heritage are inextricably linked in her childhood memories. An avid listener at first, now the passionate storyteller, she has been putting her thoughts on paper since she was Editor of her high school newspaper. Publishing a book on civil war veterans, writing articles for local newspapers, scripting jingles and ads for local radio stations, and grant writing for nonprofits has fueled her enthusiasm for sharing the history of the people where she calls home. Though not a native of Santa Maria, she nevertheless owns a pioneer heritage, and so is ideally suited to write the story of a people who forged a town so warm and remarkable as to be called the "Sweet Spot" on the Central Coast. A military spouse, she has found home in a lot of places. Listening to four children, she has heard a lot of stories. You can expect an exciting sharing of the harrowing first years in the valley, accentuated with those hearty pioneers' triumphs, on their pathway to making Santa Maria what it is today.

ABOUT THE EDITOR

MICHAEL FARRIS

Mike has lived almost three quarters of a century on the Central Coast of California. Raised in Los Alamos, he spent thirty years as a senior quality engineer for half a dozen major aerospace companies. Mike has worked with the Santa Maria Valley Historical Society for over twenty years and has been on its board of directors. In addition, Mike has been president of the Santa Maria Genealogy Society and a member of the Santa Maria Natural History Museum and the Santa Ynez Historical Museum. MIke was the editor of *The Purple Cow: A Dairy Daughters Heritage* by Laura Leigh Dias as well as three other historical books. Working on the *Historic Santa Maria Valley* has been an engaging exploration of our local history.

For more information about the following publications or about publishing your own book,
please call HPNbooks at 800-749-9790 or visit www.hpnbooks.com.